Therapy with Children and Young People

SAGE has been part of the global academic community since 1965, supporting high quality research and learning that transforms society and our understanding of individuals, groups and cultures. SAGE is the independent, innovative, natural home for authors, editors and societies who share our commitment and passion for the social sciences.

Find out more at: **www.sagepublications.com**

Therapy with Children and Young People

Integrative Counselling in Schools and other Settings

Colleen McLaughlin
and **Carol Holliday**

Los Angeles | London | New Delhi
Singapore | Washington DC

Los Angeles | London | New Delhi
Singapore | Washington DC

SAGE Publications Ltd
1 Oliver's Yard
55 City Road
London EC1Y 1SP

SAGE Publications Inc.
2455 Teller Road
Thousand Oaks, California 91320

SAGE Publications India Pvt Ltd
B 1/I 1 Mohan Cooperative Industrial Area
Mathura Road
New Delhi 110 044

SAGE Publications Asia-Pacific Pte Ltd
3 Church Street
#10-04 Samsung Hub
Singapore 049483

Editor: Kate Wharton
Editorial assistant: Laura Walmsley
Production editor: Rachel Burrows
Copyeditor: Audrey Scriven
Proofreader: Derek Markham
Indexer: Silvia Benvenuto
Marketing manager: Tamara Navaratnam
Cover design: Lisa Harper
Typeset by: C&M Digitals (P) Ltd, Chennai, India
Printed in Great Britain by Henry Ling Limited at
The Dorset Press, Dorchester, DT1 1HD

First published 2014

Library of Congress Control Number: 2013940611

British Library Cataloguing in Publication data

A catalogue record for this book is available from the British Library

ISBN 978-1-4462-0831-1
ISBN 978-1-4462-0832-8 (pbk)

Contents

About the Editors and Contributors

Colleen McLaughlin is a Professor of Education at the University of Sussex, School of Education and Social Work. For over twenty-five years she worked at the University of Cambridge, Faculty of Education, where she directed a child and adolescent psychotherapeutic programme. She has written, researched and spoken on child and adolescent care and wellbeing, which is her passion, and is also concerned with promoting the wider role of schools and teachers. She has taught in schools and worked as a counsellor. Colleen is also a Fellow of the BACP.

Carol Holliday is an Affiliated Lecturer at the University of Cambridge, Faculty of Education, where she now leads the programme for child and adolescent psychotherapeutic counselling. She is a United Kingdom Council for Psychotherapy-registered Arts Psychotherapist who works therapeutically with children, adolescents and adults, and has twenty years' experience of clinical practice and also working as a clinical supervisor. Carol has particular interests in the relationships between children and adults, and in working with images: in therapy, education, and research. Her doctoral research explored the contributions of psychotherapy to the teacher/child relationship, and she is an award-winning author of publications helping teachers to understand and work with children's feelings.

Eileen Armstrong worked for twenty years as a teacher and manager within special schools, further education and an international school before retraining as a counsellor and working in agency settings. She completed an MEd in Child and Adolescent Psychotherapeutic Counselling through the University of Cambridge, and has been working for the past few years as a peripatetic school counsellor through a counselling service. Eileen is an accredited and registered member of the BACP.

Julia Buckroyd will shortly celebrate thirty years as a counsellor and psychotherapist. In that time she has developed into an integrative practitioner with a particular interest in attachment theory. Most of her career has been spent in academic settings, so she is particularly interested in how we come to be able to learn and how our early experience affects that capacity.

Tracey Fuller is a UKCP-registered Child and Adolescent Psychotherapeutic Counsellor. She teaches on the BACP-accredited Child and Adolescent Counselling Programme at the University of Cambridge, Faculty of Education. She has many years' experience of working therapeutically with children, including with a Looked After Children's Service, with the NSPCC, and as a Schools Counsellor in numerous primary and secondary schools. She has a particular interest in developing creative approaches to forming therapeutic alliances with adolescents and extending school-based counselling. She has a particular interest in developing creative approaches to forming therapeutic alliances with adolescents and ethical issues in school-based counselling.

Clair Lewoski is an Integrative Child Psychotherapist (UKCP), Arts Therapist (HCPC) and teacher (PGCE Cantab), with Masters from Cambridge University, the Tavistock Clinic and The Institute for Arts in Therapy and Education. She set up a therapy service across 10 primary schools, integrating mindfulness practices into her work with children, teachers and parents. She has also worked in the NHS and now works in private practice, as well as teaching at Cambridge University. She has a particular interest in utilising mind–body practices in psychotherapy with children and young people.

Fiona Peacock is a BACP Senior Accredited Counsellor, as well as one of the few Certified Theraplay® Therapists currently in the UK. For over twenty years she has worked as a counsellor in various settings: colleges, schools, Child and Adolescent Mental Health Services. Currently she teaches and also runs a private practice providing therapy to children, particularly Looked After or Adopted, as well as supervision, consultation and training.

PART 1

Setting the Context

Introduction

Colleen McLaughlin

Background

The two named authors of this book have worked for many years on the accredited programme for developing counsellors to work therapeutically with children and adolescents at the Faculty of Education, University of Cambridge. Colleen McLaughlin worked for twenty-six years on this and Carol Holliday for fifteen. This is important because this book represents what both have learned from this educational journey. The other authors in this book are either part of the team who work on the programme, past students, or supervisors.

Purpose

The book is about working therapeutically with children and young people in educational and related settings. It is aimed at a specialist audience of therapists and counsellors who work, or are learning to work, with young people and those who are employed in such settings. It is now recognised that working with children requires particular skills and understanding, that this cannot be a simple transfer of knowledge and capacity from working with adults or from training to work with adults. In this book we aim to: give a comprehensive theoretical base, which we feel is highly necessary in the field; to engage with the practice of psychotherapeutic counselling; to explore the contextual and professional issues of working in a school setting; and to illustrate these matters with case vignettes of work with children in school settings delivered by highly experienced practitioners. A key feature of this book is its focus on the conceptual base for therapeutic work, and on working specifically with children and young people in educational and related settings, and especially the role of the creative arts in working with children and young people (i.e., the use of play, story and other methods of working through metaphor and imagery).

Theoretical base

There are four concepts that shape our approach. These are:

1. *An ecological or ecosystemic view of child development* This means that we engage in looking at and suggesting that the counsellors or therapists should work in the wider contexts, as well as take account of them. The ecological approach signifies that not only do counsellors have to take account of the impact of the local and distal influences on a child's development, but also that they should engage in working with these fields as well. This is different from a strictly clinical model where the work is mainly on the client and the therapy room. If counsellors adopt the wider approach, the ensuing professional issues are likely to be complex, and there is likely to be an array of these. These issues are discussed later in the book, especially Chapters 1 and 10 to 13.
2. A *developmental approach* There is an entire section that examines the implications of working with young people who are growing and developing fast. Therefore Part 2 (Chapters 2 to 5) examines child development theory in some detail and draws out the implications for practice.
3. A *pluralistic or integrative approach* (i.e., one that draws on various theoretical bases in a coherent and constructively critical fashion). An integrative approach has many elements. It takes account of all aspects of human functioning – the emotional, the behavioural, the cognitive, the bodily, and the spiritual. All of the theoretical positions and bodies of work that focus on these aspects are taken into account. It views human beings as having all the elements and needing to integrate them, so that therapy is about this process of integration: it is also the task of the therapist to integrate their approach and their understanding, so here you will find theoretical accounts that rely on the psychodynamic, client-centred, behaviourist, cognitive, family therapy, Gestalt therapy, body-psychotherapies, object relations theories, psychoanalytic self-psychology, and transactional analysis approaches, together with systems perspectives.

Each approach is viewed as giving a partial explanation of behaviour, and each is enhanced when selectively integrated with other aspects of a therapist's approach.

4. *A relational view of therapy* This is, finally, what the therapeutic process is based on. By this is meant that the therapeutic relationship is seen as central to the process of healing and working therapeutically. This is because, as Carol Holliday states, 'There is now overwhelming evidence that the quality of the therapeutic relationship generally, and of the alliance in particular, is a predictor of therapy outcome (Norcross, 2002; Cooper, 2008; Haugh and Paul, 2008). The better the quality of the relationship, the more likely the therapy is to have a successful outcome. A strong relationship predicts success and a weak relationship predicts premature ending of the therapy'. It is also because of the developmental focus of this approach and the emphasis on attachment.

These core concepts are interrogated both theoretically and practically within the book. They also drive its organisation into four parts:

- Part 1: Setting the context
- Part 2: Understanding and working with the developmental tasks of childhood and adolescence
- Part 3: Working therapeutically with children and adolescents in schools
- Part 4: Professional issues in counselling with children and adolescents

Counselling and therapy in educational and related settings

This book also focuses on therapeutic work in educational and related settings. As is explored in Chapter 1, there is a history of counselling in schools but increasingly schools are being seen as particularly effective places for therapeutic and developmental work. (The Welsh government, for example, has a large-scale strategy for this.) Schools are appropriate sites because they have a consistent view of each child over time and they are also linked to the communities in which children live and grow. Therapeutic work in these settings raises many professional and ethical issues that are fully examined in the final part of the book, as well as in Chapter 11.

Working with children and young people, as well as in schools, has many implications for theory and practice (i.e., that children are not autonomous, don't necessarily communicate their emotions verbally, and have strong connections to others who have responsibility for them and influence their development). The approaches to working non-verbally with children are examined in detail, as are the ethical, relational and practical aspects. Our aim is to offer as fully as possible all the theoretical, practical and professional aspects of therapeutic work with children and young people in educational settings.

The concepts and issues we discuss are illustrated and illuminated by case material throughout. All the contributors to this book have many years of psychotherapeutic experience to draw on, however, we would also acknowledge the complex ethical considerations that publishing work of this nature raises. The case vignettes, unless otherwise stated, are composite and draw on many cases whilst conveying examples of the kinds of issues that can arise in work with children and adolescents. The stance we have taken is to heavily anonymise the material so that individuals are unrecognisable and no person should be able to recognise him- or herself, and hence the examples offered contain no identifying features.

ONE The Child, The School, Counselling and Psychotherapy

Colleen McLaughlin

Introduction

This chapter discusses the relationship between the child, the school and counselling, drawing upon an ecological approach. We argue that counselling involves taking account of and engaging with the family, the school and the wider community, as well as the child. Research on the emotional wellbeing of children and adolescence is examined and its connections to the ecological framework explored, together with the ensuing implications for the role of the school and counselling. The final section looks in more detail at the role of counselling in schools, including describing the history of counselling therein, and the evidence for its effectiveness.

The ecological or ecosystemic approach

Human beings create the environments that shape the course of human development. Their actions influence the multiple physical and cultural tiers of the ecology that shapes them, and this agency makes humans – for better or for worse – active producers of their own development. (Bronfenbrenner, 2005: xxvii)

This quotation from Bronfenbrenner contains many of the key ideas in his ecological theory, namely that development is a dynamic process of exchange between persons and their environments, we have agency as human beings, and human relationships matter. Urie Bronfenbrenner, who studied child development, children and their families, and was the co-founder of Head Start in the USA, brought together the work of Kurt Lewin (who saw behaviour as the result of an interaction between the person and their environment) and Lev Vygotsky (who emphasised the interaction between child and adults in learning) to shape his ecological systems theory of development. Bronfenbrenner was interested in the influences in a child's life and development, and the interplay that existed between the complex systems of relationships that formed the surrounding environment. He suggested that there were critical factors in each child's development, and these were the context, time, process, and the individual's personal attributes. In doing this he was challenging the then practice of only studying 'the strange behaviour of children in strange situations with strange adults for the briefest possible periods of time' (Bronfenbrenner, 1974: 3). He saw the environment as a nested and interconnected system, similar to a series of Russian dolls, at the heart of which was the child or individual. This person would possess developmentally important personal attributes

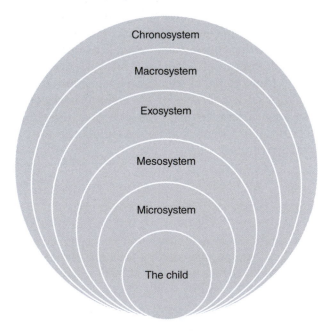

Figure 1.1   Bronfenbrenner's Ecological Systems Theory

that invited, inhibited or prevented their engagement in a sustained and progressively more complex interaction with, and activity in, the immediate environment (Bronfenbrenner, 2005: 97).

The remaining systems are both near and far, but all of these will influence a child's development. As is shown in Figure 1.1 the nearest is the *microsystem*, and this consists of the child's immediate environment (i.e., the family, school, peers, and the immediate neighbourhood). The second system, the *mesosystem*, often defines and constrains the microsystem: this is the culture or subculture of the family or the school. The third system is the *exosystem,* which in turn influences the previous two systems: this is the wider social context of the government, the education system, the economic systems, and the religious system. The final and most distant system is the *macrosystem*, which is the overarching ideology and legal system. These more distal systems clearly influence the child's immediate environment. Lastly, the *chronosystem* is the dimension of time. What we are concerned with in this chapter is the emotional ecology of each child and adolescent in school, and how this ecology works to influence children's wellbeing and development.

The emotional ecology of child and adolescent wellbeing

The topic of how society, and schools in particular, influence adolescent wellbeing is a large one, and as such it is not possible to cover this fully in one chapter (although Chapters 5 and 6 explore some aspects further). Adolescence is a unique time in the life-course because there is such huge growth and development. It is the transitional period between childhood and adulthood, and as transitional periods are a time when individuals are more sensitive to environmental inputs these assume a critical role (Mulye et al., 2009: 8). Recent research on adolescent wellbeing in the UK does however tell us something of how the systems around the microsystem work together. The Nuffield Foundation (2012; see also Hagell, 2012) has recently completed a major programme of research reviews examining how young people's lives have changed since the 1970s, and whether these could further inform our understanding of the increase in adolescent mental health problems that has occurred in the last thirty years. The main social trends identified in the UK included:

- Increases in the proportion of young people reporting frequent feelings of depression or anxiety. This figure doubled between the mid-1980s and the mid-2000s. For boys aged 15 to16, rates increased from approximately 1 in 30 to 2 in 30. For girls they increased from approximately 1 in 10 to 2 in 10.1 (Collishaw et al., 2010).

- Increases in parent-rated behaviour problems: for example, approximately 7 per cent of 15 to 16 year olds showed high levels of problems in 1974, rising to approximately 15 per cent in 1999 (Collishaw et al., 2007).
- A similar rate of increase in 'conduct disorders' (mainly non-aggressive antisocial behaviour like lying and theft) for boys and girls, and for young people from different kinds of background.
- Encouraging signs of a levelling-off in these trends post-2000. For example, there was no rise in the level of emotional problems such as anxiety and depression amongst 11 to 15 year olds between 1999 and 2004 (Maughan et al., 2008). However, there are hints that the rates of some of the underlying causes might climb with the rise in youth unemployment and growth in poverty after the 2008 financial crisis and policy responses (Nuffield Foundation, 2012: 1).

The macrosystem level was seen as having growing influence and an area for increasing research. The school was described as a key social institution, as was the family and part-time employment. The key social trends identified as affecting young people's wellbeing were: how they spent their time; education; shifts in substance use; and changes in family life. Young people spend much more time in education nowadays and this has been accompanied by a collapse in the youth labour market, especially since 2008. By 2000 the majority of young people were in full-time education rather than work. These factors affect how they experience many things and the nature of their time use. Larson et al. (2002) have highlighted some of the differences in the nature of the experience. So, for example, in work a young person is likely to experience authority and hierarchy in a different way from that of education and as a result will learn different things. They are also spending much more time with their peer group in educational settings. In addition, the nature of school experience has also changed over the last twenty years: for example, there has been a growing emphasis on testing and attainment, more participation in examinations, and young people are staying on at school longer. How these trends impact upon their wellbeing requires further work, but there are different implications for different groups. The trend towards more time being spent in education means having a different structure to the day, and young people not in education, employment or training (NEET) are those with the least structure. The implications for wellbeing of less interaction with adults, due to less time in work environments, of less structure, more unstructured time and more peer interaction, merit further research. However, we do know that there is a need for a clear structure from education to work, for managed transitions, and that this is not a straightforward pathway in our society. Transitions can be a time of vulnerability for young people, and especially for those who are most vulnerable, and in this case that encompasses those who are without education or employment (the NEET category).

Bronfenbrenner (2005) showed that factors interact and in this way the changes in how time is spent will be affected by other trends. Substance use has also altered amongst young people. There is greater availability of alcohol and other drugs, and yet there is also some evidence that levels of consumption have decreased recently. However, absolute levels of alcohol use amongst 11 to 15 year olds are higher than in most other countries and characterised by early onset, high volumes of intake, and binge drinking: 'Alcohol and substance use have been linked to depression, anxiety and conduct problems in young people' (Nuffield Foundation, 2012: 5). For the first time ever in the UK, adolescent mortality rates have overtaken those of infants aged between 1 and 4 years old (2012: 10). The emotional wellbeing of young people is also a public health issue.

Family structure has also undergone big changes (e.g., family reconstitution and increased breakdown, smaller family size, and more women going out to work). However, these are not necessarily the cause of emotional distress rather where there are high levels of conflict there is more likely to be distress. Conduct and emotional disorders increased over the last twenty years in all family types, but the rates in non-intact families tended to be higher than in intact families (20% in 2011, compared to 12% in 1999: Nuffield Foundation, 2012: 5). The Nuffield Foundation suggests that around 15 to 39% of the increased rates can be attributed to family causes and the rest to other factors. Parental stress has also increased during this time, as have self-reports on the quality of parenting. Most young people feel that their parental care is of a high quality (2012: 5).

This brief examination of the Nuffield study shows clearly the interrelationship between the various elements making up the system. The relationships described are trends and not causal, but they show the importance of looking at social trends to shape our understanding and work with emotional wellbeing in children and adolescents. So where does school feature in this landscape?

The role of the school in emotional wellbeing

General international comparisons of child wellbeing have focused upon the UK's poor record in comparison to other rich nations (UNICEF, 2007), placing the UK and USA in the bottom third on all measures except for the measure of health and safety in the UK. These statistics prompted much concern and soul searching in the UK (e.g., *The Good Childhood Inquiry* was generated from the UNICEF research; see Layard and Dunn, 2009). The part played by schools in this has also been hotly debated. There has long been an assumption that schools should be, and indeed are involved in, developing emotional wellbeing, and that as Resnick (2000: 159) has written, this involves 'the intentional, deliberative process of providing support, relationships, experience and opportunities that promote positive outcomes for young people'. There was in the late 1990s a surge of interest in, and focus upon, emotional wellbeing. The most populist example was Daniel Goleman's (1996) concept of 'emotional intelligence', which showed that in terms of success in life and work the place of emotional or social competence is more centre stage than academic attainment. Recently there has been a move to promote healthy development through schooling and to go beyond a problem-based focus (Resnick, 2000).

There have been both heated debates and policy initiatives related to the school role: some have argued vehemently that there is a rise in 'a therapeutic ethos' within schools, and that this is 'turning children, young people and adults into anxious and self-preoccupied individuals rather than aspiring, optimistic and resilient learners who want to know everything about the world' (Ecclestone and Hayes, 2009: i); other responses have included major policy initiatives aimed at developing emotional wellbeing, and placing counselling services within schools as part of mainstream provision for young people.

Policy makers have seen school as an important site for the development of emotional and social wellbeing, with the last Labour government's policy *Every Child Matters* (DfES, 2003), the *Social and Emotional Aspects of Learning* (DfES, 2005) programme from the Department for Education, and the Department for Health's (2004) wellbeing initiative the most recent prominent examples. The 1988 Education Reform Act (ERA) set education within the context of the spiritual, moral, cultural, mental and physical development of pupils and society, and also imposed a requirement to care for young people and 'prepare them for the opportunities, responsibilities and experiences of later life' (Department for Education, 1988: 2). There is currently some discussion about whether personal, social and moral education should be statutory, however this is a highly debated and contentious area of both the curriculum and schools' role.

. As has already been shown, we have a body of research on young people and the changes in their behaviour and emotional 'problems' (e.g., Rutter and Smith, 1995; Collishaw et al., 2010), and we also have a body of research on young people and schools' role in shaping identities and academic performance. However, we have little highly focused research on the contribution that schools make to adolescent mental health or wellbeing. This is, Gray et al. (2011: 1) argue, largely due to omission and the lopsided nature of research on educational outcomes. So what exactly do we know using the research we have to hand?

We know that when young people are asked, they rate school as playing a crucial part in their social and mental lives (Rudduck and Flutter, 2004: 76; Pople, 2009: 17–18). They value friendships and their relationships with teachers, as well as opportunities to have good experiences of mastery and learning. They are concerned about the school environment and the difficulties that can arise from relationships, especially bullying (McLaughlin et al., 2012). The school as a site for social developmental and interaction is a key one for young people.

We know also that effective schooling is a key asset for young people, enhancing their personal, social and emotional wellbeing and efficacy, and that school has an educative role of in terms of the personal and social aspects of development. We know as well that the capacity to form friendships and be engaged with school life and learning impacts upon wellbeing, but we also know that schools can intervene to improve those aspects of development, especially for vulnerable groups who may not have the resources that have encouraged this development elsewhere (McLaughlin et al., 2012.) This interconnection between the psychosocial and the academic or cognitive aspects of learning and schooling was first shown when Rutter (1991) demonstrated the long-term psychosocial effects of successful schooling, showing the chain reactions that occur. If a child leaves school with a sense of mastery and competence in skills, this will have an effect on their later capacity to be employed, be a good enough parent, and have a good enough partnership. Thus engaging in school life and learning is in itself emotionally and socially important. Research by Smith (2006: 4) showed the long-term implications and power of good attachment in schools. In his study of youth transition and crime in Edinburgh, he found that the attachment to school was:

> related to young people's behaviour more widely in school and more widely to delinquent and criminal conduct. Amongst these variables the most important dimension was attachment to teachers, but the belief that school success will bring later reward was also important. Attachment to teachers at age 13 was (also) related to lower levels of misbehaviour and delinquency at age 15. (2006: 4)

This has been more fully discussed elsewhere (McLaughlin and Clarke, 2010), but it led Roeser and colleagues to conclude that 'Perhaps the best mental health intervention teachers can implement in middle schools is good teaching' (2000: 458). If a young person feels that they belong in the classroom and school, that they are being successful in some aspects of learning, that they have some mastery and agency, then it is likely that they will have good feelings about themselves both as learners and people. They may then develop some resilience in struggling with problems and require some support along the way.

We know that schooling and learning are emotional and that emotion plays a large part in whether children can learn effectively. Views on learning now acknowledge the personal, social and emotional nature of learning (Greenhalgh, 1994; James and Pollard, 2006) and how emotional difficulties can affect this. We know that teaching is also a deeply emotional experience (Salzberger-Wittenberg et al., 1999) and that such emotion is not a problem area in teaching and learning but a central dimension to school life.

Gray et al. (2011: 21–43) concluded that despite the need for much greater research on the part that schools play in the development of emotional wellbeing there was evidence to support the notion of the 'supportive school' having a relationship to emotional wellbeing. The supportive school was characterised by students having a good connectedness to that school. There were five identified aspects to school connectedness:

1. Supportive relationships with peers and teachers.
2. Levels of young people's satisfaction with schools.
3. Young people's sense of membership of a learning community.
4. How schools handle academic pressures and the stresses associated with them.
5. Whether schools can make themselves accessible to young people by 'thinking small', and creating units that embue them with a sense of connection.

These elements emerge as having a strong part to play in emotional wellbeing, and suggest that paying wider attention to the school as a whole is necessary if emotional wellbeing is being considered.

From the preceding discussion it is clear that there is a strong, formative and long-lasting relationship between what happens in school between people, in the classroom and in the general school processes, and young people's social and emotional wellbeing. So what part does counselling in schools play in developing good mental health and emotional wellbeing?

Counselling in schools, mental health and emotional wellbeing

Counselling in schools has been seen to have a key role in emotional wellbeing and this has existed in different forms for many years. This section begins by describing the historical trends in counselling in schools over the last sixty years and then explores the issues around definition, role and effectiveness. It also draws heavily on historical reviews by Baginsky (2004) and McLaughlin (1999). What can be discerned from these two reviews is that there are many ideas and models that are deeply interconnected. How in different times the role of education, and particularly the role of the school in relation to the care of the child, is perceived, acted out and measured; all these elements have impacted upon how counselling is seen and defined. How one constructs the role of counselling in schools is heavily dependent upon a connected view of the purposes of education, the role of the teacher, and the nature of care in schools. It is also linked to the wider conceptions of boundaries and professionalism in the socio-political context of the time. Increasingly, the adopted or dominant model of the nature of knowledge and research effectiveness is impinging on counselling practice too.

An historical account

The notion of counselling in schools grew out of a tradition of 'pastoral care', or the notion that schools had some responsibility for the emotional wellbeing of their pupils (King, 1999; Baginsky, 2004). Child guidance and educational psychology preceded the arrival of school counsellors in the 1950s, while the 1960s saw a growth spurt in the employment of counsellors in schools. A government report on raising the school leaving age (the Newsom Report in 1963) proposed counsellors in schools, and thus training courses at universities in Keele and Reading were established, and the seminal ideas of Carl Rogers and others in the USA began to shape viewpoints in the UK. In addition, many people had gone out on scholarships to study counselling practices in the USA. Therefore, in the 1960s there was a growth of counsellors in schools, the beginning of a training network, and a deep interest in pastoral care in schools, and this was seen as part of the teacher's role that needed developing (McLaughlin, 1999; Baginsky, 2004). This continued throughout the 1970s and into the 1980s with an expansion in centres of counsellor training, and by 1977 Baginsky had reported that published research showed there were 351 counsellors employed in schools in England and Wales, though with 54% of them located in nine local education authorities (2004: 2).

Come the mid-1980s there was a huge change in the political context. The new Conservative government had a philosophy of education that did not include an expansion of the personal and social education occurring in schools, or an increased emphasis on a wider role for teachers. This was seen as a highly contested area of education, and together with huge financial cuts the outcome of this pincer movement was a huge reduction in school counsellors (McLaughlin, 1999).

During the late 1990s and into the 2000s there was an increase in, and development of, counselling and counsellors in schools. There was also an increased 'professionalisation' of counselling. The growth in counselling provision was connected to developments within and outside of schools. During this period the pressure on teachers and teachers' time grew, largely due to increased centralised control and bureaucracy. In 2003 the unions and the government negotiated a shift in terms and conditions. This agreement with the DfES (entitled *Raising Standards and Tackling Workload: A National Agreement*) aimed to improve the work-life balance for teachers after many years of rising concerns over excessive teacher workloads. As a result of this national agreement they would work a directed number of hours, classroom assistants would be employed, and many of them were given pastoral duties. There was also an emphasis on the 'teaching' aspect of being a teacher which gave rise to a change in many teachers' perceptions of the boundaries of their role: and this could be said to have become more restricted and narrow. Schools therefore had to find different ways of responding to the needs of young people, and one way in which they did that was to employ support staff. Many of these were given pastoral roles, and in addition counselling and support services became the province of specialists.

The 1990s were a time of extraordinary educational change. The educational reforms brought with them numerous impacts and many of these fell on vulnerable young people. Exclusion rates rose and this can be credited to an array of complex factors: competition between schools; the aforementioned changes to teachers' conditions of service; changes to the curriculum; and an increased emphasis on standards and standardisation (Baginsky, 2004; McLaughlin, 1999; Watkins, 1999). The high inspection regime, accountability and competition between schools had made vulnerable pupils, particularly those with emotional and behavioural difficulties, less able to be maintained in 'comprehensive schools', and so many vulnerable children were located in specialist units and schools which were outside the mainstream school system. Recently there have been very different trends and these could be said to be pulling in various directions. There has been a greater increase and acceptance of counselling and counselling approaches in schools, greater use of specialist counsellors, and less incorporation of what Hamblin (1974) and others have called 'applied counselling skills', or 'first level skills', which he saw as the province of all teachers. However, this is not to say that the relational aspects of teaching are not highly valued today.

The other big change, which mirrors the field of practice generally, has been the shift from person-centred approaches towards a wider array of theoretical models and techniques. The use of cognitive approaches has increased in schools and many of the techniques are widely understood. There has also been the large-scale adoption of counselling in various parts of the United Kingdom, and most notably in Wales where in April 2008 the Welsh government rolled out the National Strategy for School-based Counselling Services, informed by Pattison et al's (2007) report, which had identified 'standards of practice and the frameworks needed to deliver high quality and sustainable services'.

The Welsh strategy aimed to ensure that counselling services were available in all Welsh secondary schools, along with the piloting of primary school services in four local authorities. This is the biggest systematic attempt to adopt counselling in schools in the UK to date. There are many other organisations (such as the Place2Be and Kids Company) that are engaging in therapeutic work, but the Welsh example has been large scale and evaluated at the various stages. The conclusions of the evaluation were that:

> Participation in counselling was associated with large reductions in psychological distress; with levels of improvement that, on average, were somewhat greater than those found in previous evaluations of UK school-based counselling. Key recommendations are that permanent funding mechanisms should be established to embed counselling in the Welsh secondary school sector, with consideration given to its roll-out into primary schools. (Hill et al., 2011: 6)

In this strategy school-based counselling is viewed as 'a skilled way of helping young people with personal and developmental difficulties provided by professional practitioners' (2011: 7). It aims to give them opportunities to:

- discuss difficulties in a confidential and non judgemental atmosphere
- explore the nature of their difficulties
- increase their self-awareness
- develop a better understanding of their difficulties
- develop the personal resources needed to manage their problems
- develop strategies to cope with change. (2011: 10)

The work of counselling is mostly with individuals, but includes working closely with school staff and agencies to provide a complementary service to other interventions in school 'that support and promote young people's emotional health and wellbeing' (2011: 10).

In the most recent UK study of counselling in schools Cooper reviews the field and acknowledges that the term counselling in schools is 'Increasingly ... being reserved for the activities of professionally trained counsellors (2013: 3). He also cites the British Association for Counselling and Psychotherapy's definition of school-based counselling, which is 'a professional activity delivered by qualified practitioners in schools. Counsellors offer troubled and/or distressed children and young people an opportunity to talk about their difficulties, within a relationship of agreed confidentiality' (2013: 3). Counselling in the UK is characterised by a relational approach, as opposed to the guidance emphasis of US counsellors in schools, and is mostly individual rather than group or family focused.

Cooper concludes that 'school-based counselling is one of the most widely delivered forms of psychological therapy for young people in the UK', that it is highly valued by young people and those involved in their care, and it 'appears to be producing positive effects (2013: 22). The strength of school-based counselling is that it can provide 'an easily accessible mental health intervention for:

> any young person struggling with difficulties in their lives, and particularly those who may have no-one else to turn to'. (2013: 22)

At the beginning of this section, the question of the part counselling in schools plays in developing good mental health and emotional well-being was posed. There is now strong evidence to show that counselling in schools is successful in reducing the distress of young people and is successful as a site for this work. There are also well developed models now for working in schools and on a large scale in both primary and secondary schools.

Conclusion

If we take a critical look at the field and return Bronfenbrenner's ecological approach, what other reflections can we make? Twenty years ago (McLaughlin, 1993) I argued for three elements: an *educative* function (i.e., to develop students personally and socially in the context of the school); a *reflective* function (i.e., an exploration of the possible impact of and contribution to personal and social development and mental health of practices in the classroom and other aspects of the school community); and a *welfare* function (i.e., the responsibility to plan for and react to issues which impact on students' welfare). These functions are still very important, but the words we use today may well have changed in the interim, and thus 'welfare' is not much in evidence nowadays, and instead we have the 'care or therapeutic function'. It is this third function which seems to have become dominant and largely the province of a specialised service made up of professional counsellors. Paralleling this is a shift in terms of the language in which counselling in schools is discussed, with a move towards a more medicalised language and model. There has also been a shift towards the dominance of the medical or experimental mode of research, so the NICE model as the benchmark of good research is threaded through much of the discussion in BACP documents for example.

I began with a quotation from Bronfenbrenner, who argued that:

> Human beings create the environments that shape the course of human development. Their actions influence the multiple physical and cultural tiers of the ecology that shapes them, and this agency makes humans – for better or for worse – active producers of their own development. (Bronfenbrenner, 2005: xxvii)

If this is the case then the function that needs most development, and which has largely disappeared from the discussions on counselling in schools, is the *reflective* one. In a greatly altered educational landscape dominated by accountability and measurement, one which is affecting the wellbeing of our young people (Gray et al., 2011), this reflective function is a brave one for counsellors to engage in. It is interesting to note that many of the early pioneers in counselling and counselling in schools became interested in, and wrote about, the learning process and schools as organisations for health or good guidance communities. Examples of this are Rogers' *Freedom to Learn for the 80's* or William Glasser's *Choice Theory in the Classroom*. These books go beyond a discussion of working with individuals and engage in a wider discussion of how schools and their values and processes can engage in, and impact upon, the wellbeing of young people in their care. This element of the discussion is not very visible and given the research on the power of the school as an organisation to impact upon the wellbeing of young people, then this is a significant loss.

PART 2

Understanding and Working with the Developmental Tasks of Childhood and Adolescence

TWO Infancy: The foundations of learning and relating

Julia Buckroyd

These foundations [of how human beings become fully human and how they learn to relate emotionally to others] are laid during pregnancy and in the first two years of life. This is when the 'social brain' is shaped and when an individual's emotional style and emotional resources are established (Gerhardt, 2004: 3).

This chapter will discuss the emotional development of children up to 2 years old and consider the likely significance of this period of life for learning and later formal education. The chapter will consider three major topics: the environmental setting, both physical and emotional, into which the child is born; the child's genetic inheritance, including inherited personality traits; and the relationship between the child and its primary caregivers. These three areas constitute the matrix within which the child develops and are mutually interactive (Gerhardt, 2004).

The environmental setting

Trainee therapists are sometimes given an exercise to make them more aware of the material and emotional environment into which they were born and how those circumstances are relevant and have effects on all of us: they are asked to imagine the situation in which they were conceived; their parents' attitude to the pregnancy; the material circumstances into which they were born; the support available to their mothers; and the meaning of their birth to their parents. Of course this exercise involves considerable imaginative re-construction for most people, but it is not difficult to see that there can be major differences in circumstances. A 17 year old from a deprived background, whose unplanned child was conceived in a short-term relationship and who has no means of earning her living, may depend heavily on her own mother, who may or may not be willing to give the intensive support that such a young woman will need to look after her baby's insistent demands. That child may be seen as a disaster for the mother, standing in the way of her opportunities for education and employment, and even as a disaster for the grandmother who has been drawn back into intensive child care. Alternatively, that child may be the means for the mother to separate from her own mother, to gain status and attention as the mother of a child and perhaps to have meaning for her life. At the opposite end of the socio-economic spectrum, a baby born to a woman in her mid-thirties in a stable relationship, whose partner can support her financially and emotionally in caring for a much-wanted child, will have far fewer stresses on her, especially if she is also supported within a social (think Mumsnet, the NCT, a mother and baby group) or wider family circle. Conversely, that mother may be desperate to return to work and may find the task of attending to a tiny baby boring and frustrating. A mother who is living in a war or refugee situation will have extraordinary anxieties and difficulties to contend with in caring for a newborn, when the most basic requirements of food, shelter and safety may all be in short supply. Whether she can begin to manage a baby adequately will depend greatly on what support is available to her in these demanding circumstances (Macksoud and Aber, 1996; Dybdahl, 2001).

Jaffee et al. (2006) are among those who have emphasised that adequate material circumstances and extensive support can enable mothers to be more responsive to their children. It stands to reason that mothers who are preoccupied by difficult material circumstances or taxing emotional conditions will have less energy to devote to their children. And this environment is all the more important if the child in question is unwell or handicapped in any way: at the same time as adjusting to a new role as a mother, the woman and her partner may well be grieving the loss of their hoped-for perfect and healthy child (Sinason, 1992). It is hard to make major adjustments in different directions at the same time. It would be surprising if such a mother did not find that her resources for looking after her baby were under strain.

Uterine and neonatal development

What that exercise in reflecting on their beginnings implied for trainees was the importance of what happened to mother and baby before that baby was even born: 'Too often in our approach to the newborn we deal with him as if he is exactly that, "brand new". We neglect the fact that the neonate is really the culmination of an amazing experience that has lasted 40 weeks' (Brazelton, 1982: 2). In recent years, however, it has become much clearer that the nine months making up a pregnancy and the development of the foetus are profoundly affected by the mother's social and emotional wellbeing. At the extreme end of the spectrum are conditions such as foetal alcohol syndrome, when the child's development *in utero* will be severely affected by the mother's alcohol misuse (Hanson et al., 1976). At a more ordinary level, the foetus will be the recipient of nutrition and a whole range of biochemicals delivered across the placenta via the shared blood supply. Deficiencies in nutrition will predispose an individual to illness in later life (Barker, 1998). In an optimum situation the mother will be at ease with her pregnancy, will have no pressing anxieties and be relaxed and content. Her nutrition will be good and so the baby will develop physically in a normal way. She is likely, because she feels content, to deliver oxytocin to her baby, which will both soothe the foetus, engender a baby that is easy to soothe after birth, and prepare it for continuing to produce oxytocin after birth. Conversely, if the mother is anxious and under stress – financial, relational – she will be producing significant amounts of cortisol, the stress hormone, and will produce a more agitated baby *in utero* and one who will be more difficult to soothe after birth (Wadhwa et al., 2001; Gerhardt, 2004).

At birth the child will already have had an extensive experience of the birth mother (Liley, 1972). In the nine-month process of pregnancy the foetus experiences the mother's heartbeat and bloodflow and internal physical processes of digestion, and in later months hears the mother's voice (Trevarthen and Marwick, 1986). While still *in utero* it practises sucking and swallowing the amniotic fluid and may also suck its thumb (Popescu et al., 2008). It will respond to stimuli, for instance music (Gerhardt and Abrams, 1996), and be capable of greater activity or what seems like sleep (Peirano et al., 2003). It seems that via the mother's diet, the foetus will even have developed taste preferences by the time it is born (Mennella, 2013). When the child emerges from the womb, therefore, it is already accustomed to the mother. Immediately after birth the baby will prefer the smell of the mother to other smells, and the sound of the mother's voice to other sounds. From birth the baby will also be focused on its mother's face (Braten, 1998). Not surprisingly, a baby who is taken away from its mother at this early stage, for health reasons or for early adoption, will register this separation, not cognitively perhaps, but in some nameless feeling of loss or absence: 'The unresolved grief around the loss of the first mother gives the child an underlying sadness that manifests as low-grade depression.

The fear of another abandonment is expressed as an ever present anxiety' (Verrier, 2009 [1993]: xvi).

Genetic inheritance

However, this baby also comes with a genetic inheritance that is both physical and temperamental. That inheritance will determine much of what the child looks like and probably its susceptibility to illness. The science of epigenetics examines how genetic inheritance is translated into active characteristics via a person's interaction with the environment (Egger et al., 2004). The capacity to put on weight easily and lose it with difficulty is, for example, probably characteristic of the genetic inheritance of 70 to 80% of us, but this has only been translated into very high percentages of overweight and obese people because our environment now provides inexpensive and accessible food in a way that is new for human beings (Barness et al., 2007). Likewise, some of us will be vulnerable to mental illness. When that genetic inheritance meets prolonged cannabis use, it will greatly increase the risk of resulting mental illness (Semple et al., 2005). Genetics will also determine much of a child's temperament (Saudine, 1996). Resilience, for example, seems to be largely innate. I had a colleague who was adopted at the age of five months. For those five months he lived in an institution and since we are talking about the 1940s it is hard to imagine that the quality or consistency of his care was good. Nevertheless, he was able to recover from that very adverse beginning, bond to his adoptive parents and live a productive and satisfactory life, making friendships and intimate relationships. Surely this was a child who was born with an unusual degree of resilience, although he was also exceedingly fortunate in his adoptive parents. Cognitive capacity is also innate, but is a very obvious example of a characteristic that can be modified for better or worse by the environment. In particular, it is clear that a benign and enabling environment (such as may be provided by a secure attachment) will have the best prospect of maximising cognitive functioning (Howe, 2011).

Attachment

Whatever that uterine experience or genetic inheritance, babies are born, with rare exceptions, ready, willing and able to relate (Trevarthen and Aitken, 2001). They will use their eyes and their feet to register interest and engagement and seem to be primed to interact – to be prosocial (Hay, 1994). Treatment of depressed mothers has shown how a baby in these circumstances will try hard to engage with its mother. As humans we are born with an immature brain and will be extraordinarily dependent on our mother, indeed far more so than other mammals (Howe, 2011). In these circumstances our innate capacity, known as attachment behaviour, to attach to our mother is a vital survival instinct. (It seems that babies need one, or at most a few, primary caregivers. This person is usually the mother, however many babies/children are cared for by persons other than the mother, for example, a grandmother, older sibling, foster or adoptive mother. For the sake of brevity the primary caregiver will be called the mother in this chapter, but the reader should remember that there are other possibilities.)

John Bowlby was the author who first provided a coherent account of attachment behaviour (1969, 1973, 1980). He built on the work of ethologists who had observed animal behaviour and the attachment of animal young to their parents and those who had observed children's relationships with their primary caregiver, such as the documentary makers, the Robertsons (www.robertsonfilms.info). They filmed the effect on toddlers of separation from their primary attachment figure – in their case, the mother. The heart-rending images of small children attempting to cope with sudden separation and the chronicling of the dramatic and lasting harm done to them was one of the influences which began to change policies about visiting hours in hospitals for parents and children, and made researchers such as Bowlby acutely aware of the importance of the mother-child relationship.

Bowlby proposed that attachment behaviour on the part of the child was innate and an evolutionary benefit designed to maintain its safety. He identified the child's major need as proximity: when a small child is near its mother, it is much safer than if it strays away or if the mother leaves it unattended. This behaviour evolved when home was no more than a cave and the ground was unprotected by coverings, but it is still visible and active in us now. So, for example, if a mother moves from one room to another, her crawling/toddling infant will follow her, and her immobile baby will soon register a protest. Attachment behaviour's second purpose is to enable the child to use the mother as a refuge from perceived danger, so, for example, if a stranger comes to the house, a small child will hide behind its mother until it feels safe enough to venture away from her. Any fright or upset, for instance a loud noise, or a fall, will make it immediately seek the comfort and safety of its mother. The third purpose of attachment behaviour is to enable the child to use the mother as a safe base from which to make expeditions, so, for example, if they go to the park, the child will play in the sandpit with the mother nearby, but will make return visits to her to ensure that the safe base is still there, before venturing out again.

The next phase of Bowlby's work involved distinguishing between the various forms of attachment that were observed between child and parent. This was the work of Bowlby's colleagues Mary Ainsworth and Mary Main. Ainsworth developed an experimental situation called the 'Strange Situation' (Ainsworth et al., 1978; Wallin, 2007), designed to place mild stress on the young child's attachment bonds with the idea of being better able to evaluate how those bonds were operating. This process involved creating a laboratory situation where the child was left by the mother for a brief period when a stranger came into the room, and who when later left the mother returned.

What Ainsworth discovered was that not all infants responded in the same way and not all mothers interacted with their child in the same way (Wallin, 2007; Howe, 2011). Approximately 60% of toddlers demonstrated what Ainsworth called 'secure attachment'. In this scenario the mother was able to play and interact with her child in a way that showed her capacity to engage with it and enabled the child's play. She neither ignored the child, nor was over-directive; she allowed the child to determine the activity and developed the play in a positive and enjoyable way. So, for instance, if the child was playing with a train she might make train noises and show them how to hook a carriage to the train. She might then create a story round the train – 'Where shall we go today in the train? Shall we go to the park?' In the words of Daniel Stern (1985), a later developmental psychologist, she encourages 'proximal development', reaching for a further stage that is still within the child's capacity. When the stresses of the Strange Situation make the child (mildly) distressed, she comforts it quickly and appropriately, and when the child is comforted allows it to return to play. The secure child can be readily comforted and will return to play easily.

The characteristics of a mother's caregiving that will enable her child to be securely attached are that she is available (physically and emotionally) responsive, 'attuned', (Stern, 1985), and consistent. The child can rely on her rapid, appropriate, consistent response to its need and especially to powerful feelings, such as anger, distress or fright. The result is likely to be a relatively happy and contented child: 'Well-managed babies come to expect a world that is responsive to feelings and helps to bring intense states back to a comfortable level; through the experience of having it done for them, they learn how to do it for themselves' (Gerhardt, 2004: 19).

This child can engage freely with others in its world and begin to learn the vast number of skills that small children need to acquire, such as gross and fine motor control. It is likely to be curious and interested in whatever stimulus is presented, having learned from its caregivers that investigation and exploration will produce rewarding results. This experience will provide the ideal foundations for learning at playgroup, nursery, and eventually school. At the same time the child is learning that other people can be counted on to help and respond to its needs and desires. When it cries it will be attended to; when it is hungry it will be promptly fed. This baby will be stimulated by play and engagement with others and will learn how to initiate as well as respond to contact with those in its world. As a result its brain development will be optimised and it will have internalised the benign caregiver and the capacity to self soothe by the production of soothing brain chemicals (Schore, 2003a, 2003b). By the time this child goes to playgroup it will have a positive disposition towards others and be able to interact with the care staff at the playgroup, as well as enjoy the company of other children. Well before it is 2 years old this baby will be capable of creativity, games and jokes, have an increasing command of language, and will be using that language to express its needs and desires in progressively more sophisticated ways. In this fashion it will participate in the relationship with its caregivers and enable the development of that relationship.

Unfortunately all of this still leaves about 40% of the population who are not so lucky, for whom the general label is 'insecurely attached'. The circumstances which produce various styles of insecure attachment have been divided into three groups: avoidant attachment; anxious or ambivalent attachment; and disorganised attachment (Wallin, 2007; Howe, 2011). These differing experiences are likely to have a huge (and often lifelong and damaging) impact on how a tiny child will then live its life (Gerhardt, 2004).

The current concensus suggests that about 20% of us will develop an avoidant style of attachment, although some research suggests as many as 25%, and cultural differences also exist (Prior and Glaser, 2006). The message we get from our caregivers is that they are unable to attend to our (physical and) emotional needs and we must manage these ourselves. This message may be conveyed verbally by expressions such as 'Stop crying for goodness sake, you never leave me alone', or 'Don't make such a fuss, I'm coming as fast as I can', but with an infant this will more often be conveyed by slowness and a reluctance in attending to the child. A child may be left to cry, for example, or not fed promptly enough, or not picked up and soothed enough, or not played with and stimulated enough. This does not necessarily imply that the mother is actively hostile or ill-disposed towards the child (although it can mean that), but usually that she is overwhelmed by what she has to deal with herself, and will also reveal how her own needs were attended to as she grew up. Many women with small babies are managing demanding situations which will overwhelm their coping capacity.

As a trainee counsellor I worked in a neurosurgery unit as part of a chaplaincy team, offering a listening ear to the patients and relatives there, who very often were facing life-threatening illnesses (Buckroyd, 1992). Part of the unit was devoted to the care of babies and small children with neurological problems. The parents of these children varied enormously in how they coped with the situation. Some were able to offer sustained soothing and comfort to their tiny children: they spent many hours with their child and according to its capacity offered stimulus and comfort. Others, presumably demonstrating an ongoing pattern, were incapable of focusing on their child: they would retreat to the dayroom and the company of other mothers, leaving it alone to cry and survive as best it could on its own. At the time I felt very judgmental about these mothers, but since then I have been able to reflect on their lack of resources in a testing situation, and speculate about their inability to engage with their child's pain in this extreme situation. These are mothers who, for whatever reason, have learned to cut themselves off from their child's feelings (and probably from their own). Doing so is a survival mechanism.

In less extreme circumstances the children of mothers who cannot bear their infants' distress will learn not to show it. In the descriptions of the Strange Situation, for example, the avoidantly attached child seemed not to be aware of their mother's leaving and returning, and would even turn their back on her. However, heart monitors revealed such children were just as distressed as those who more obviously showed the effects of the experience: 'Their heart rates during the separation experience are as elevated as those of their visibly distressed but secure peers while the rise in their level of cortisol ... pre- to post-procedure is significantly greater than that of secure infants' (Wallin, 2007:19).

I once watched a mother and her small child in a carpark. The child was trotting alongside the mother who was busy with her mobile phone. He then tripped and fell – bare legs on gravel – and must have been both hurt and frightened. Despite this, the mother did not halt her conversation for a second, instead she wordlessly picked the child up and stowed him in the back of the car. She made no acknowledgement whatsoever of his experience. He looked distressed but made no sound – he already knew what he must do.

But what does this experience do to an infant? David Howe (2011) is emphatic that children will develop whichever attachment pattern is most likely to achieve the goal of maintaining proximity to their mother. If protesting and crying are counter-productive, a child will learn to keep quiet in the hope that with this strategy the mother may be induced to keep him with her, rather than remove him from her. As a preparation for learning, however, this is not a good strategy. Infants need all sorts of help (reaching for things, finding things, and manipulating things for instance); if a child has already learned by the time it goes to playgroup or nursery that others are unlikely to help, then its learning will be limited. This is the toddler who sits passively on the edge of the group watching other children, who makes no demands on the carers, and who will probably be ignored while more vocal children in the group capture those carers' attention. At this stage such a child is incapable of conscious calculation, but the experience will have already led him to expect very little from others.

Of the 40% of insecurely attached infants, 15% or so are said to be ambivalently or anxiously attached. The experience these children will have had will be one of intermittent care: they have 'now you see me, now you don't' caregivers, mothers who are sometimes available (physically and/or emotionally) and sometimes not. This means the child's experience is one of inconsistent, unreliable care. This mother may well have many demands on her: even though she wants to attend to her child, and is capable of doing so, other factors prevent her from doing so consistently. This child has had enough care to know that there is something more to be had, some good experiences of being with the mother. The response that child will give, when she is intermittently absent or unavailable, will be to 'turn up the volume' (Howe, personal communication) to protest, in the conviction that this will persuade her to demonstrate the care the child knows she can give. These infants learn early on to watch out for times when the mother can attend to them and will take advantage of such opportunities. Mothers in this situation will often feel guilty about their failure to offer more consistent care, and guilt may bring about impatience – 'Just a minute, for goodness sake'. This is the mother who may well have many other responsibilities: perhaps she has financial problems which mean she can't be there as much as she would like, or maybe she has many other demands on her time – other children, sick or elderly parents, a demanding partner.

A current advert on television shows a harassed young mother trying to look after her infant, a dog and someone on the phone, all at the same time. In her haste and distraction she gives the dog the child's food and the child the dog's food. More serious circumstances can however have more serious effects. Nicola Horlick, the well-known hedge fund manager, had six children: we can imagine that hedge fund management did not leave her huge amounts of time to spend with her children. Tragically, her eldest child contracted leukaemia and she made the decision that she would have to prioritise this child's needs – which of course meant that in the circumstances the needs of her other children were relegated to second place. In the year before her eldest child died, those other children must have experienced much less of their mother's attention than would have otherwise been the case.

Strange Situation research shows that these kinds of carers are less attuned to the needs of their infants than those whose care produces secure attachment. Presumably, because they are distracted by other demands, and/or have little experience of attuned care themselves, they will tend to misjudge children's play, and indeed their interventions may over-ride a child's initiatives. If that child is playing with a train, a less-attuned mother may say 'Oh, let's play with the racing car'. This then requires the infant to abandon its own game in order to achieve its attachment aim of maintaining proximity with the mother. Understandably this makes for less calm and contented infants, and also undermines the child's clarity about its own desires (i.e., I was playing with the train; oh, no, that wasn't right; I need to play with the car). Our capacity to know our own desires and wants is central to the development of the self. I work with many adolescent girls who have been over-managed since they were tiny children, and the effect by their mid-teens is that they will have absolutely no idea about their own authentic desires and preferences, but they are able to speak volumes about what others want *from* them and *for* them. The roots of such uncertainty lie in very early experiences.

Anxious/ambivalently attached infants are harder to manage. They have the prevailing feeling of never having quite enough of what they need and so they can be clinging. Alternatively, they can be the kind of child who makes a great deal of fuss, presumably in an attempt to secure their carer's attention for as long as possible. Unlike the avoidantly attached child, they have discovered that protest is effective in ensuring the carer's focus, but in doing so they can give that carer the feeling that their needs can never be satisfied. The relationship can then feel less rewarding to the carer (i.e., a lot of hard work) which may in turn increase that person's lack of consistency and availability. One mother told me that before she returned home from work in the afternoon she would stop off at a local pub to fortify herself against re-entering her relationship with her 'difficult' child.

Thus far all of these attachment patterns I have described are along a continuum. At the extremes of a lack of response or inconsistency children will demonstrate significant effects, which will be enough to interfere with their capacity to relate to others or learn. There is, however, a further type of attachment experience that by definition is likely to cause serious damage to the emotional (and perhaps physical) development of the child, and that is disorganised attachment (Shemmings and Shemmings, 2011). This category was first observed and articulated by Mary Main and describes those children whose caregivers, instead of offering help, are actively hostile towards them. These are the parents/caregivers whose children are abused or even killed by the parents themselves. Accounts of the tortured lives of these infants are usually only available from court records or case notes where abuse has come to the attention of social workers or the police, yet it is a dynamic which can also be seen on the streets and in the supermarkets of any town in the UK. I can think of two examples that I have observed in the past: a small child in a pushchair, protesting at something, whose mother came round to face him and then hit him in the face; and another small child who was similarly being wheeled along protesting in a supermarket trolley whose father lifted her out of the trolley and then smacked her. In both of these situations neither of the children could have been more than 2 years old.

From a child's point of view, behaviour that has been designed to elicit help, to manage powerful feelings (of anger, distress, discomfort, etc.), has been met by harm and violence and the parent's equally dis-regulated feelings. The result is that the child cannot adopt any rational course of action to meet its attachment needs and is at a complete loss as to what to do with its distress: '[In the Strange Situation] the research-ers noticed that some children behaved oddly when their carer returned. They saw children who, on reunion with the parent, would begin to approach the carer, but then stop suddenly in their tracks and not move for 15–20 seconds; or they would hold up their hands in front of their face ... They noticed that many of the children had been abused and/or neglected' (Shemmings and Shemmings, 2011: 33). These are the tod-dlers who will have huge difficulty fitting in to playgroup or nursery; whose behaviour is likely to be randomly violent or passive; whose capacity to interact with other children will be grossly inept; who will have little expectation that carers will soothe, protect and help; and whose capacity to learn will be badly damaged. Such a child will prob-ably by 2 years old already be failing to make developmental mile-stones, will have poor concentration, and be retarded in its speech development. Sadly, these are also the children who, if removed from neglectful or abusive parents, will often find it difficult to attach to foster or adoptive parents and may never be able to trust others.

The importance of all this work on infant attachment is that the experience of the young child is powerful in establishing 'templates' or explanatory models for the way that child approaches the world and particularly other people. As Gerhardt (2004) emphasises, these early experiences create patterns for life which will be difficult to modify, even in very young children, and will have a huge influence on their capacity to learn and relate. Even more fundamentally these will also affect brain development: the more gross the early experience, the more obvious is this effect (as we saw for example in the damaged brain development of Romanian orphans left unstimulated and unloved; see Chugani et al., 2001). It seems that if an appropriate stimulus and relationship are absent until the age of 3, the chances of mending the damage are very poor.

However, at this very early stage careful and informed reparative parenting can have some hope of repairing less profound early damage, which may then leave the child with a relatively intact capacity to learn. A recent novel, *Unexpected Lessons in Love*, described how a grandmother, Cecelia, had taken charge of a child abandoned by his mother at two months, and how her care enabled him as a toddler to recover from that trauma:

> There was an abiding sense of their having survived, survived something that could have been fatal for him, and survived it together; and a sense that it was because of her that he was unscathed, and had a mind that was able lightly and joyously to fasten completely on his little cars, and how to make them run, one by one, down a tilted board, each in turn received by Cecelia. (Bishop, 2013: 210)

It is hard to believe, and indeed perhaps we don't want to believe, that so much happens in a child's life in their first two years. We might prefer to believe that children do not know and cannot remember, yet all the evidence suggests that the matrix of genetic inheritance, material circumstances, and the nature of the care given will together determine much of a child's future. Later experience can and may modify that original template, so we must hope that children are fortunate and that the relationships they encounter and the environments in which they learn can maximise the possibility of optimum development.

THREE Pre-school and the Early Years

Fiona Peacock

In this chapter we look at the developmental phases that coincide with the pre-school and foundation/early years experiences of children, roughly from 3 years old through to age 6. This period in a child's development will be referred to as 'pre-latency'. Infancy is seen as the pre-verbal stage of children's development, and latency as traditionally related to the time in a child's life when infantile sexuality was repressed (Mitchell, 1986): this can generally be seen to start around the age of 6 or 7. Teachers will often recognise the term 'the magic 7', which is a point around about 7 years of age when children's thinking seems to change quite dramatically, and they seem more able to manage concepts and abstractions.

We will examine what happens for children during pre-latency where there is a good-enough attachment experience. We will also consider the significant challenges that children face when their attachment experiences have, for whatever reason, left a mark through anxious or disorganised attachment behaviours. In particular, the chapter will look at Theraplay® as a model of intervention.

Developmental tasks for early years children

Erikson (1995) identified the second of his eight ages of man as being occupied with issues of shame and doubt versus autonomy. Through the experiences in this stage Erikson suggested that the growing child works through issues of 'love and hate, cooperation and wilfulness, freedom of self expression and its suppression. From a sense of self control without loss of self esteem comes a lasting sense of good will and pride; from a sense of loss and self control and of foreign overcontrol comes a lasting propensity for doubt and shame' (Erikson, 1994: 228). This stage of development is followed by one of initiative versus guilt.

Shame and doubt versus autonomy would seem to be predominant in the early stages of pre-school settings, where as the child progresses through to the foundation/early years and year 1 the issues of initiative and guilt begin to predominate.

Here we have to consider the central role of shame, and following on from this guilt, in the expression of a child's attachment experience. Kate Cairns (2002) writes about reintegrative shame as significant in the attachment process and sees shame as an affect, something that precedes feeling or emotion. Shame is undoubtedly an uncomfortable affect and most infants would have a drive to reduce shame affects. In essence, this enables a child to curb some of their impulses in order to retain emotional proximity to their caregiver through not stirring up a negative reaction from that individual.

A toddler, exploring the world as is natural and necessary at this stage of development, gets very close to an electrical socket. To the child this is just another thing to explore and there is no sense of danger. The caregiver, in anxiety shouts 'Stop it, that's naughty!' The attunement between child and caregiver is ruptured; the toddler drops her head, hides her face, and lowers her gaze. She cries.

For the securely attached toddler, in an environment that gives a good enough daily experience of affective attunement, this shame-based affect is quickly addressed through a reparative process between child and caregiver. Mummy might say 'Oh I'm sorry I made you feel bad by shouting but I was worried you'd get hurt. Electric sockets are dangerous' while holding the toddler in her lap and soothing her disregulated and shame-filled child. In this way the child's personhood is restored. They will not attempt to stick their fingers in the socket again, not because their under-developed prefrontal cortex has processed that this is not safe, but because they wish to retain that emotional proximity to the caregiver. At the same time, however, their curiosity to explore the world (safely) is not impaired. This process of shame followed by reparation Cairns calls 'reintegrative shame'. Where there is no reparation the child is left with a sense that it is they themselves who are shameful and there is a sense of disintegration rather than reintegration. Such internal feeling may then incline the child to give up exploration or, alternatively, continue with dangerous exploration if that at least gains some attention from the primary caregiver.

The process of the shame-inhibiting impulse is at its most active in individuals between 9 and 18 months old (Hughes, 1998). However, it is still a significant function in the early stages of transition from the family group to new groups of peers and other adults. Such patterns, as with all the early attachment experiences, will once again be activated when the child is under stress. Starting pre-school or 'big' school could be such times.

Winnicott (1965: 16), drawing on Freud's writing, connected guilt with the anxiety that was felt because of the conflict between love and hate: 'Guilt-sense implies the tolerance of ambivalence'. Guilt could, therefore, be conceptualised as a reaction that holds the potential for a connection with others, and unaddressed shame is an experience of separation.

Winnicott (1965a), in exploring other relevant developmental process in pre-latency, suggested that there was a progression from absolute dependence in infancy to relative dependence and then independence. Relative dependence starts to occur when the mother (or primary caregiver) sensitively fails the child followed by appropriate reparation for those failings. For Winnicott, relative independence coincided with the beginning of intellectual understanding.

This seems to connect to the neurobiological understanding that right brain functions predominate in infants, but the left brain comes into greater play when language is used to convey meaning. Chiron et al. (1997) found, by measuring cerebral bloodflow, that between 1 and 3 years of age this bloodflow showed a right hemispheric predominance. However, this would then shift to the left after age 3. Schore (2011b) has also highlighted similar processes. As the process of relative independence continues perhaps the child develops a capacity to process loss out of a growing ability to manage complex emotions through conceptualisation (e.g., they might form more of an intellectual container for the loss: 'Mummy has just gone for a bit but I know she will be back soon').

The process towards independence is not a cutting-off of ties with the primary caregiver but a widening of relational ties and the establishment of interdependence. Significant in the process towards independence is the capacity to communicate (e.g., a teacher or peer saying 'Mummy will be there at the end of the day').

This shift from needing the object to be physically there to being able to hold on to an internalised image or construct of the mother gives the child a growing sense of their inner life being independent of the mother object, and also enables them to feel that this inner life, external events and reality interact with one another.

If emotional developmental processes are met in a good-enough way then a child will be able to identify with society and a widening social circle. Winnicott (1965) suggested these processes were active pre-latency and again in puberty.

Work by people such as Allan Schore (2012) and Bruce Perry (2006) has focused on when the child's developmental processes are compromised by poor attachment experiences, alternatively known as developmental or relational trauma. Schore (2012) points out how the development of the right brain is compromised by relational trauma and how this then impacts on children's subsequent development. Perry (2006) examines the neurobiological sequencing of treatment to address the impact of relational trauma (i.e., the therapeutic repair work needs to start at the age/stage where the damage occurred in relational/neurobiological developmental terms).

From these ideas, one might suggest that supporting the right brain developments of all children pre-latency may give a positive foundation for a fruitful and creative interdependence between people, adults and children in the learning environment.

Play as a tool for development

In infancy Winnicott (1971) suggested that play would be a way of showing the outside world the inner world of the child. In infancy, when a child is still in a state of absolute dependence, it is the facilitating environment through the relationship with the primary caregiver that provides an external ego to shape and give meaning to this 'play'. However, as infancy and absolute dependency moves to pre-latency and relative dependency play then takes on a more personal role in enabling a child to discover the self.

Culturally and linguistically it is easy to minimise the importance of play. Cattanach (2008) suggests some professionals see play as being of less value than talking or undertaking a focused activity in a therapeutic encounter, with 'What did you do today?' rather than 'How were you today?' often being the greeting as the child or group of children return to the formal learning environment from a therapeutic encounter. The learning environment in school tends to have a greater focus on cognitive achievement as is shown by a focus on 'what you are doing' or WALTs (we are learning to). Even in therapy, Cattanach (2008) suggests play can sometimes be viewed as a background task, something that is there to facilitate the talking, and therefore a 'proper' therapeutic process.

Vygotsky (1933) challenged the whole idea of objects in play holding a symbolic function for children. He suggested that 'in play the child creates the structure meaning/object, in which the semantic aspect – the meaning of the thing – dominates and determines his behaviour'. Through play, word meaning replaces objects and Vygotsky argued that by school age play will have enabled the transition from real objects being needed, to things shifting to internal processes and internal speech, logical memory and abstract thought. He suggested that 'this is the transitional nature of play, which makes it an intermediary between the purely situational constraints of early childhood and real thought that is totally free of real situating'.

Vygotsky never fully developed his ideas around the zone of proximal development (ZPD) but described it as 'the distance between the actual developmental level as determined by independent problem solving and the level of potential development as determined through problem solving under adult guidance, or in collaboration with more capable peers' (1978: 86). Following his death others took up his ideas and added to the notion of a ZPD the idea of 'scaffolding', or the way in which an adult or more 'competent' peers would support someone to take that next step in development and understanding.

The expansion in the pre-school and early years provision has shifted the pre-latency child's world from being predominantly focused around developmental tasks that are met via a dyadic primary caregiver relationship (addressed in the historical writings of practitioners such as Winnicott, Klein, and Vygotsky). Pre-latency children are more visibly now having to process and manage a range of relationships with peers and adults, and adults in group environments cannot remain focused on a single dyadic relationship.

Children's friendships and their role in emotional wellbeing and development

Judy Dunn, in her book exploring children's friendships, starts by trying to define what constitutes friendship, suggesting that it is 'a reciprocal relationship between two people with both affirming it' (2004: 2). Friendship, Dunn argues, includes qualities of companionship, intimacy and affection, and while *fully fledged* friendships showing loyalty and commitment are not likely to be present in pre-latency children, the seeds for these are cultivated and explored in this developmental stage of a child's life.

Dunn makes a key distinction between good social skills and the development of friendship as a bond of intimacy, although good social skills can certainly help in the formation of friendships. Friendships, she suggests, are protective in that they may enable children to experience support in stressful situations such as transitions, and are there in a way that parents or siblings can't be as children move towards becoming independent.

For the child whose early attachment relationships may have been far from ideal, can the friendship of other children offer developmental 'catch-up' opportunities via the ZPD where there are right brain deficits from the early relational trauma?

Dunn points to the first signs of intimacy being apparent in the friendships of pre-school-aged children (2004: 155). This would suggest that during the phases of development when right brain functioning starts to lose predominance, the role of sharing in imaginative play, and exploring feelings, humour and justice will all contribute to the development of the potential for understanding others. The friendships between pre-latency children can also provide scaffolding to enable peers to develop within their ZPD in terms of emotions.

Dunn (2004) does note that children who have had difficulties in the relationship with their primary caregiver are more likely to have troubled relationships with their peers. She links this with the loss of early reciprocal relationships and exchanges and argues that there is much less capacity to play seen in such children. Therefore it would seem important to identify such children early on and support their relational abilities.

The school counsellor at a primary school was doing one of her fairly regular playground observation sessions. This was an opportunity for pupils to approach her easily and without formal referral. Being embedded in the school culture clients were used to this and how to manage these times were negotiated with clients as part of the contracting discussion.

On this occasion one of the Year 6 'buddies' came up to the counsellor and said she thought that a Year 1 boy didn't have any friends. When the buddy tried to talk to him he seemed to be quite rude to her and prodded her arm. The counsellor thanked the buddy and said she would look out for the boy.

On observation of him in the playground the counsellor could see he was 'running around the fringes' of group activities, sometimes 'interfering' in a way that provoked verbal annoyance from his peers. The counsellor's sense was that he was trying to join in but didn't know how to do so. After a while he went off and walked along the white line that marked out the netball court on the playground.

Following up with his teacher the counsellor was told he was just a bit eccentric and was quite lovable even if he was a bit of a handful in class. The counsellor intended to monitor the boy, but with the pressure of other children being 'real problems', he slipped under the radar until Year 4 when he again came to her attention when he lashed out and hit another boy.

Looking at the case it seemed that difficulties had slowly escalated over the previous three years, with the boy now being seen by his peers as a bully and teachers finding his behaviour in class disruptive and increasingly difficult to contain. Home had also noticed that he had become increasingly angry and destructive, but as this had increased slowly over time it wasn't until they were invited to reflect on this that they registered the change.

He did agree to see the counsellor but was hard to engage. Sandtray work led the counsellor to the hypothesis that the boy swung from feeling that he was nothing and nobody and feeling ashamed, to taking a position where he made himself 'somebody' by bullying those around him. He seemed somewhat clumsy in his bodily movements and was left-handed. The counsellor also noted his restlessness when she tried to talk to him while he was making a sandtray or drawing. This restlessness lessened when he was allowed to do one thing at a time. He always wore shorts even in the cold winter months. When the counsellor reflected back to him on this he said he didn't like the feel of trousers on his legs.

Putting all the pieces together, the counsellor suggested that it might be helpful for him to be assessed as possibly being on the autistic spectrum. However, before this could be thought about the boy was removed from the school, as his parents felt he was always the child who was being blamed for things when he was as much a victim of bullying as being a bully.

Schore (2012) focuses on the impact of relational trauma in the development of right brain functions in infancy, and the consequences for relationships with caregivers and on the restorative relationship of therapy. It would seem to fit that his understanding of the neurobiological impact of relational trauma will impact on children's ability to make and keep friends. Equally, undiagnosed or undiagnosable neurological impairments can also impact on children's attachment capacities/experiences even when no maltreatment is present. The interdependence that Winnicott saw as significant in the experience of independence is lost when something makes relationships difficult for a child to enjoy.

Difficulty in making and keeping friends in the pre-school and early years environment should be taken seriously as a possible symptom of relational trauma, thought about sensitively, and early intervention provided where necessary. Peer support on its own seems unable to address these difficulties. However, peers can offer very age-appropriate support once the recipient is able to emotionally let them in to some degree. Perry (2006), in his book *The Boy Who Was Raised As A Dog*, gives a lovely example of how educating a child's peers about the difficulties that a child was facing changed the way his peers responded to his difficult behaviour.

Siblings and other lateral connections

Juliet Mitchell (2003) raises some interesting and thought-provoking ideas about how siblings may play a part in the development of children.

Writing from a psychoanalytic perspective, she highlights that the role of siblings appears to have been written out of the traditional psychoanalytic approach to providing therapy for children. She writes about Klein's Narrative of a Child Analysis and how Klein consistently interprets the child's talk about his brother as his feelings about his father. Mitchell suggests that Klein missed the possibility that in the transference she could be a sibling.

Mitchell's questioning of why sibling relationships have not been an active part of psychoanalytic thinking can lead us to think about the nature of these relationships, particularly in a world where many children may find the most consistent person in their life is their sibling.

A 9 year old boy self-referred to counselling saying he felt really tired and upset but didn't know why. He used the sandtray to make a representation of his world. The tray held no objects but a scattered and fragmented pattern of sand. In exploring this image it emerged that his parents had separated when he was 3 years old. The separation was amicable and the contact arrangements were never in dispute. He and his older sister spent one week with Mum and the next week with Dad. He loved both parents, had his own room in each home, and both his parents took a significant interest in his activities and schooling. However, his sister had just finished her GCSEs and had decided to go and live with another family member in order to be closer to the college where she was undertaking training. His sister had been the one consistent person in his life from the time his parents separated. She hadn't undertaken any actual caring role for him, but her absence had destabilised him and left him feeling bereft. When asked he'd said he had no feelings for his sister, just that sometimes she annoyed him.

The nature of the relationship was beyond friendship and more like attachment. It appeared to have some sense of 'fit' at a non-verbal level, a sense of belonging even when that belonging could be characterised by arguments or jealousies.

Where there is an absence of consistent parenting it may be that these lateral sibling, or sibling-like relationships, are something that promotes significant resilience in children. It could also help us understand why it is that children who have attachment-based difficulties always seem to be drawn together in school: 'It's almost like they can sniff each other out' one teacher commented to me.

Such reflections point to our need, as counsellors, to keep an open mind about the material a child presents, and not fall into the traditional trap of only thinking about the attachment relationships between the adult caregiver and child but also recognise those that exist with other potential attachment figures.

Theraplay as a treatment modality for pre-school and early years

The above exploration of the developmental tasks of this period of a child's life suggests that the child and their environment bring great fluidity and creativity to 'growing up well'. It is a time when issues and difficulties can be spotted at an early stage and when early intervention can prevent emotional and psychological challenges becoming future mental health problems.

It is vital to keep in mind that the child at this stage is still dependent on the family group that they are living in. While traditional individual therapies may enable a child to explore different inner working models, to do this without addressing the context in which that child is still dependent could be counterproductive or minimise the amount they can 'safely' change without catastrophically disrupting the system they live in.

Working with a child in their environmental setting therefore seems a very appropriate model for the pre-latency child. In this way therapeutic intervention can support 'normal' developmental processes by supporting and extending 'ordinary life experiences', rather than pathologising difficulties in the younger child.

Therapies such a Systemic Family Therapy, Filial Therapy and various group approaches to working therapeutically all have their place in providing suitable treatment for children and their families. I would suggest, however, that for the pre-latency child, where the right-brained processes of connecting with people are still very active and accessible, a treatment methodology that specifically works in a right-brained way would be a good starting-point.

Theraplay is a method of engaging children that is fun and easy to adapt to classroom and family settings. It has as yet not gained a great deal of recognition in the UK, although it is being seen more widely as a suitable method of working with children who are adopted or Looked

After and are displaying significant attachment-based difficulties. A thorough assessment and reflection on the needs of both child and family are of course essential before determining the suitability of any treatment methodology.

Theraplay began in Chicago in 1967 when Ann Jernberg saw that the need for psychological services for treatment of children far outstripped the availability of such services. Out of the need to find a treatment that addressed this need, and addressed it rapidly, as well as taking that treatment to the child and family rather than them having to travel to where it was available, Jernberg developed a new approach that could be understood and used by relatively inexperienced mental health workers, one that was based on her understanding of healthy parent-infant interactions.

The model drew on work by Bowlby that specifically enabled a child to change their inner working model of themselves through the positive and playful interaction they had with a Theraplay therapist. A central element of Theraplay is that the emphasis is placed in affirming the child's health, potential and strength, and by extension this positive regard is also helpful in respect of the adult's capacity to find within themself the ability to provide a positive developmental experience for the child.

Theraplay is a methodology that, like counselling, lends itself to working across the therapeutic spectrum. As with the application of counselling skills, Theraplay based ideas can enhance the practice of other professionals in the performance of their core activities, and the Level 1 Theraplay training can prove very valuable to teachers, nursery nurses, social workers, speech and language therapists, nurture group leaders, etc. As with the provision of psychotherapeutic counselling, Theraplay can also be used to address the 'heavy end' of the spectrum of presenting difficulties in children, those that can spring from attachment disorders or issues such as a pervasive developmental delay or Autistic Spectrum difficulties.

Core concepts of Theraplay

Figure 3.1 gives a diagrammatic representation of the Core Concepts of Theraplay. It is reproduced by the kind permission of The Theraplay Institute.

Theraplay identifies the key qualities that are present in high quality, emotionally healthy relationships, and then translates these into the core concepts that are applied to enable therapeutic change through Theraplay. It is, therefore:

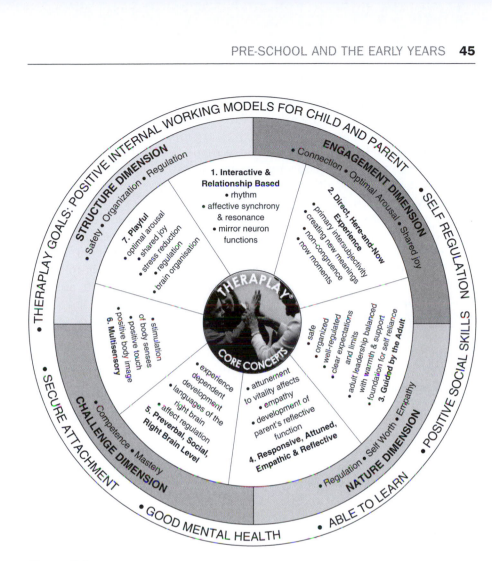

Figure 3.1

- interactive and relationship based;
- a direct here-and-now experience;
- guided by the adult;
- responsive, attuned, empathic and reflective;
- geared towards the preverbal, social, right-brained level of development;
- multi-sensory, including the use of touch;
- playful (Booth and Jernberg, 2010).

Booth and Jernberg (2010) review how the methodology, developed over forty years ago, fits well with the neurobiological understanding that is emerging through the work of Bruce Perry (2006) and Alan Schore (2012). Theraplay explores the strengths and difficulties that a child and adult have in their relationship by looking at four different dimensions of relationship behaviour, namely the pair's capacities to work with Structure, Engagement, Nurture and Challenge.

Structure looks at the adult's ability to organise the child experience and enable them to internalise a sense of regulation through appropriate limit-setting, and their capacity to accept those limits. *Engagement* explores the child's/adult's joint ability to let themselves playfully and positively connect with each other. *Nurture* activities explore again the capacity in the relationship to appropriately show to a child that they are worthy of care. These activities support the development of empathy as well as self-esteem and so seem uniquely connected to the developmental tasks of the specific age group this chapter is focusing on. *Challenge* activities support and explore the child's ability to achieve at a developmentally appropriate level as well as the adults capacity to adapt activities to make them achievable for this child on this occasion.

These dimensions can't be viewed as totally separate entities, as within the process of engaging with a child an adult may need to be aware of structuring activities in a way that engagement doesn't become over-stimulating to the child and leads to disregulation. Activities are developed to try to address the difficulties that a child/parent may be facing by identifying their strengths and then working from these to address the more difficult elements of the relationship.

Application of Theraplay in the school setting

Working with the child and family

The formal Theraplay protocol can be used in a school setting where appropriate.

In an early years class staff noticed that one of the girls was unwilling to try the range of activities on offer. Her paintings were mono-coloured and she seemed afraid of getting paint on herself even though coveralls were provided. Gentle encouragement from staff hadn't made a difference and the girl's peers were giving up trying to invite her to take part.

Staff discussed this with the girl's parents who were very concerned, although they said that the girl was 'no trouble' at home. The parents agreed to meet with the school counsellor to think whether her input might be helpful.

At the initial interview with the parents, without the child being present, the counsellor took a developmental history for the child. Mum said that she had been significantly depressed when the girl was 2 years old following a miscarriage. She acknowledged that during that time she hadn't been able to cope with the energy and exploration of her daughter and said 'I felt that I just kept saying no and then would cry'. She then confided that she had just found out that she was pregnant and was really worried about whether she'd be able to carry the baby full-term. Teasing out what the family meant by the girl being 'no trouble', the counsellor heard that the girl would spend time in her room watching television or DVDs.

A Marschak Interaction Method (MIM) was offered to the mother and girl (the father was unable to participate due to work commitments). In the MIM the mother and girl were given various activities to do together, such as the adult taking a squeaky toy and giving another one to the child and together they would make the two animals play or the adult would teach the child something they don't know. Included in the eight to ten activities would be the adult being asked to leave the room without the child for one minute. This acts as a way of observing how child and adult negotiate separations. The MIM is videoed and, if possible, is also watched via a two-way mirror or a video link.

In viewing the MIM and recording, the counsellor could see that for this child and mother pair there were significant difficulties in the dimensions of nurture, engagement and challenge while their strongest ability was to manage structured activities. The counsellor showed parts of the MIM to the mother, who said that seeing herself and her daughter on the screen made her really sad as they looked so unhappy together. She hadn't realised how 'flat' they were, and how much the relationship they had developed while she was depressed had continued.

A very gentle Theraplay programme was worked out for the mother and child, given the mother's pregnancy. Mum played 'round and round the garden' on the girl's hand, singing to her at the same time. She made lots of eye contact with her daughter and responded to any 'lighting-up' of her daughter's face by exaggerating that expression back with words of delight: 'Oh how your eyes sparkle when you smile like that!'. She and her daughter also snuggled together on a sofa and Mum fed her daughter small snacks such as grapes or savoury biscuits. Slowly the girl became able to let herself enjoy these nurturing and engaging activities. Mum carried on doing their favourite ones at home and taught some of these to Dad. This phase of the work continued for about ten weeks. Mother and daughter would have three sessions with the counsellor and then Mum would meet with the counsellor on her own, looking at some of the key moments on video recordings of sessions and thinking about how she felt the relationship between her and her daughter was changing.

By this time Mum was clearly pregnant but her daughter was ready to start to enjoy more boisterous games in the Theraplay work to help her manage challenge and learn how to regulate and enjoy arousal. At one of

(Continued)

(Continued)

the parent meetings Mum came up with the idea of Dad taking a day off work to come to a session and learning some games he could play with the girl at home.

Dad came to a session and he and the girl, observed and supported by Mum, learnt games like 'Magic Carpet' where Dad towed the girl around the room on a blanket, watching for signals from her as to when to stop and start (one blink meant stop, two meant start, and the girl then spontaneously said 'three blinks means go really fast!'). Dad and the girl worked together helping her balance on a pile of cushions and then jumping into Dad's arms. He then swung her around and hugged her. They also played balloon tennis together, and then the session ended with both Mum and Dad snuggling up and feeding their daughter.

Mum reported that the girl spent less time in her room and seemed keen to come and play her 'special games' with Mum and Dad each evening. One day she asked 'Do I have to go to my room after tea?' Mum said she went and gave the girl a big hug saying 'Of course not if you don't want to'. It was another point of realisation for Mum about just how her depression had 'squashed' her daughter.

At school staff reported that the girl was less withdrawn and more able to join in with group activities when these were structured.

Theraplay with groups

Theraplay can also be offered to small groups of pupils. By helping them take turns, engage, learn to look after each other's needs and have fun together by tapping into their right-brained non-verbal skills, they seem to effectively retain these skills outside of the Theraplay session. There are three simple rules for Theraplay groups: Have Fun, No Hurts and Stick Together. These readily become part of the way children manage their actions in other parts of school life, particularly the No Hurts rule. This is explained to children as not only 'no hurts' to bodies but also 'no hurts' to feelings. If 'hurts' happen we'll stop, but it doesn't mean we can't play the game, we just have to work out how to play it in such a way that people don't feel hurt.

The counsellor was walking towards a classroom to collect a group. On the way she passed two boys who were also coming to groups. They didn't see her but as she passed one boy picked up the other's coat and was about to throw it. The other boy looked him in the eye and said 'No Hurts!' The first boy handed him the coat and walked away.

Groups can also be run with parents and children together or with whole class groups. The Theraplay Institute's Sunshine Groups programme is designed with whole class groups in mind, and is not a therapy as such but fosters a positive environment in the classroom where attachment skills can be practised and allowed to thrive. This helps the deeper therapeutic work (of whatever modality) enormously when children return to classrooms where the environment facilitates their development as part of the normal daily process.

Conclusion

At this age, more than any other, the distinction between therapeutic work, preventative work and just 'good growing up' is very slight. Even children who have experienced significant trauma and distress in their lives still seem to have an emotional flexibility and capacity to take in new and different experiences. With gentle, calm repetition these new, often more positive experiences can go on to change such children's inner working models.

Notes

Theraplay® is a registered service mark of The Theraplay Institute, Evanston, IL, USA. See www.theraplay.org for more information.

All the examples in this chapter are fictionalised, drawing on the many children I have worked with and the many schools I have worked in over the years. No individual should be able to recognise themselves from these examples. If any of my former clients wish to discuss the examples with me I would be delighted to hear from them. They have all taught me so much and I thank them.

FOUR The Primary School Years

Clair Lewoski

The primary school years, spanning the ages between 5 to 11 years old, mark a stage of vast emotional, social and cognitive development. This begins with a transition from the smaller, personalised environment of home or nursery to the larger, more formal setting of school. It ends with a similar transition to something larger and more formalised. In between, an extensive range of developmental milestones and experiences are struggled with and negotiated. During this time children become progressively more immersed in school, where they can forge out an identity and life of their own, separate from their family. They form their first attachments to adults such as child minders and nursery workers, who are not known in such an intimate way as family members, and have to negotiate a set of new relationships with peers. These relationships bring new opportunities to explore how to be one of many in a class, how to get one's needs met in a group larger than a family, how to manage feelings of rivalry or envy, and how to see things from many different people's viewpoints. Friendships with other children can similarly provide experiences of managing envy or rivalry, as well as those of intimacy and empathy. As the years progress friendships will become increasingly gender specific, stable groups of friends can form, and 'best' friendships can become significant. Play, which can cement friendships, changes from being fantasy dominated and informal, to something governed more by rules and structure.

These changes in play parallel changes in children's thinking during this period. Children of 5 years old are just beginning to be able to 'mentalise', namely to reflect upon their own and others' mental states (Fonagy et al., 2003; Midgely and Vrouva, 2012). Often they will struggle to maintain this ability in the face of real situations and instead will manage these reflections more readily during fantasy play. A child of 5 may easily regard what they think and feel as being the only reality felt by everyone. As they get older this capacity to mentalise becomes more stable and sophisticated, so that thinking about the motivations, intentions and mental states of others increases their ability to empathise and their understanding of why people behave the way they do.

The backdrop to all of these changes will be the dramatic bodily changes that are occurring during this period. Children begin this phase often unable to tie shoelaces, zip up a coat, write with a pencil, ride a bike or swim independently. By the time they reach the end of this phase most of these milestones will have been met as their body will have evolved in terms of its strength and dexterity. Baby teeth will have been replaced by adult teeth, just as fantasy figures such as the Tooth Fairy and Father Christmas will have been replaced by reality-based figures, such as pop stars or famous footballers. The body starts to become a site of preoccupation again in a way that it has not done since infancy, as changes begin to occur beyond one's control.

A common thread running throughout this period of enormous change is the desire for mastery and the importance of learning. Erikson called this phase the Age of Industry versus Inferiority, as he appreciated what was at stake if one was unable to successfully negotiate this phase and experience oneself as a 'worker' with skills. Between the ages of 5 and 11 years old much of a child's energy will be focused upon amassing knowledge and acquiring skills. They will be eager to keep pace with the skills and knowledge acquired by their peers, in order to maintain a healthy self-esteem and feel they have something to contribute outside of the family.

What impacts upon this capacity to learn, and to thus experience oneself as masterful, is something to which we now turn.

The primary school years and the development of the capacity to learn

If we recall our own experience of this stage of development, we may say that many of the key developmental tasks involved learning (i.e., learning to read, write, do mathematical tasks or the traditional 3 'r's of reading, writing and arithmetic). We might remember learning our times tables and reciting them repetitiously until we knew them 'by heart,' or memorising dates from history or the names of countries and their capital cities. We might feel impressed or even overwhelmed when we recall the amount of knowledge we managed to 'collect' or accumulate during this period of our lives. Yet we will also recognise that these learning 'about' tasks were not the only, or necessarily the most important, tasks we encountered at this stage of our development.

In addition, we might recall *how* we responded to these tasks. What did we learn from our experience of primary school, being part of a class, making friends, getting to know our first teacher, learning to read and write? Psychoanalytic child psychotherapist and teacher Biddy Youell believes learning involves 'the capacity to *learn from experience*' which enables children to 'use their minds to think and to feel' and thus be prepared for life's challenges and opportunities (2006: 9). This is a view of learning that places a child's emotional experience at its centre. It sees the link between learning and emotional experience as the means by which learning has meaning and contributes towards a child's developing sense of identity and how they see themselves in the world. It rests upon their capacity to make use of the academic and social learning opportunities that the primary school years provide, in order to develop a sense of trust in their own mind as a resource. A key developmental question therefore is whether a child's mind and thinking can evolve through the learning experiences of these years into a rich source of nourishment and creativity? Can their mind and their thinking provide a solid yet flexible platform from which they can then approach adolescence and adulthood? As we shall see, much depends upon the type of learning that has occurred during a child's early years and infancy, and how this now influences their responses to new learning opportunities.

In this chapter we shall consider what impacts upon developing this capacity to learn from experience and to think about this in relation to the primary school years and the particular learning challenges these years present.

Learning about and learning from experience

The primary school years are often referred to in psychoanalytic literature as 'the latency stage'. This was a term first used by Freud (1962), who saw the psychosexual instincts as being repressed during this phase but remaining 'latent', only to re-emerge later during puberty. For Melanie Klein, a follower of Freud's and a pioneer in psychoanalytic child therapy, these psychosexual instincts were not so much repressed as channelled into the controlling, somewhat obsessional, and yet perfectly ordinary activities of children of this age through their collecting and ordering of things, including knowledge and learning. Hence this is the phase of children collecting and swapping superhero, football or action figure cards, rubbers, marbles or whatever forms the latest craze, and of listing and knowing all the different facts and details of their collections. As Meltzer, a follower of Klein has stated, for the latency child this thirst for knowledge is more about power and control and the feeling of mastery that can come through naming and knowing about things, rather than primarily understanding (1973: 159).

This form of learning that focuses on collecting or the acquiring of knowledge, has also been referred to by Wilfred Bion (1962), another follower of Klein's, as a 'learning about' as opposed to a 'learning from experience'. Although the latency child may be dominated by a learning-about type of thinking, alongside this, if a child has had a good enough experience in infancy, there will be the capacity to learn from experience. Bion differentiates learning from experience as involving an emotional link between the learner and what is learned. He traces this back to the earliest learning experiences between mother or main carer and baby, where an emotional link is formed through the mother's containment of the baby's communications. The mother, through her own thinking or reverie, emotionally digests the baby's communications and hands them back to the baby in a more digestible and manageable form, as we shall see with Sam below. (This returns us to the ideas discussed in Chapter 3.)

Sam aged 6 weeks old

Mother sits on the sofa to feed Sam, but after just a few minutes he pulls away from the breast crying, drawing up his legs to his tummy. 'It's your tummy, I know', says mother gently, sitting him up to wind him. He is sick and whimpers, tears filling his eyes. After winding him, she cradles him in her arms rocking him softly and placing a dummy in his mouth. His eyes fix on hers and she begins to talk to him about his tummy, empathising with his discomfort, whilst stroking his cheek. As she speaks, she raises her eyebrows and he responds by raising his eyebrows and smiling widely so that the dummy falls from his mouth unnoticed. As she continues to speak his breathing quickens and he begins to make noises in turn with her voice, and they appear to have a conversation about his 'poorly tummy'.

Sam is literally experiencing indigestion of his mother's milk but through her own thinking his mum enables this raw, indigestible experience to become thinkable about and understood: 'it's your poorly tummy I know'. We cannot know how much Sam understands of the content of what his mother is saying to him, but we can see that her ability to continue thinking in the face of his distress soothes him and gives his experience meaning. What was previously for Sam a raw, painful and confusing experience now becomes something that can be thought about. Repeated experiences like this will mean that over time Sam will introject not only these now 'thinkable thoughts' from his mother, but also the apparatus for thinking itself.

This 'making a thought thinkable' for the baby occurs through a process of 'projective identification', where the baby projects their feelings into the mother, who receives these communications, processes them through her own thinking or reverie, and then communicates back in such a way that the baby experiences their communications as having been understood. Neuro-psychoanalyst Allan Schore (2010) has stated that this is an unconscious communication process between the right brain of the baby and the right brain of the mother, and represents a link between them where the mother's mind functions as the link. The baby thus experiences their emotional communications as having been contained through the regulation of their affect, and over time the baby introjects this capacity to contain or regulate themselves via this thinking capacity.

The latency or primary school-aged child who has experienced, like Sam, time and again their thoughts made thinkable by their main carer, will have their own apparatus for thinking and learning securely in place. Through internalising the container-contained experience, Bion (1962) argues that a state of mind is developed that is flexible and open to new learning, as a 'link' between new ideas and the knowledge and learning from experience that has gone before can occur in a meaningful way.

We could think about the child who has had these experiences as the securely attached child who comes to school ready to learn, as their mind is not pre-occupied with attachment issues and they have the apparatus for thinking already well established.

Sam aged 5 years: Reception class/Foundation Stage

Sam is working alone on a floor puzzle with many pieces. He has managed to put together the bottom section of the puzzle but is now working on the top two corners. He selects a piece and turns it round to see if it will fit. He frowns a little, looking perplexed, and when he cannot make it fit he puts the piece down. He searches carefully through several other pieces and then chooses one and tries to see if this will fit. Again it doesn't, and he looks a little confused and surprised. Just as he is about to put this piece down he seems to have an idea, picks up the previous piece, and finds it fits together perfectly with the one in his hand. He looks delighted and smiles and almost laughs to himself. He then looks at the two pieces in his hand and tries to see where they fit with what he has done on the floor. He moves them around several times but cannot make them fit anywhere; he then sits scanning the other pieces on the floor. His teacher approaches and shows an interest in what he is doing. He shares that he cannot find where these two pieces go. His teacher suggests he finds all the pieces with long, hard edges and then tries to fit them into the two remaining corners. Sam seems excited by this idea and enthusiastically begins looking for all the pieces with long hard edges. He keeps the two joined pieces close by his side, as if keeping them ready to slot into place at the right time.

Here we can see an older Sam using his thinking capacity to manage the challenge and frustration of completing a complex jigsaw. It is not an easy task and yet he steadily and patiently tries different strategies and is not defeated by the challenge. His state of mind seems open and flexible and he is willing to try out a variety of approaches. One might see reflected here Sam's internalisation of his mother's patient and flexible thinking when she managed his poorly tummy, that she did not collapse or despair when faced with this challenge in feeding Sam. Yet what of the children who have not had the sort of experiences that Sam had in infancy? How does this impact upon their capacity to learn from experience and make use of what school has to offer?

Learning from relationships in school: relationships with school staff

As Giana Williams (1998) has stated, for children who have experienced emotional deprivation or a lack of consistent emotional regulation, they face the challenge of possibly never having sufficiently developed this apparatus for thinking and emotional regulation, and so will arrive at school unable to fully make use of the learning opportunities presented to them, as the following case example illustrates.

Carl aged 8 years old/Year 3

Carl's teacher is talking to the whole class about the next activity. Carl is sitting rigidly in his seat and he fixes his gaze upon her as if hoping she will notice him. When she meets his gaze briefly his body relaxes, then when she returns to focusing on the whole class his rigidity turns

(Continued)

(Continued)

to wriggling and tapping his pencil. The teacher tells the class they need their maths books from the centre of the table. Carl grabs his before anyone else and instantly fixes his gaze back on his teacher ready for the next instruction. She tells the class to fold a page in half and number the lines 1 to 10; they are going to have a test. Carl frantically completes this instruction and then once again checks he has done this before anyone else and fixes his gaze upon the teacher. The test begins and Carl looks anxiously at the other children on his table and begins tapping his pencil. As they start to write their answers he leans back on his chair to look at the book of the girl next to him; seeing her answer he swiftly copies this in his book. She realises he is copying her and she places her arm around her book, firmly obscuring his view. With each question Carl looks up at the children around him, as it is clear they are working out the answers on their fingers or are silently mouthing their counting. He has a look of blind panic and confusion and seems totally lost. He suddenly puts up his hand and says he needs to use the toilet.

Here we see a child struggling to think. Carl, like many children who have not had the containing experiences in infancy like Sam, where their feelings, bodily sensations and communications were given meaning and thus became thinkable about, arrived at school with what Gianna Williams (1998) has referred to as 'faulty equipment' for thinking. In the language of neurobiology we might say that Carl has a sensitized stress response system, meaning that he experiences mild stressors such as this maths test as hugely dysregulating. As his body goes into a flight response it 'shuts down' the higher thinking functions of his cortex. Many children like Carl therefore feel dependent upon their relationship with their teacher in order to think: they will look to their teacher to offer them the emotional regulation they need in order to make use of their higher thinking functions. We can see this with Carl: when he feels he is kept in focus by his teacher, communicated by her gazing at him, then he physically relaxes and enters a state where it might be possible to think. The gaze facilitates Carl feeling an emotional link between him and his teacher, much as we saw happening between baby Sam and his mother. Yet once Carl's physical connection with his teacher is absent, it is as if he feels dropped from her mind and cannot rely upon his own mind to think through the task. He then resorts to what Margot Waddell (2000) has referred to as an 'adhesive' type of learning, where he tries to almost 'stick' to himself the knowledge that belongs to the girl next to him, by copying her work. When this adhesive learning is made impossible, one can feel the emotional dysregulation building within Carl as he enters a 'flight' response, and needs to flee the situation and evacuate his anxiety in the toilet.

For Carl, the anxiety of being unable to think means he is unable to learn from the experience presented to him in this situation. He cannot link it with his previous knowledge or thinking, and the experience becomes one of panic and confusion instead of meaning and understanding. Winnicott held that children like Carl came to school looking for what their home had failed to provide: 'They do not come to school to learn but to find a home from home' (1964a: 20). Or we might say that they have not come to school primarily seeking a 'learning about' sort of learning, rather a learning that comes from their experience of relationships. Winnicott went as far as to say that the main purpose of school was to provide a structure and a network of relationships in which 'experiences can be lived through' (1964: 20). For children like Carl this may provide a second chance at learning from the experience of relationships, as the work of Heather Geddes has demonstrated. Geddes (2006), along with Barrett and Trevitt (1991), has described how significant the attachment relationship formed between a pupil and their teacher is, and how this relationship impacts upon a child's learning and general functioning in school. Geddes cites research by Scroufe (1983) which shows how the attachment relationship pattern between a child and their parent becomes replayed between teacher and pupil. So a child like Carl, for example, who cannot focus on the learning task, but instead is preoccupied with his relationship with his teacher, might be said to have an insecure-ambivalent attachment relationship with his teacher that replicates or mirrors his attachment relationship with his main carer. Whereas a child like Sam, who can balance his focus between the learning task and his teacher's direction or support, might be said to have a securely attached relationship with his teacher.

Geddes' work offers teachers guidance on how they might respond and structure tasks and their relationship with their pupils dependent upon each child's attachment style. How much a child like Carl, or children with an insecure-avoidant or insecure-disorganised attachment style, will be able to make use of the experience of a relationship with their teacher will depend upon that teacher's capacity to provide the type of containment shown by Sam's mother. How much can Carl's teacher digest his inability to bear frustration and the need to be first, and yet not respond with frustration herself? Can she help Carl find ways to bear the gaps when he does not have her full attention? This is no easy task, and unlike Sam's mother a teacher has many 'babies' to contain and digest communications from, which is perhaps why teaching is such an emotionally complex and taxing task. For some children like Carl specialist intervention and support for teachers may be invaluable, which may be provided by child counsellors with their knowledge of children's emotional development and its impact upon learning. 'Educational psychotherapists' have developed a particular expertise in supporting teachers in their thinking about children's emotional blocks to learning, as well as providing an individual therapeutic relationship for a child that puts the process of learning at its centre (Barrett and Trevitt, 1991; Geddes, 2006; Salmon and Dover, 2007).

Whether a child is securely or insecurely attached to their teacher, what is apparent is that the relationships formed between children and school staff during the primary school years are formative experiences. For some children like Carl these relationships present opportunities to work through relational experiences and from these learn about what may not have been possible in their families. Thus a learning support assistant, lunchtime organiser, school receptionist or after school club leader may for some children become their first experience of a secure attachment relationship. For children like Sam their relationship with a teacher or other members of school staff may represent their first important relationship outside of the family.

First day at primary school

It is the first day at primary school and the children are waiting outside their Reception classroom. Amy is hopping on one leg excitedly as she holds onto her father's hand, asking him how much longer do they have to wait. Her father patiently shows her his watch and says that it is nearly 9 o'clock. Nearby is Carl. He is holding onto his mother in a monkey-like grip around her waist, nestling his head into her side. She holds him tightly to her whilst she strokes the top of his head and looks nervously towards the classroom door. Ellie then appears and rushes up to Amy, and both girls squeal and jump up and down hugging each other. Ellie's mother smiles, pushing a buggy holding Ellie's 2 year old brother. Sam looks up briefly at Amy and Ellie and then returns to fingering a small acorn he has in his pocket. He notices another acorn on the playground nearby and picks it up to compare them. His mother comments it is just like the one from their garden. Just then the door opens and the teacher appears. There is a sudden flurry of activity as Amy, Ellie and the other children rush enthusiastically towards the teacher. Some children like Carl seem to be retreating as far as they can from the teacher and the classroom door, burying themselves in their parents' bodies. Sam hands one acorn to his mother to look after and putting the other in his pocket and walks to join the children who are now lining up by the classroom door. Sam's mother watches as he enters the classroom and shows his teacher his acorn. His teacher responds with interest and says perhaps he might like to show it to the rest of the class later.

In this rather typical snapshot of the first day at school we can see a range of responses from both children and parents. Winnicott (1965a) referred to this moment of starting school as the 'leaving of the enclosure' of home, where the environment of home (when all has gone well enough) has been personalised and specially adapted to the child. Yet with the start of primary school this personalised environment is substituted for one that is governed by the needs of the group or class, although there may be some personal adaptation made to individual children in their early weeks in Reception. Even for children that have attended nursery or a playgroup, or have been with a childminder full-time, there will still be a personal adaptation to the child to some degree, which makes the experience of starting primary school quite different and significant.

Children will approach leaving their pre-school enclosure in a variety of ways, which will depend upon a combination of their individual temperament and what has occurred earlier in their development. And here we can see Sam again, who seems to be managing this moment with the help of his mother to find a link and a familiarity between home and school that is represented by the acorn. His mother taking the one found in school, and Sam keeping the one from home, seems a way for him to feel he is remaining linked to his mother as he makes this transition away from her: the acorn functions as a transitional object to help them both manage this separation. Sam can do this as he has developed object constancy where his mother has been internalised as a resource within him, or to use the language of attachment theory, he has an internal working model of his mother as a constant secure base even when they are separated. Yet at this moment when his object constancy needs reassurance, he finds a transitional object as an external reminder of his mother's *internal* presence within him. Trusting in his mother as a secure base enables Sam to transfer this expectation from his internal working model onto his teacher. He expects her to show an interest in him and he is rewarded (even at this busiest of moments for his teacher) with her curiosity. From here on Sam's teacher provides a figure outside of the family for him to identify with. We can see this in children Sam's age when their teacher suddenly becomes the 'font of all knowledge' and is frequently quoted at home: 'But Mrs Jones says ... or Mrs Jones thinks'. This is an adjustment for parents who until now have been a child's main world and figures for identification.

Yet what of children like Carl, what is the experience of their relationship with their teacher at this stage? Carl represents the response of many ambivalently attached children who struggle to manage the separation from a main carer when going to school. We can see him retreating and clinging to his mother but we can also see his mother holding tightly onto Carl. Winnicott (1965a) stated that in order for a child to be able to separate and leave their main carer to go to school, they are dependent upon that carer to let them go, to allow them to leave the enclosure of home. How this leaving will be negotiated will often mirror in some way how past separations have been managed. If a child senses their parents' desolation at being separated and they fear their parents will not survive emotionally or psychically without them, then a child may feel responsible for their parents' state of mind and struggle to separate from them. Similarly, if a child feels that their parent will quickly fill the space that *they* had filled in their mind with other activities, perhaps in response to finding the separation so difficult, then again the child may struggle to let go and enjoy an independent existence at school. Children can feel guilty about forgetting a parent whilst enjoying school and disloyal if they enjoy their relationship with their teacher. The stronger the relationship between a parent and their child's teacher, as well as a child feeling the parent's ability to let them go as well to welcome them back, then the easier it will be for that child to immerse themself in school life.

A parent's relationship with school can hugely influence how their child feels about going to school. Parents 'transfer' feelings, expectations, hopes and fears onto their child's teacher as well as onto the school as a whole, based upon their own school experiences. Perhaps in the example of Carl's mother we can see someone who had negative experiences of school, which are now re-evoked through her son starting school. The projection of her own school experiences may make it difficult for her to separate out how it could be different for Carl. If we look at this ambivalence from an attachment perspective, we can see Carl as a child with an ambivalent attachment who has perhaps experienced his mother as not always able to be consistent and reliable in regulating his emotions. It is therefore hard for him to experience her as a secure base from which he can launch and explore the wider world represented by school and his teacher.

Some children will present like Carl when they start school, not because of an ambivalent attachment, but because developmentally they may not be ready to leave the enclosure of home given they are nearly a whole year younger than some of their peers. It may be no coincidence that we see Amy and Ellie eager to immerse themselves in the experience of school, when they are both born in the autumn and therefore are nearly 5 years old on starting school. There are of course those children who initially respond with enthusiasm and an eagerness for school like Amy and Ellie, but who later on may show reluctance once their idealised fantasies of school, or the stark reality of it being a permanent fixture in their lives, dawn upon them. For some children, the learning from experience that is a feature of school life is not what they had anticipated. Instead there may have been an unconscious hope that the knowledge of reading and writing and 'being clever' like an older sibling or parent might magically occur in a rather omnipotent way, without the struggles that are inherent in the knowledge that comes from experience. These may be the children who as babies, for various reasons, found frustration difficult to tolerate (Waddell, 2000).

Learning from relationships in school: relationships with peers

The experience of developing peer relationships at school can help a great deal with the transition involved in leaving the enclosure of home. For the first time many children will develop significant relationships outside of their family. The sense of having one's own social life and separate existence beyond the family can compensate for the loss of the personal enclosure of home or pre-school. Developing one's own friendships and having something 'good' of one's own may also support a child like Amy, for example, who may be leaving a younger sibling at home with mum, with all its potential to stir up understandable feelings of sibling rivalry.

As Scroufe's (2009) work in particular has demonstrated, children will also display secure and insecure attachment patterns in their relationships with their peers, and therefore they may or may not be able to make good use of the opportunity to form friendships with those of their own age. Those children who have experienced secure attachment with their main carers are more 'attractive play partners', as they show more positive affects and less negative behaviours in their interactions with peers (see Scroufe, 2009: 135). As the primary school years progress the capacity to make close friendships takes central importance for both boys and girls as peers become figures for identification, as well as intimate supporters and allies as social and academic pressures increase.

Learning from experiences of mastery

Erikson (1951) has referred to the primary school years, or latency stage, as the Era of Industry, where the key experiences that will lead the child to feelings of competence are those of skilful mastery. In the absence of these mastery experiences, the child is left feeling inferior to others. So what are the sorts of learning experiences that contribute towards feelings of mastery? Carol Dweck's (2000) research outlines extensively what she believes gives rise to a 'mastery-oriented' response to learning, where students/pupils are seen as 'Engaging fully with new tasks, exerting effort to master something, stretching their skills and putting their knowledge to good use'. This strongly parallel's Bion's ideas about learning from experience: namely, that this is a struggle and involves frustration but contributes to a sense of self worth as the knowledge gained has been given personal and emotional meaning.

What Dweck's research shows is how these mastery experiences are mediated. How a child's view of their intelligence and performance, often gained through the types of praise and criticism they receive from teachers and parents, significantly influences whether learning is imbued with feelings of mastery and competence, or inferiority and low self worth. For those children who see their intelligence as a 'fixed entity' that cannot be increased, and link this to whether they perform successfully in exams, their sense of self worth is utterly dependent upon whether they perform successfully or not. These children will have often experienced performance-related praise from teachers and parents that supports this fixed entity theory ('Well done for getting such results. *You're* so clever'). As they are dependent upon good 'results' in order to feel intelligent and competent, they may be risk averse, choosing to narrowly apply themselves to subjects and tasks at which they can easily be successful. Dweck (2000) has shown how this can significantly limit what we can feel masterful at. She has demonstrated that girls in particular can feel successful at primary school where the curriculum requires more 'safe rote learning' and less risk taking, but once they go to high school they often retreat from the challenge of subjects that they cannot easily master, such as maths and science (Dweck, 2006).

Children who develop an incremental view of their intelligence believe they can 'grow' their intelligence through effort, and thereby incrementally build mastery and skill experiences. These children will have received feedback that has focused more upon their strategies and effort and are able to show resilience in the face of not performing well in exams or tasks, as they are focused upon how to try harder, what different strategies to use, and crucially, *what can be learnt from the task*. When they leave primary school and meet the challenges of the high school curriculum they are thus more likely to persist in the face of these challenges and overcome them.

Dweck's research also emphasises the vulnerability inherent within fixed entity views of intelligence, namely that one only feels as masterful and intelligent as one's last test result. She has also shown how IQ and self-confidence do not mitigate against this vulnerability (2000: 57). The vulnerability that may be hidden beneath intellectual mastery is also discussed by Winnicott in his concept of the False Self (1960). He delineates the vulnerability of a self that is false as it locates itself in the mind as a 'split off intellect', cut off from the body (2000: 30). Winnicott traces the source of this vulnerability in a different way to Dweck. He believes that the child who has achieved 'unit status', has a self where mind and body are integrated and where they experience themselves as a whole person, and separate from others. These would be children who have experienced a good-enough facilitating environment with their main carer as we saw with Sam. A child with a false self, however, has not achieved unit status and locates their identity solely in their intellect or mind. Like Dweck, Winnicott argues that a high IQ therefore does not provide resilience, and in fact may mean that a child appears competent and masterful in terms of their intellectual capacities, but this may be a false self that is vulnerable to breaking down. Children in the primary school years who have over-relied upon a split-off intellect for self worth, may find this no longer serves them well when they reach secondary school and encounter the social, emotional and bodily challenges of adolescence.

Conclusion

> As a child goes through the classroom door what lies behind is infancy; what lies ahead is puberty, adolescence and adulthood. (Edwards, 1999: 79)

As we have seen, the learning that occurs in the primary school years is to some extent dependent upon what has occurred previously in infancy. Similarly, what is or is not learnt from the experience of the primary school years becomes the platform adolescence is built upon. This view (enshrined by Erikson in his psychosocial theory) shows how cumulative learning or not learning from experience is. The primary school years mark the half-way point in his Eight Ages of Man, and by this stage a child will have learnt trust or mistrust, autonomy or shame, and initiative or guilt, all of which will contribute to how well that child will be able to make use of the opportunities and challenges the primary school years provide. Yet it is through attending primary school that children's worlds extend beyond family, and so these earlier crises in development now have new opportunities to be revisited and re-negotiated as there is a second chance for learning.

The implications for therapy of our understanding of the primary school-aged child are that the quality of the relationship is of crucial importance. It is also vital to communicate and model within the therapy relationship that it is fine to make mistakes, to be uncertain or to not know. Therapists can offer age-appropriate information or psychoeducation if necessary and encourage self-discovery and self-acceptance.

Starting primary school and leaving primary school both involve leaving 'enclosures', which Winnicott has stated can feel both exciting and frightening. This process is a part of life, which could be viewed as 'a long series of coming out of enclosures and taking new risks and meeting new and exciting challenges' (1964b: 52). What is central in this recurring process is the ability to 'get back to the enclosure', and therefore it remains important throughout life to retain a link with what has gone before, so that a false, pseudo maturity does not set in. Retaining a link with the primary school years through what has been called a 'latency state of mind' (Edwards, 1999) facilitates a type of thinking that is often very useful in both adolescence and adulthood. The ability to name, sequence, order, and organise, alongside a general 'knowing about' things, plays a key function throughout our lives. However, if this state of mind cannot exist alongside an ability to learn from experience, then it may become rigid, obsessional and restrict other types of learning and experiences. Ultimately, the primary school years should be allowed to live on within us as a nourishing lifelong resource.

FIVE Working with the Developmental Tasks of Adolescence during the Secondary School Years

Tracey Fuller

Introduction

In this chapter we intend to explore how counsellors can work help-fully alongside young people at secondary school. The 11 year old child who stands at the gates of their new secondary school is about to join a highly demanding social world. If this transition is successful they will eventually leave as young adults who are ready to enter the world of work, or seek higher education, perhaps having equipped themselves not only with qualifications but also with a more settled identity. They may have developed clear ideas about themselves as friends, boyfriends or girlfriends, as well as a healthy understanding of their parents as imperfect human beings who will not be able to meet all their needs. This is the voyage from a childhood dependence on family to the autonomy of an adult identity and self-concept (Mabey and Sorensen, 1995; Coleman, 2011). During secondary school young people are moving towards their integration into wider society at the same time as they are exploring inwards, developing a sense of their own uniqueness and differentiation from others (Frankel, 1998). In this complex process of internal examination and external exploration, relationships are central, as adolescents can only construct a personal identity in relation to others (Geldard and Geldard, 2004).

We will start by considering the transition to secondary school. A brief discussion on making successful therapeutic alliances with adolescents will follow, and the implication of recent developments in neuroscience on our understanding of adolescent brains. We will continue by exploring how adolescent development is viewed as a psycho-social stage in the work of Erikson, and how we can support young people through the process of individuation and the development of autonomy whilst promoting communication with parents and peers. We will also investigate ways to work therapeutically with the different identities and powerful emotions that adolescence gives rise to. The chapter will then conclude with an overview of current trends in young people's wellbeing and mental health, focusing briefly on those experiences that may cause the greatest concern for school counsellors.

Transition to secondary school

The transition to secondary school is perhaps considered a rite of passage for young adolescents. Although the majority of children will meet the challenge of transition successfully (Gray et al., 2011) some researchers question whether the transition to secondary school is becoming more demanding (Hagell, 2009). The sudden complexity of making multiple new relationships with peers, older students and many different teachers at once after leaving the security of one class teacher in primary school can be daunting, especially for those students who have an internalised model of relationships as anxiety provoking and unreliable and hence have an 'insecure attachment' (Bowlby, 1988). The impact on brain development of insecure or neglectful parenting during infanthood can leave these young people less resilient and also less able to cope with stress (Schore, 2003b).

Bomber (2009) describes the transition process as the 'survival of the fittest', where insecurely attached young people struggle in their new environment and multiple transitions of rooms, subjects, groups and staff are the norm (Winnicott, 1965a; Bomber, 2009). Thus vulnerable Year 7s can feel overwhelmed, confused and abandoned in the first weeks, months, or even years of secondary school.

> ## Dawn/Year 7
>
> Dawn has been at secondary school for six weeks. She takes my box of shells and evenly spaces 40 or 50 shells across the surface of the sandtray. There seems to be no groups, just lots of fragmentally placed individual shells filling the space. She works in silence and I notice that there is no shell to identify with, just lots of different shells with no connections. The image feels lonely, confusing and over-crowded. She talks about all the new faces, endlessly talking at her, and feeling lost in the crowd.

For children like Dawn, reliable adults who take an individual supportive interest in their experience can be safe harbours in what can seem an otherwise huge and treacherous ocean. There is not sufficient space here to explore useful strategies in supporting young people with insecure attachments in school environments, but we would refer those interested to the work of Bomber (2007, 2009), Delaney (2009b), and Geddes (2006).

Difficulties during transition can develop into longer-term problems that will affect students' wellbeing through secondary school and beyond (Gray et al., 2011). Research suggests that young people regard schools, and relationships with teachers in particular, as greatly affecting their wellbeing (Pople, 2009). A detailed exploration of the importance of school relationships on early adolescence wellbeing can be found in McLaughin and Clarke (2010).

Before we proceed to discuss how adolescence is theorised as a developmental stage, there follows a brief reflection on the process of establishing therapeutic alliances with teenagers.

Making therapeutic alliances with adolescents

There is much evidence that the therapeutic alliance is crucial to both process and outcomes in therapy (Horvath and Symonds, 1991; Gelso and Carter, 1994). Kazdin (1990), who surveyed child and adolescent therapists, suggested that 90% of them regarded the therapeutic relationship as the most crucial variable influencing change. According to Frankel, despite adolescents' perceived tendency towards secrecy and concealment from adults, 'Adolescents are yearning to be made visible', (1998: 4). How then do we as therapists accompany young people helpfully through this paradox in order to make authentic and helpful relationships with them?

Traditionally, adolescents have been regarded as a difficult group to engage with therapeutically (Church, 1994; Di Giuseppe et al., 1996), yet young people are highly capable of making warm and effective therapeutic alliances. Creating an authentic and accepting relationship that conveys empathy and warmth is a highly active part of the therapeutic process (Rogers, 1957). The challenge is to remain congruent whilst adapting to the developmental and relational needs, communication style and social uniqueness of each young client. It can be helpful to match the more intense and direct communication style of adolescents (Geldard and Geldard, 2004; Hughes, 2009). This echoes the affect attunement process of earlier infancy (Stern, 1985), the significance of which is emphasised by recent developments in neuroscience as reviewed by Schore (2011b). It has been suggested that such matching promotes a more inter-subjective relationship where counsellors are also open to being affected in the encounter, thus promoting deeper communication (Rowan and Jacobs, 2002; Hughes, 2009). There is some evidence that young people find it easier to be trusting where they feel the counsellor is more of an ally rather than an authority figure for example (Diamond et al., 1999; Everall and Paulson, 2002), although this aspect perhaps warrants further research.

Understanding teenage brains

The secondary school years mark the development of thinking with increasing degrees of abstraction (Piaget, 1966). Young people can reflect more symbolically and imagine multiple outcomes from events, as well as solve problems involving deduction and hypothesis and detect contradictions (Flavell, 1977; Knight, 1985). Maturing adolescents have a growing capacity to think critically about other people and themselves in context.

Neuroscientists such as Cozolino (2006) and Nelson et al. (2005) have described the continuing plasticity of teenage brains and suggested an active reorganisation of the neural pathways from age 12 to 16. There are three fundamental social transitions underpinning this rewiring:

1. Moving away from the family of origin.
2. Establishing an identity and a connection with a peer group.
3. The creation of new adult relationships and eventually a family (Cozolino, 2006).

Recent research also suggests that adolescent risk taking may be the result of an increase in feelgood receptors in the brain during early adolescence, at a point when the inhibiting pre-frontal cortex is still developing (Steinberg, 2008). However, much of the progression in our understanding of physical changes in the adolescent brain is still the subject of current debate (Males, 2009; Sercombe, 2010; Coleman, 2011), so perhaps it would be most useful to take from this developing research:

1. An awareness of the increased sophistication of teenage brains in understanding self and others.
2. Adolescents' innate capacity to create new and significant relationships.

In the next few sections I will go on to explore the implications for therapeutic practice with adolescents of Erikson's developmental framework.

Adolescence as a developmental stage: exploring the Erikson model

Erik Erikson is one of the most formative thinkers in the field of identity development, and therefore offers school counsellors significant insights into working helpfully alongside adolescent clients. Erikson's (1967) theory suggests adolescence is characterised by identity formation brought about through the resolution of a series of crises that mark the process of transition to a separate adult identity. This second individuation process mirrors the transition for an infant from symbiosis with the mother to becoming an individuated toddler (Blos, 1967). A young person may alternate between seeking independence and rejecting their parents, with an intense need to be supported and comforted by them (Frankel, 1998).

For Erikson (1967) the key emotional themes of adolescence are the development of identity versus the danger of role confusion. With the advent of puberty all the sameness and continuities that were relied on earlier are questioned again. A fear of fragmentation arising from this process results in an over-concern with how adolescents are seen by others and an intense identification with peers and cultural heroes (Erikson, 1967).

Adolescence is a time of both change and consolidation in a young person's sense of themselves (Coleman, 2011). Changing bodies in the form of puberty, and changing minds in terms of increasingly complex cognitive abilities, result in an inevitable rise in self-consciousness. At the same time there is a greatly increased cognitive capacity with which to carry out this self-scrutiny and introspection. Young people become able to identify the roles they play in different contexts, and with different people, and how those roles may interact with each other (Marsh et al., 1988; Kroger, 2004).

Erikson implies that in order to progress successfully through each developmental stage of life a psychosocial crisis must be faced, which for adolescents will centre on this development of identity (Kroger, 2004). A young person may struggle with the following aspects (see Figure 5.1).

Intimacy. The adolescent may fear their increasing capacity for close relationships and the possible loss of a separate identity. They may find themselves isolated or, alternatively, they may rush headfirst into a variety of potentially unhelpful relationships with little discernment.

Time. They associate the future with an unwelcome change to adulthood and they therefore will avoid all future planning.

Industry. An adolescent may find it hard to make best use of their resources in order to complete their studies. This may result in either them pursuing one subject in unrealistic depth to the exclusion of other areas, or dropping out of courses just before they take their exams.

Negative identity. The young person seeks to create an identity which is in direct opposition to their parents.

Figure 5.1   Adolescent psychosocial crisis (adapted from Erikson 1968 and Kroger, 2004)

Identity Diffusion
- These adolescents are not yet displaying any signs of commitment to any set of beliefs or values.

Identity Foreclosure
- Premature identification with the beliefs and cultures that have been chosen by those around the young person.

Moratorium
- Young people are involved in an active engagement with the search for possibilities of identity by experiment with different options and are therefore seen as working towards a settled adult identity. Thus this is seen as a necessary stage.

Identity achievement
- Young people have a new settled idea about who they want to be as an adult.

Figure 5.2   Stages of identity formation (adapted from Marcia, 1993, cited in Kroger, 2004)

In this space between childhood and adulthood young people will have an opportunity to try out and experiment with different identities before moving to a more settled position. Marcia (1993), cited in Kroger (2004), further developed Erikson's ideas into the notion of four identity forming stages: identity diffusion; identity foreclosure; moratorium; and identity achievement (see Figure 5.2).

There has been much debate about whether these stages are necessarily sequential and whether their existence is supported by research into adolescent wellbeing (Kroger, 2004; Nurmi, 2004). Coleman (2011) suggests that initial findings from these studies imply that adolescents in the diffusion stage exhibit the greatest severity of psychological and emotional difficulties, whilst those in foreclosure display greatest conformity and least autonomy and greatest need for social approval. Those in the moratorium stage display the greatest anxiety and opposition to authority. By contrast, young people in the identity achievement stage seem to be psychologically healthier and to have clearer career goals and a greater motivation to reach these goals. This, if true, has implications for our work with them, as it has been suggested that the moratorium stage of trying out different identities is a necessary step towards eventual identity achievement. This suggests that increased anxiety and perhaps oppositional defiance are normative and necessary parts of the developing process.

Later researchers have criticised Erikson's lack of acknowledgement of the multiplicity of the adolescent experience, and the impact of culture and ethnicity, and have argued that we need to move towards a more pluralistic understanding of adolescence as a developmental stage (Larson et al., 2002; Coleman, 2011). These criticisms are certainly valid, but we believe that Erikson's ideas remain a helpful framework that can support our reflections on clinical work with adolescents: for example, we may reflect Erikson's categories of psycho-social development of 'Intimacy' and 'Industry' and normalise and support our adolescent clients' struggles to make intimate relationships or organise their studies.

Working with the emerging and separating self

1. Encouraging communication with parents

Adolescents want to start making their own choices of friends, image, and culture, as well as detach themselves from their earlier childhood idealisation of their parents. This transition to a separate identity is often marked by high levels of confusion and ambivalence. Reiner describes adolescents' desire to denigrate their parents as a way of destroying the childhood need to rely on and idealise parents (see Frankel, 1998). The resulting feelings for parents of isolation, rejection and powerlessness can cause them to withdraw from their adolescent children at a time when, although striking out for independence, they are still vulnerable, and in need of parental support (Geldard and Geldard, 2004; Steinberg, 2008b). However, much research suggests that resilience in adolescence is promoted by positive relationships with peers, parents and others (Garmezy and Rutter, 1983; Wentzel, 1998) and recent studies have refuted the psychoanalytic view that adolescence is centred on autonomy and individuation. Larson (1996), for example, suggests that although the overall time spent with the family decreases in adolescence, individual time with mothers and fathers remains relatively unchanged. Autonomy may be important for young people, but so is their connectedness with family ties.

The most vociferous criticism of parenting styles that I have encountered was in a therapeutic group for young women who criticised parents who 'let their teenage children go out and do what they like'. These young women described their need for appropriate freedom to be balanced with continuing daily support, care, and guidance.

Young people are not simply separating from their parents, rather they are redefining their relationships with them.

2. Encouraging communication with peers

Many workers, from Erikson (1967) through to Pople (2009), would acknowledge the fundamental significance placed on friendships and peer relationships during adolescence. Peer relationships are vital in developing self-esteem (Harter, 1990). Often adolescents can talk to each other in a more reciprocal and less pressured way and they can provide a rich potential for mutual support. Young people who have had abusive experiences may also find it easier to trust people of their own age. Therefore, it is important to acknowledge and promote the resources in these relationships. Working alongside adolescents there will often come a time where there is a shift from talking primarily about family to talking about friends. We need to recognise this shift as a healthy signal as ultimately it is relationships with peers that will prove to be the most appropriate future focus for any adolescent.

Working with autonomy: the importance of being seen and being hidden

One of the central paradoxes in working alongside clients of secondary school age is their drive to be both recognised and to keep themselves hidden. Winnicott (1964) suggests that the self-consciousness and introspection of adolescence are in reaction to a desire not to have a still developing self intruded upon. An image for this concept is one of the pupa stage of butterfly development: this drawing into itself is necessary for the chemical soup inside the chrysalis to do its development work. As such the walls of a teenager's bedroom may perform the same containing role: adolescents are resistant to being intruded upon and uncovered before they have had a chance to discover what lies beneath. Many young people will enter therapy because they have experienced a violation of their core self in the form of physical or sexual abuse (Frankel, 1998), and therefore to intrude upon an undeveloped sense of self may represent a repetition of earlier traumatic violations. Simple phrases that reinforce their right to be the arbiters of what they reveal can be helpful, such as:

'You are in charge of what you talk about or share with me'.

In contrast, there are also parts of adolescents that are longing to be affirmed and recognised. Young people may often progress in therapy by exposing increasingly those more challenging parts of themselves, which can then be accepted and potentially integrated (Frankel, 1998).

Towards the end of working with adolescent clients they can be asked 'how much' they have been able to share in counselling. This can be represented metaphorically as a group of pebbles or shells in a sandtray or as a diagram showing the divisions of a circle. They can then decide how much they want/need to reveal in any remaining sessions. It can be helpful to acknowledge that they may want to keep some material private, or perhaps share these feelings with a friend or family member instead. This models a holding process that is flexible and acknowledges the significance of other relationships.

Holding the gaps

Although many secondary age clients will come regularly to sessions exactly on time, the seesaw balance between autonomy and dependence is often symbolically represented in the work by frequent gaps between sessions. During these times it is important to continue to keep open the therapeutic space. Being a 'good enough' therapist for secondary school clients can mean allowing for the 'moving away from' and 'return to base' nature of adolescent development.

3. Working with angry, confused, and shameful adolescents

In this section we will explore the feelings of shame, anger and confusion with adolescents. There are many other feelings that will be powerfully present for young people, but these three emotions seem to me to be actively related to adolescence as a developmental stage.

Confusion

The idea of role confusion is synonymous with our idea of adolescence (Erikson, 1968) and indeed young people may try out different identities and peer group and cultural affiliations. All of this is happening at a point where the rising production of sexual hormones in conjunction with changing relationships and social experiences may give rise to intense emotionality and mood swings (Geldard and Geldard, 2004). Intense confusion can often provoke a feeling of being overwhelmed. Having thoughts and feelings mirrored and named in counselling can allow young people to gain distance and clarity. Image making in particular can offer the opportunity to externalise contradictory feelings through which greater clarity and understanding may emerge.

Anger

This is equally associated with adolescence. Oaklander (2006) suggests that anger is vital to express needs and hence it is essentially an assertion of the self. For adolescents who are actively forming and defining their selfhood anger is perhaps a natural vehicle, yet this is the emotion around which there is greatest prohibition. The repression of anger can be experienced as rejection (and thus if I am angry, and anger is considered bad, therefore 'I must be bad'). Oaklander suggests that the repression of natural anger is at the root of most referrals to therapy for young people. Anger may be misdirected, projected, turned back in, and end up erupting in a variety of social, behavioural or even physical symptoms that seem to be removed from the original source: from the 15 year old boy in foster care causing fear and powerlessness by deflecting his anger into acts of aggression, to the withdrawn and compliant 11 year old girl, whose anger only finds expression through her constant scratching in response to chronic eczema. There may be infinite numbers of reasons why adolescents are angry, but there are perhaps some common development themes (see Figure 5.3).

Loss of idealised views of parents. *Sometimes young people need space to mourn the loss of their idealised parent image. This can be complicated by family separation or conflict.*

Re-emergence and recognition of earlier trauma. *Sometimes with increasing maturity and social pressure, and lessening idealisation, young people come to see their earlier inadequate parenting, or abuse, as 'not okay'.*

The need to re-negotiate patterns of parenting from those appropriate to younger children to those appropriate to teenagers.

The need to define and assert a separate identity from parents and other adults.

Figure 5.3 Anger in adolescence

Angry teenage clients first need to be given permission to be allowed to feel angry. Sometimes a young person may have experienced such active disapproval of their anger expression that they have lost contact with any awareness that they are angry. Alternatively, they may deflect their anger outwards into acts of aggression that are far removed from the original provocation for the feeling. Reframing the feeling of anger as a force for change is helpful, while minimising acting on anger in such ways as is hurtful for others or self-destructive. It can be useful to explore whether a client usually directs their anger outwards or inwards and the consequences for them of both these options. A young person who has had an opportunity to dialogue the really angry things they would like to say to their dad is likely to find catharsis and containment in such expression. This may also promote an expression of the vulnerability that may underpin such angry feelings. It is important to convey an interest in anger, and therefore send the message 'Your anger is okay and therefore you are okay'. Decreasing confusion by explicitly giving permission for love and anger to co-exist can also be very helpful.

Shame

This has also often been described as a feature of adolescence (Erickson, 1967; Frankel, 1998; Bomber, 2009). Adolescents can be highly self-conscious and fear exposure. Comments about their personality or appearance by peers, adults or parents can be experienced as excruciatingly painful. The concern about how they are perceived is also echoed in the attention they give to how they dress and speak, and their niche within social hierarchies and groups. A sense of inner badness can overwhelm some young people in the face of over-exposure, which can then give rise to a profound toxic shame that can leave young people in despair (Bomber, 2009). Frankel warns against therapists becoming 'ultra-sound technicians', indiscriminatingly using counselling techniques to 'uncover a definite image of the self before it is ready to be born' (1999: 128). The development of an adolescent's psyche requires some level of concealment and so a degree of therapeutic 'lightness of touch' is often helpful with these clients. This is the therapeutic equivalent of the off-side rule in football, namely that to be effective and protect the working alliance we never want to get too far in front of our adolescent clients.

Working with adolescent configurations of the self

It has been well established in psychotherapy that the self can be experienced as a community of voices (Mearns and Thorne, 2000; Stiles, 2005). For adolescents with their active experimentation with different identities this may be a very normalising concept. From Jung the idea of a 'persona', or masks worn in different groups and situations, can be helpful to teenagers struggling with their sense of identity as can the idea of a 'shadow' or destructive side (Winnicott, 1968; Samuels, 1985). There may be a part of a young person that feels aggressive or nihilistic (the 'not for growth' part as identified by Mearns and Thorne, 2000). This young person then has an opportunity to establish healthy connections and dialogue between these sub-personalities and hence live in a less 'split-off' way (Frankel, 1998; Stiles, 2005). As counsellors we have an opportunity to accept and offer empathy to different parts of the self, and especially to those parts that the young person (or others) would find difficult.

The following creative activities can be useful:

1. Discussing the roles clients play in different contexts and making masks to represent these. *This provides opportunities to explore the feelings behind the mask.*
2. Using sandtray figures or animals to represent the various sides of a young person's personality. *Providing an opportunity to dialogue between figures and discuss who sees each side of their personality.*

3. Personifying in close-up particular parts of the self or persona by drawing or painting these. *This gives a client an opportunity to externalise a more problematic sub-personality and have it recognised and accepted.*
4. Depressed young people often experience an inner critic (Stinckens, 2002). *It can be helpful to separate this out by making an image of this, and encouraging the young person to dialogue with it.*

We will now conclude this section by giving a brief outline of adolescent wellbeing and mental health.

Overview of current issues in adolescent wellbeing and mental health

Adolescence is a decisive time in the development of lifelong mental wellbeing, as most lifelong mental difficulties usually develop before the age of 25 (WHO, 1998). Today's young people are growing up in a period of rapid social changes and the impact of these changes on their wellbeing is the subject of much current research and debate. There is only sufficient space in this chapter to give a brief overview of what are considered some of the key changes affecting adolescent wellbeing. In-depth investigations of adolescents' changing social lives can be found in work by Gibson-Cline (1996), Larson et al. (2002), Coleman (2011), and Hagell (2012).

A UNICEF study reported that young people in the UK scored very low in five out of six measures of wellbeing in comparison to those in other wealthy countries (Adamson, 2007). The implication that teenagers in the UK are comparatively worse off in terms of their emotional wellbeing has prompted much concern. There is some evidence that the rising rates of emotional and behavioural difficulties that were increasing worryingly in the 1980s and 1990s have plateaued in the twentieth century thus far (Collishaw et al., 2004; Hagell, 2009). However, a recent review suggests that young people in Britain still suffer from poorer life experiences and emotional health than their counterparts did living through the 1970s and 1980s (Nuffield Foundation, 2009).

The reasons for this situation are still the subject of ongoing investigation, but the following suggestions have been raised by Rutter and Smith (1995), Collishaw et al. (2007) and The Nuffield Foundation (2009):

1. The increasing rate of social and economic inequality in British Society. *The gap between the resources and opportunities available to wealthier young people and their poorer counterparts is widening.*

2. Changing family structures. *In addition many young adults may face an increasing period of dependence on parents.*
3. Changing educational expectations and opportunities. *Especially for those young people who usually struggle in academic tests.*
4. Changing patterns in youth employment.
5. The impact of differences in the current youth culture.
6. The impact of changes in how young people spend their leisure time and the nature of peer relationships. *Do young people spend less time with adults than they used to?*
7. Particular factors pertaining to social changes for young men in terms of relationship patterns, the availability of drugs and alcohol, and an increasing risk of imprisonment.

Coping with difficulty is also necessarily influenced by inner self-esteem and confidence (Sandler, 1997; Dumont and Provost, 1999; Haine et al., 2003). Difficulties can arise where young people have too many things to cope with at the same time, and especially when important decisions or changes need to be made around key 'turning-points' (Graber and Brooks-Gunn, 1996).

John

John (aged 18) was studying for his 'A' levels when his best friend killed himself. Three months later his mum was diagnosed with cancer and his dad became depressed. The resulting stress and anxiety greatly affected his studies and his decision not to go on to university.

There follows an outline of some of the major mental health disorders that young people can experience. There is insufficient space here to outline every possible mental health difficulty that might arise, so I shall instead mark out the most worrying difficulties that counsellors working with adolescents may encounter.

Depression

Many adolescents will exhibit symptoms of mild depression from time to time. Low mood can be a feature of dealing with the developmental and social demands of maturing towards adulthood. Occasionally, however, this low mood can deepen into a more significant or major experience of depression. It has been suggested that up to 3% of adolescents can experience significant depression in one year that impairs their ability to function (National Institute for Health and Clinical Excellence, 2005a).

The features of depression typically include sadness, irritability, a loss of interest and social withdrawal, as well as more physiological factors such as difficulty sleeping, changes in appetite and difficulty concentrating, as well as pervading feelings of guilt, shame, worthlessness, and possibly a preoccupation with thoughts of suicide (BMA, 2006). Depression can be connected with major or multiple losses that young people have experienced. A settled sense of powerlessness, hopelessness and isolation can be a feature for depressed youth. Young people need opportunities to express their feelings of loss or anger, but also need to increase their sense of connectedness in relationships along with their sense of personal power and agency.

Self-harm

Self-harm in young people is often connected with other emotional difficulties and can be a form of release, or a method for numbing painful or overwhelming feelings. It can also be a way of taking control or managing problems (BMA, 2006). It can act as a method of coping which adolescents feel they have ownership of. It may be connected with thoughts of suicide, but conversely it is most often a method for ensuring survival (NSPCC, 2009). Self-harm can take many forms, including cutting, burning, scalding, scratching, self-poisoning, hair pulling or punching walls. There is evidence that the incidence of self-harm is increasing for young people in the UK. Ougrin et al. (2012) suggests that 10% of adolescents will have self-harmed by the time they finish secondary school, while Madge et al.'s (2008) anonymous European survey suggested that 70% of 15 to 16 year olds reported that they had self-harmed at some point. It is more common for girls (11.2%) than boys (3.2%) (Hawton et al., 2002), and the average age for beginning to self-harm is 12 years old (MHF/CF, 2006). Self-harm can also be a way of mitigating the pain felt in the aftermath of sexual abuse or other major traumatic experiences (Van der Kolk et al., 1991; Klonsky, 2008).

Self-harm can be misunderstood in schools where the accusation of 'attention seeking' or 'copy-catting' belies this often highly secretive and shame-laden experience. The act of cutting, for example, can provoke powerful feelings of anxiety, disgust, anger, shock or horror that can cause others to recoil at a point where maintaining relationships is vital. Young people are often fearful of disclosing self-harm for fear that their parents will be informed, as is common practice in schools (MHF/CF,

2006; NSPCC, 2009). This leaves counsellors with dilemmas about how to work safely, and ethically, in order to best support self-harming clients. Sometimes conversations with young people about reducing the frequency of cutting, or minimising the risks of infection, can be helpful. However, it is not often therapeutic to give a focus to the self-harming behaviour as self-harm is the means of managing a difficulty rather than the underlying cause of the distress.

Suicide

Working alongside young people who have thoughts of suicide can cause huge anxiety. Suicide and attempted suicide are very rare for under 11s and more of a risk in later adolescence (from 15 upwards; see BMA, 2006). Young men between the ages of 15 and 24 are most at risk due to the more dangerous methods that boys tend to choose, although there has been some levelling-off of this trend in recent years (Samaritans, 2012), however, girls are more likely to attempt suicide. Between 2 to 3% of girls will do so at some point during their adolescence (BMA, 2006). Young people are considered to be at greater risk in the following situations:

- Where there have been previous suicide attempts.
- Where there is substance abuse.
- Where there is associated serious mental illness, particularly depressive illness.
- Where there has been the previous suicide of a close friend or family member.
- Where there is social isolation (WHO, 1998; BMA, 2006).

There is also some evidence that adolescents who attempt suicide have stressful lives and fewer coping skills, and often a poor school performance (Dacey and Kenney, 1997). Suicidal ideation can be a common experience for adolescents who are severely depressed. Intense hopelessness is strongly associated with thoughts of suicide and coming into contact with such powerful feelings can have a paralysing counter-transference effect on us as counsellors. We would advocate actively using supervision to contain anxiety and create a separate thinking space aside from our clients. It is beneficial to consider the network of other professionals, friends and family who may also work to support the young person. Having a supervisor who is willing to accept 'emergency' phone calls in response to concerns about suicide is also important, as there is sometimes an immediate need to discuss the potential risks if clients are to be kept safe. It is also vital to recognise the limits of our own competence and make onward referrals to the local Child and Adolescent Mental Health service (CAMHs) where there is serious suicidal intent or risk, as this will allow young people to be further supported by a multi-professional team. If we as counsellors allow ourselves to become isolated and hopeless in response to these feelings in our clients, we are unlikely to prove helpful to this most vulnerable group.

Eating-related distress

Changing bodies during adolescence, increasing self-consciousness and awareness of peer judgements, as well as an increasing prevalence of media hyper-concern with body image, can all make young people become highly sensitive to insecurities about their body shape and uncomfortable with their relationship with food. For some young people who feel deeply powerless their most natural self-assertion is to control their food intake. Intense feelings of shame can lead them to focus their care on others and want to starve themselves, or conversely hide their inner sensation of badness in food and fat. Food is often used to communicate that which is unsayable in family relationships: there is significant evidence, for example, that eating disorders can be associated with sexual abuse (Hall et al., 1989; Welch et al., 1997). I believe that eating difficulties are primarily a metaphor for the true origins of distress.

Anorexia (starving oneself) can often be accompanied by excessive exercise to increase weight loss. Bulimia involves a cycle of bingeing and vomiting or the use of laxatives. Both conditions can be hazardous with severe weight loss potentially causing other severe health issues such as osteoporosis and cardiovascular disease and potentially, death (BMA, 2006). Seeking the support of the local CAMHs or specialist eating service is appropriate here. The average age for the onset of anorexia is 15 whilst for bulimia it is 18 (Mind, 2005). To further explore the relationship with food as a manifestation of distress I would recommend helpful work by Buckroyd and Rother (2008), and to explore the wider social construction of body hatred in our twenty-first century society I would suggest Orbach (2009).

Post-traumatic stress

Trauma may be the result of a single incident or the result of a series of incidents taking place over months or years, as is often the case in physical, emotional or sexual abuse or the witnessing of domestic violence (Royal College of Psychiatrists, 2012).Trauma may leave young people secretly stuck in the past, constantly reliving the terror in their bodies and minds but often failing to be able to fully express and integrate the events that have overwhelmed them (Van der Kolk, 1994: Herman, 2001). Post-traumatic stress is the label for a group of common reactions to frightening experiences. These include:

1. *Intrusive memories of the event*, often in the form of flashbacks.
2. *Hyper-arousal that can pervade the person's present life.* High cortisol levels evoke an almost constant state of fear arousal (Rothschild, 2000).
3. *Avoidance of stimuli associated with the trauma.* Clients may feel generally numb, unable to feel positive emotions. Amnesia may also prevent them from recalling aspects of their experience (American Psychiatric Association, 2001: NICE, 2005; Royal College of Psychiatrists, 2012).

Experience suggests that sometimes the physical, social, cognitive and sexual changes in adolescence seem to evoke a re-connection with, and a re-evaluation of, earlier traumatic experiences. These young people may seem distant, numbed or switched off, and may experience an on-going everyday mood of constant low-level fear (Perry, 2005). They may also have very short fuses, especially in situations where they feel frightened, trapped, powerless or shamed (Bomber, 2005), and perhaps experience powerful feelings of guilt, shame, anger, confusion and anxiety (NICE, 2005).

Attending to clients' ability to cope in the present is vital as there is the real possibility of re-traumatisation in the face of such overwhelming feelings. It is helpful to discuss strategies for managing flashbacks, such as positive visualisations or 'anchors' of safe people or places as described by Rothschild (2000), or develop other strategies for self-soothing. Some young clients can be encouraged to imagine a simple red no entry sign as a symbolic way of blocking intrusive images. Often just the hope that it is possible to lessen the frightening experience of flashbacks can help clients feel more in control. Image work is very helpful as this allows for processing the unspoken and this happens in the right brain, which it is suggested is responsible for the regulation of extreme fear reactions through its connections with the limbic and autonomic nervous systems (Schore, 2011b). Detailed description of approaches to working creatively with young trauma survivors can be found in Carey (2006) and Bannister (2003). Young people may feel like they are going 'mad' and therefore it is vital to convey that these confusing symptoms are a normal psychological reaction to frightening or powerfully shameful experiences.

Early onset psychosis

Psychosis is a loss of contact with external reality through withdrawal into a private unreal world of hallucinations or strange beliefs in the form of delusions and behaviour in response to these beliefs (see *DSM-IV-TR*, American Psychiatric Association, 2001). Although serious psychosis is more often experienced by young adults, the first signs of a later, more ongoing difficulty can appear from about age 15 onwards (Royal College of Psychiatrists, 2012).

Hallucinations

These are perceptual experiences that do not exist in reality. They can be experienced as visual or kinaesthetic (e.g., feeling things crawling on you) or auditory (hearing voices). Such voices can often be highly persecutory and denigrating in nature (BMA, 2006).

Delusions

Young people may develop beliefs that seem out of step with their cultural and social context. They may become overly religious or superstitious, they may feel they are being inexplicably persecuted, or they may feel like they deserved to be punished for some imagined crime. Alternatively, they may perceive themselves in a grandiose way as especially significant or powerful (Royal College of Psychiatrists, 2012).

These experiences will often cause great anxiety for parents and teachers as well as huge distress in the young people concerned. Conversely, they can also be regarded as 'everyday' and usual by some clients. These elements may be combined with a withdrawal from social interactions and school work, extreme emotionality, and unexplained behaviour.

Such experiences are common from time to time in young people. However, where there are serious concerns about ongoing unusual perceptions, beliefs, behaviour and hallucinations, we would recommend a referral to CAMHs for further assessment. Hallucinations can be associated with a compulsion to self-harm or attempt suicide, as when young people hear voices telling them to hurt themselves in particular ways. These experiences may be early indications of longer-term mental illness, such as schizophrenia or bipolar affective disorder, or brief intense periods of mental disturbance such as acute psychotic disorder (*DSM-IV-TR*, American Psychiatric Association, 2001). Such conditions may require treatment with medication that suppresses the psychotic symptoms and allows the young person to continue to function. Substance abuse is also closely related with hallucinations and psychotic experiences (see below). Young people may also initially present with descriptions of strange perceptual experiences that they will cease to talk about once they feel more secure and start to express their feelings about themselves and others.

Substance abuse and mental health

Mind-altering drugs such as alcohol, glue-sniffing, aerosols, amphetamine and cannabis can trigger and significantly worsen young people's mental health. Using certain substances can likewise induce hallucinations and paranoia. A study during 2004 found that 11% of 11 to 15 year olds had taken cannabis (National Centre for Social Research, 2005). The survey also found that 4% of 11 to 15 year olds had taken Class A drugs in the previous year. The effects of using drugs during the teenage years, where young brains are still developing, are the subject of ongoing research. For example, early use of significant amounts of cannabis has been heavily linked to mental illness and psychosis in later life (Hall, 2006). Alcohol can also worsen the effects of suicidal ideation in young people and make suicide attempts more likely (BMA, 2006).

Conclusion

Students at secondary school are experiencing profound developmental changes in their bodies, minds, emotions and social identities. The clients who enter our counselling rooms may have experienced early developmental deficits, trauma, loss, attachment difficulties or multiple stressors, and they deserve support from counsellors who are sensitive to their emergent and often multi-faceted identity and appreciate their capacity for resilience. We have outlined how adolescent development is viewed by Erikson as a stage focused on identity formation and confusion, and looked at some of the implications for clinical practice. We have also explored working with the powerful feelings of anger, confusion and shame. Recent developments in our understanding of young people's wellbeing have been overviewed and some of the most worrying conditions that adolescents may experience discussed. If twenty-first century secondary students in the United Kingdom have poorer life-experiences and more emotional difficulties than their counterparts in previous decades, they deserve access to high quality support (Adamson, 2007; Hagell, 2009). The recent report into the Welsh school counselling programme is an indication of the sucessful impact on young people's wellbeing of increasing access to school-based counsellors (Hill et al., 2011). Our tentative hope is that this programme can be a trailblazer that gives rise to an extension of this kind of provision to other parts of the UK.

We would just like to add how energising it can be working with secondary school clients. It is impossible to generalise about the uniqueness of these therapeutic relationships but some themes do emerge: for example, adolescents' 'down to earthness', their honesty and feistiness, and on occasion their sense of drama. Above all, in working with young people's developing identities, we are engaging with possibility, movement and change that when taken together are profoundly exciting.

PART 3

Working Therapeutically with Children and Adolescents in Schools

SIX The Therapeutic Relationship: Building a working alliance with children and adolescents

Carol Holliday

This part of the book begins by discussing the various strands of what constitutes a therapeutic relationship and in particular explores the factors that make a difference to children's emotional wellbeing. Concepts from the main approaches to child therapy are examined and related to evidence from research and practice. In separating the strands of the therapeutic relationship for the purposes of discussion we do not mean to imply that these are indeed separate. Examining relationship via the metaphor of strands is a useful means of analysis and helps us to think about the whole (many theoreticians and researchers use this device e.g., Gelso and Hayes, 1998, Clarkson, 2004 and Jacobs, 2010). In reality, these strands interpenetrate each other and are seamlessly interwoven to form the fabric of the therapeutic relationship. The 'threads' we examine below are the working alliance (this chapter), the real relationship, and the transferential relationship (Chapter 7).

There is now overwhelming evidence that the quality of the therapeutic relationship generally, and of the alliance in particular, can be a predictor of the therapy outcome (Norcross, 2002; Cooper, 2008; Haugh and Paul, 2008): the better the quality of the relationship, the more

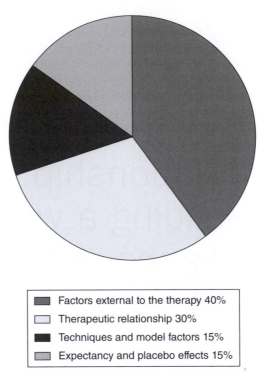

Figure 6.1   Factors that influence therapy outcome

likely the therapy is to have a successful outcome. A strong relationship predicts success and a weak relationship predicts a premature ending of the therapy. Asay and Lambert (1999), in a much quoted study, have suggested that of those factors under the influence of the therapist, the nature and quality of the therapeutic relationship accounts for the largest percentage of improvements in clients.

Subsequent literature research by Wampold (2001) concludes that there is no evidence to suggest that any specific ingredient is responsible for the benefits of psychotherapy, whereas an examination of the common factors convincingly demonstrates that the quality of the therapeutic relationship is a key component.

Norcross (2002) shows that the most demonstrably effective factors in psychotherapy are the quality of the therapeutic alliance, goal consensus and collaboration, and empathy. The majority of research in this area is that which takes place with adult clients, and the construct of a therapeutic alliance was originally articulated in relation to therapy with adults. However, more recent investigations of processes in child and youth therapy indicate similar correlations (Creed and Kendall, 2005; Zack et al., 2007).

Based on the knowledge articulated in Part 1 of this book, where the emotional environment is identified as being a key factor in human development, we can make the informed supposition that relational factors are even more significant in child and adolescent therapy than in adult work.

We note here that terms are used inconsistently in the literature. Some authors see the therapeutic relationship as being a constituent of the therapeutic alliance (e.g., Creed and Kendall, 2005). In this book we are following Gelso and Hayes (1998, 2007) and the majority of practitioners in viewing the therapeutic relationship as the overarching concept and the working alliance as a component of it.

Succeeding chapters in this part of the book focus on the various interventions available to therapists. We explore working with feeling and thinking and the importance of working with the body. We then reflect on the significance of play, image and working with the arts. These chapters demonstrate that therapeutic work needs to be particular and contingent, that it is not a case of one size fits all. The work needs to be adapted and tailored to the needs of the child, not the child to the therapy. Child therapists, therefore, have to be creative, spontaneous and flexible in order that they can devise and offer the particular intervention that a particular child needs at a particular time and place. They also need to have a broad and deep theoretical base to help them think through the unique situations they will find themselves in. Fiona Peacock completes Part 3 by pursuing the relational theme and considering how to work with other relationships in children's lives.

This next section explores the theory and practice of creating a working alliance in a developmentally appropriate way. It also examines the boundaries of the work. The concept of containment is key here and we explore what this means for child therapy. The practical features of how to build an alliance will be discussed and examples will be given.

The working alliance

The working alliance is a concept initially articulated by Bordin (1979) as involving tasks, goals and a bond. Gelso and Hayes (1998) define the working alliance as 'the joining of the reasonable part of the client with the therapeutic aspects of the therapist for the purpose of the work' (i.e., it is about collaboration and a commitment to the work). Although the working alliance can be conceptualised in varied ways (O'Brien and Houston, 2007), and different theoreticians and practitioners will have differing emphases, there is a broad agreement that it involves two key elements:

- An alliance/collaboration with particular boundaries that provide a structure for the work.
- An emotional bond.

We will now examine these elements in relation to child therapy.

Collaboration

Taking an integrative stance means that the therapist 'needs to work from a coherently organised reflexive philosophical and theoretical position within a relational framework' (Gilbert and Orlans, 2011). This means the therapist is continually reflecting on and evaluating relationship issues and the client's needs. This standpoint makes their collaboration with the client a central feature of the work. With adult clients this is a matter of talking it through: with children a therapist will need to find developmentally appropriate ways of doing this by using a developmentally appropriate vocabulary as well as utilising symbol and play.

Building a working alliance in a developmentally appropriate manner

The working alliance is a collaborative venture and the therapist may need to explain to the child the nature of the work. Children are often referred to therapy by adults and might perceive therapy as a punishment, a remedial educational activity, or sometimes as an art and craft activity. They may simply not know what to expect. Sometimes they will have been given erroneous or even misleading information about therapy. It is important to clarify the child's understanding at the outset and attempt some kind of agreement for the journey ahead. Ascertaining that the child understands and then, if necessary, helping them reframe their notion of therapy is often a first session, or at least an early session task. This, of course, requires us, as therapists, to be clear in our own mind about the nature of the work.

Sally, aged 8, was referred to therapy for her aggressive behaviour at school and her increasing isolation in the playground, as her peers didn't want to play with her. Her teacher and her parents were worried and at home she often fought with her sister. She believed there was something

wrong with her and that people didn't like her. In our first session I won-
dered out loud what she knew about me and about what we would be
doing in our sessions together. She said we would be playing and that I
was going to help her stop fighting.

I have a set of Russian dolls (male and female) in my therapy room
and I sometimes use these as a visual aid for explaining what we do in
therapy. Alternatively, I could use a different containing object such as a
basket or treasure chest. I open the biggest doll and empty her. I suggest
that the inside of the doll is like our minds and that when things happen
in life we have thoughts and feelings and memories about those things
that go into our minds.

I say, 'This is Mildred and inside her is her mind where she has feelings and thoughts and memories. One day something frightening happens
to her and she has some very big feelings that go into her mind'. I put an
object in the doll. 'Then something sad happens and more feelings go into
her mind'. I place another object in the doll. Then I place a few more and
give them feeling labels (e.g., angry, jealous). 'After some time, there are so
many feelings in Mildred's mind that there isn't much room for thinking
or schoolwork or playing nicely with friends'. I put more things in Mildred
and now she doesn't close properly. The feelings all start jostling about and
getting in the way of Mildred's life. I agitate Mildred gently. I say, 'Mildred
needs some help to sort out her feelings and find them a place so that they
don't have to get in her way anymore. In this room, this is the work that we
do. We work with feelings and thoughts and memories and we try to sort
them out. We feel them and think about them. When they have been felt
and thought about they don't cause so much trouble'. I suggest to the child
we do this by talking, telling stories, painting, working in the sand, playing
and lots of other ways. In listing the kinds of things that might be troubling
it can be useful to include something about the child's presenting problem,
in this case playing nicely with friends. Using a male Russian doll for a
boy would also be appropriate as there is some evidence that gender and
cultural matching can be beneficial (McLaughlin et al., 2013). This pertains
both to using toys and when matching client and therapist.

Another useful method for explaining the nature of the work is to
crumple sheets of paper and place them in a suitable container to represent unprocessed thoughts, feelings and memories.

Taking each crumpled sheet out, smoothing it, folding it neatly and
replacing it, can illustrate the sorting-out of feelings that we are
attempting in the work. This metaphor conveys the idea that processing feelings creates more space in our minds with which to think and
it is a metaphor I often use with adolescents. It chimes with the notion
of being 'messed up'. Again, I will talk about the task of feeling and
thinking and say that this can be done in a number of ways.

In trying to create a collaborative alliance I will also flag up the possibility of difficulties on the journey ahead, and try to gain a commitment to continue when the going gets tough. This makes it easier to talk about whatever difficulties arise along the way and weather them. Once an agreement has been established this provides with a warrant for the work that as therapists we can refer to later.

The many-handed contract

In working with children it is not so simple as to establish an alliance with a child, but as therapists we need to develop a working alliance with the parents and any other relevant adult (e.g., a teacher, social worker or health professional). This can be a very complex business, as each relationship is likely to be accompanied by anxieties about the child and/or phantasies about the therapy, which are likely to distort the relationship via projections, transferences and defences.

There is evidence that a parent-therapist alliance is significantly associated with decreases in youth externalising symptoms (Zack et al., 2007) and regular meetings with parents are often a feature of working therapeutically with children. We explore working with parents, and the other adults in children's lives, later in Chapter 10.

Boundaries

Metaphors used by theoreticians to describe therapy include:

- A crucible (Jung, cited in Sedgewick, 2001).
- A temenos (Abramovitch, 2002).
- A safe container (Winnicott, 1965a).
- A frame (Milner, 1950; Gray, 1994).
- A vessel (MacKewn, 1997).
- A vas (Clarkson, 2004).

These all have an idea of containment and a sense of being watertight and leakproof. This is seen as essential in most psychotherapy schools. The boundaries around the therapy are a prerequisite for the work and have many purposes:

- They provide safety and reliability, and facilitate trust.
- They magnify things that would otherwise be invisible (e.g., without a definite start-time perpetual lateness would not be noticed).

- They illuminate/constellate the shadow (e.g., separation distress).
- They provide containment for the therapist and protect against acting out (Gray, 1994).

When working with children the boundaries cannot be watertight. This has been brought home to me, particularly, in my role as supervisor. On several occasions I have been supervisor to a therapist who has graduated from a generic counselling or psychotherapy programme and has obtained employment or a placement in a school setting. There have invariably been difficulties as the therapist is working to one set of assumptions and an idea of watertight boundaries, whereas the school will be working to a different set of assumptions. This lack of mutual understanding has then caused difficulties.

There will be times when it is in the child's best interest for the therapist to talk to parents (or others). There can be a constant tension between the paramount ethical principle of confidentiality and other ethical principles (BACP, 2012) and/or the need to communicate with parents or others. Children are not autonomous in the way that adults are; they cannot divorce, or move home or get a different job. The boundaries around the work of therapy with children need to be semipermeable rather than watertight. I think about this as being like osmosis, namely a transfer of material from one side to the other and back as the relative conditions dictate. The boundary needs to be flexible, elastic, and able to breathe. My preferred metaphor here is that of skin. Skin is protective, it is a barrier that keeps out bacteria and dirt: it also contains and gives form to its contents. Healthy skin keeps in what needs to be kept in and keeps out that which needs to be kept out. Skin is discriminating, sensitive and communicative. It is alive.

I am not arguing that boundaries are not important in work with children. I think they are of great importance and that clarity of boundaries is paramount. Skin is extremely strong and in a healthy organism it has no holes. When skin is broken there is harm and pain. What I am arguing is that the boundaries around work with children are different from those when working with adults and there is no one-size-fits-all approach. This work brings with it an additional ethical responsibility for therapists. Those who work with children need to have a deep understanding of both ethics and the law, which will permeate all they do, not only in regard to safeguarding but also in all other things. For example, they need to be familiar with the various models of children's rights (Daniels and Jenkins, 2010) and able to think about the assumptions they are making about children. They also need to be aware of children's emotional and developmental age, which might be different from their chronological age.

Finally, skin, like the other metaphors for therapy, is supportive, holding and containing. The containment required in child therapy is multi-dimensional. It involves the administrative, ethical, physical, temporal and psychological dimensions of life in particular, and with young children especially it also involves behaviour. The boundaries around therapy are particular and create a space inside them that needs to be free and protected (Kalff, 1980) for therapy to happen. The next section discusses the nature of these boundaries and the spaces they create.

Administrative

This covers who the alliance is with (i.e., the child, parents, teacher, school, social services and/or agency), how the communication will happen (by letter, telephone, email, text, etc.); what will happen with answering machines; whether it is okay to leave a message or not; whether there is a link person in the school; if the professional roles are clearly defined; and how any changes will be made to the initial agreement.

Ethical

Ethical boundaries around the work are paramount. The therapist's central task is one of fidelity or faithfulness, to be trustworthy, honour their word, and protect the child's confidentiality as appropriate. This is a huge area for discussion and will be analysed further in later chapters.

Physical

The physical boundaries of the work involve the walls, ceiling, doors and windows of the room, and the environment in which the room is set. The space these boundaries enclose is the physical setting of the work. The physical environment will have an impact on the work and it is important to think about the message that the setting communicates both about the work and the therapist. Windows through which peers can see in, or doors that could burst open and through which people may intrude, will not promote a space where sensitive feelings can be safely expressed. Rooms that ooze dilapidation or neglect will also not confer a sense of value or respect on either the child or the therapist. Many troubled and troubling children will be familiar with deprivation, emotionally and/or physically. What they need is a reparative experience and it is hard to see how this might happen in a deprived physical environment. This does not mean that the setting must be lavish, rather that it is 'good enough'. This goes for the toys and materials that are provided as well. Battered and broken toys, and stubs of crayons, will convey a lack of care. Likewise, a vast array of multitudes of newly minted toys will be overwhelming. You are aiming for a warm, clean, calm, inviting space with adequate and appropriate materials. In this way you will communicate care, worth and respect for both yourself and your clients.

These physical boundaries can prove symbolic of the therapeutic relationship itself, becoming more than merely the walls and so on, and acquiring a larger meaning.

Temporal

Therapy in school settings is normally bounded by the constraints of the school year and school timetable. There are fixed holidays and a fixed school day. As therapists working in school settings will normally offer a series of sessions the pattern of which will be agreed between us, the child and the school. The time boundaries around the therapy session protect the time inside, which is to be focused on the good of the client. The child's response to the time boundaries can give important information about them and perhaps their families. What is the meaning of always being late or early? Is there a communication of chaos or anxiety?

Our reliability as therapists, being where and when we say we will be, is a key part of the work as it facilitates the development of trust. As with the physical boundaries, the temporal boundaries can become symbolic and acquire a larger meaning. If we can keep clear physical and temporal boundaries we are more likely to be experienced as someone who can provide psychological containment.

Psychological

Psychological containment is the capacity to internally manage troubling thoughts and feelings: as a concept it was first discussed by Wilfred Bion (1970). In early life the mother of an infant is the container for his or her feelings, and through a process of feeling and thinking about them she metabolises them into something that can be tolerated and have meaning. The infant is soothed by her communication of toleration and meaning. The infant is therefore contained, and over time, through a continuous repetition of this process, begins to contain him- or herself. We saw this happening with Sam in Chapter 4 (see page 53). Containment means the adult takes in the feelings and projections of the child and thinks about them, and then conveys to the child a sense that these are bearable, understandable and meaningful.

This idea of containment is related to Winnicott's (1965a) concept of holding. Here, the attentive mother meets the needs of her totally dependent infant and this is referred to as providing a holding environment. It involves physical holding but goes beyond it to include all aspects of meeting the baby's needs, including psychological needs.

Behavioural

In child therapy we take a permissive and accepting stance towards children. However, there are limits to acceptable behaviour and there will be occasions when you will have to set boundaries around this. It is essential to be clear here: the thoughts, feelings and desires of the child are to be fully accepted no matter how aggressive or destructive, but harmful behaviour is not permitted. By firmly holding this particular boundary you are helping the child to feel safe and find more appropriate means of self-expression.

My experience of supervising beginning therapists suggests that holding these boundaries and setting limits to behaviour are anxiety provoking and difficult. We have to tread a fine line that balances the need for acceptance and permissiveness with safety and containment. Setting limits is facilitated by being clear and calm, able to think about what limit is required and why, and having an appropriate vocabulary and form of words.

The boundaries that are set regarding behaviour are those that are also required to ground the therapy in reality. Dee Ray (2011) suggests that the following questions should guide a therapist when deciding which boundaries to behaviour are required:

1. *Is the child's behaviour physically hurting themself, the therapist or other people?* Harm is not allowed. The feelings behind wanting to cause harm and the strength of the impetus to harm are to be accepted, understood and acknowledged. The actual behaviour is not. There is an implication here for the timing of the intervention and boundary setting. Premature boundary setting might interfere with the expression of the desire to hurt and therefore miss an opportunity for understanding and empathy.
2. *Will the behaviour interfere with the provision of the therapy?* This question links with issues relating to the physical and temporal

boundaries. The child might push these boundaries in a way that interferes with the provision of therapy, for example by not wanting to leave at the end of a session or wanting to visit the toilet repeatedly during the session.

3. *Will the behaviour harm the continued use of the room for other clients?* In normal practice a therapy room and its equipment will be used many times in a single day. If one child covers all the toys in paint then it will not be possible for successive clients to use these. Therefore for reasons of practicality this cannot be allowed.

4. *How will the child's behaviour affect the relationship between them and the therapist?* There are some particular child behaviours that might interfere with the therapist's ability to be accepting and to maintain a therapeutic presence. For example, a child picking their nose and then eating the contents might disgust a particular therapist so much that she is not able to do her job. In this case the behaviour is affecting the relationship to the point that a limit must be set. These issues are particular and personal and another therapist might not be at all affected by such behaviour.

Thinking through these four questions will help us decide which boundaries need to be drawn. We can see from these questions that there is not a 'one-size-fits-all approach'. Each case is unique and timing how we set limits is important. The play therapy literature (Axline, 1989; Landreth, 2002; Ray, 2011) is helpful in providing forms of words for drawing boundaries around behaviour. It is likely that all therapists will need to hold these boundaries:

- 'I am not for hurting'
- 'You are not for hurting'
- 'I am not for touching in private places'
- 'In this room you are not for touching in private places'
- The walls are not for painting, gluing or throwing water on'
- 'Sand is not for throwing'
- 'Your clothes are not for taking off'
- 'My clothes are not for taking off'
- 'This room is not for pooing or weeing in'
- 'My hair/clothes are not for cutting'
- 'Your hair/clothes are not for cutting'
- 'Glue/paint is not for drinking'

(Ray, 2011)

In child therapy the therapist's role is to be the containing adult. The details of the processes involved in this role are examined in the next chapter.

The emotional bond

'The bond component of the alliance consists of the affective qualities of the relationship' (Safran and Muran, 2000). The quality of the bond influences the degree of collaboration that can be achieved and vice versa and this is an ongoing process. This idea relates to Winnicott's (1965b) sense of 'fit' between a mother and her infant. Similarly, in therapy there has to be a certain chemistry or a 'good-enough' emotional fit between therapist and child for there to be a 'good-enough' alliance. There needs to be a liking between the therapist and child. The child needs to feel understood, valued, and needs to develop trust and confidence in the therapist. These needs are met by the provision of the boundaries discussed above, the provision of facilitative conditions (Rogers, 1957), and the provision of a secure base (Bowlby, 1988; Holmes, 2001).

Factors that facilitate the working alliance

The chemistry and fit between the therapist and the client, the quality of the understanding of the collaboration and the client, and the clarity and reliability of the boundaries, have each been associated with a strong working alliance and thus better outcomes (Gelso and Hayes, 1998; Cooper, 2008). Other factors identified by these authors include:

- The therapeutic presence of the practitioner.
- Personal preparation of the practitioner.
- The capacity of the therapist to be non-defensive.
- The capacity of the therapist to offer core conditions.
- The expectations of both parties.

These factors and allied processes are covered in the next chapter, which examines further aspects of the therapeutic relationship.

SEVEN The Therapeutic Relationship: Conditions and processes

Carol Holliday

This chapter considers in more detail the various conditions and processes involved in a therapeutic relationship. It will identify key concepts, explain what they mean and why they are important, and illuminate them with case examples to demonstrate how to work with them. Understanding these concepts is necessary because, as we will see, a therapist's conceptualising and thinking skills are essential in managing countertransference and in purposely utilising the therapeutic relationship.

The chapter is organised into three sections. The first looks at that strand of the therapeutic relationship termed the 'real relationship'. Here we examine the core conditions, affect attunement, selective attunements and misattunements, affect regulation, and those aspects generally emphasised by humanistic therapies. The second examines the transferential relationship and the ideas of transference, countertransference and defences, which are ideas traditionally identified with psychoanalytic/psychodynamic approaches. In the third section we explain the attachment relationship and emphasise the importance of supporting other relationships in a child's life, such as those between the child and its parents, grandparents and teachers.

The real relationship

According to Gelso and Hayes (1998) this strand of the therapeutic relationship has two defining features:

- A realistic perception and reaction (i.e., it is more or less uncontaminated by distortions such as transferences).
- A genuineness (i.e., 'the ability and willingness to be what one truly is in the relationship').

There is in the real relationship mutual respect and liking, and the more positive the real relationship the better the process and outcome of therapy (Gelso and Hayes, 1998; Cooper, 2008).

The real relationship also has support from a number of psychotherapy orientations and is encapsulated in the literature under the following concepts:

- Person to Person Relationship (Clarkson, 2004).
- Core conditions (Rogers, cited in Mearns and Thorne, 2007).
- Dialogic encounter – Gestalt theorists.
- I–thou meeting (Buber, 2004).
- Now Moments and Moments of Meeting (Stern, 2004).
- Intersubjectivity (Stolorow and Attwood, 1992).

The therapist's theoretical orientation plays a significant part in how they contribute to the real relationship and humanistic therapists will tend to emphasise this strand of the therapeutic relationship. As the name implies, this aspect is about being human and being real: it involves an emotional contact and empathy on the part of the therapist that is free from the distortions of transference and other internal processes, and when working with children this aspect comes very much to the fore.

Virginia Axline (1989), who developed non-directive play therapy from Carl Rogers' theory and practice of client-centred therapy, established eight basic relational principles for play therapy that would guide a therapist in how to be with a child:

- The therapist must develop a warm and friendly relationship as soon as possible and build a rapport.
- The therapist must accept the child exactly as they are.
- The therapist needs to establish a feeling of permissiveness so that the child feels sufficiently free to express all their feelings.
- The therapist is alert to recognising the feelings the child is expressing and reflects those feelings back to the child in such a manner as they gain insight into their behaviour.

- The therapist maintains a deep respect for the child's ability to solve their own problems if given the opportunity to do so. The responsibility to make choices and instigate change is the child's.
- The therapist is non-directive (i.e., the child leads and the therapist follows).
- The therapist allows the child to go at their own pace and does not hurry them.
- The therapist establishes only those limitations that are necessary to anchor the therapy in reality and to make the child aware of their responsibility in the relationship.

These principles are rooted in the relational conditions Carl Rogers (1965) identified as being necessary and sufficient for therapeutic change in the client. Of Rogers' six original conditions, the therapist provides three, and we now examine these further. They are unconditional positive regard, congruence, and empathy, and these are interrelated, interdependent and interpenetrate each other. We separate them here for ease of elucidation.

Unconditional positive regard

'Unconditional positive regard is the fundamental attitude of the therapist towards the child. The therapist who holds this attitude deeply values the humanity of the client and is not deflected in that valuing by any particular client behaviour' (Mearns and Thorne, 2007). This attitude is demonstrated in the therapist's enduring acceptance of and consistent non-possessive warmth towards the child. This attitude prizes the child for their very humanity and existence in the world. It is fundamentally accepting and non-judgmental.

The research evidence as reviewed by Cooper (2008) concluded that positive regard was modestly related to the outcomes of therapy. Conversely, a lack of unconditional positive regard was associated with negative outcomes. These findings held regardless of the theoretical orientation of the therapist. There is also evidence from several sources that 'genuine care' on the part of the therapist is an important contributor to positive therapeutic outcomes (Cooper, 2008).

Congruence

Congruence is the state of being of the therapist when their outward responses to the child consistently match the inner feelings and sensations that they have in relation to the child (Mearns and Thorne, 2007). Here we are talking about being genuine or authentic (i.e., what you see is what you get).

Rogers believed it to be the most important of the three conditions, however the research evidence has been more ambivalent, with some studies showing no significant relationship to outcome and one third showing a positive relationship. Several studies do cite trustworthiness as being significant and it is difficult to conceive of trust without authenticity (Cooper, 2008). The interpenetrative nature of the core conditions is such that it is unlikely that a child will experience acceptance and empathy unless these are authentically offered.

Empathy

Rogers sees empathy as one of the core conditions of psychotherapy that are necessary and sufficient for change and growth. It is defined as a continuing process whereby the therapist lays aside their own way of experiencing and perceiving reality, preferring to sense and respond to the child's experiences and perceptions (Mearns and Thorne, 2007). It is about tuning in to the child's emotional experience (i.e., feeling with, without being sucked in). It is properly understanding the child's reality and communicating that understanding to the child. It also means entering the child's frame of reference. This is not the same as sympathy, which implies a sense of merging or fusing: the empathic therapist retains their sense of being a separate self.

Most approaches today would concur with the necessity of these facilitative conditions but some would debate their sufficiency. Moursund and Erskine (2003) advocated that therapists should proceed with clinical competence and therapeutic intent. Therapeutic intent ensures that the welfare of the client is paramount and clinical competence allows the therapist to find a response that is appropriate and contingent. For example, if they are amused by a child's anger it would not be helpful to express this, even though it is authentic, as the child might be belittled and shamed. An overprotective parent might perfectly well understand their child's emotions and respond very genuinely but this would not be helpful.

Kohut (1984) also places empathy centre stage. For him, it requires 'vicarious introspection' and the therapist must delve inside themself to imagine what it feels like to be the client, and from there attempts to resonate with the latter's emotional state. A mature self is gradually developed through empathic contact with someone who has mature self-structures, in conjunction with an explanation of what is going on. Thinking and feeling are therefore required.

There is much discussion of empathy in the literature, with Rowan and Jacobs (2002) describing three levels of empathy from level one empathy (a simple cognitive understanding), through level two empathy (a more affective and direct knowing), to relational depth (Mearns and Cooper, 2005). Relational depth is defined as 'A state of profound contact and engagement between two people in which each person is fully real with the other, and able to understand and value the other's experience at a high level'. Here, the space in the relationship between two people is fully occupied and there is no distance between them. The experience is one of time standing still and there is a sense of unity.

There is a common understanding across theoreticians that empathy consists of a cognitive and an affective aspect, an understanding of thoughts and a 'feeling with'. Empathy involves not only experiencing the child but also communicating that experience to them. It moves beyond understanding and includes an appropriate response.

The research evidence shows that therapists' levels of empathy are closely associated with outcomes. The more empathic the therapist, then the better the outcome. Conversely, the characteristic most consistently associated with negative outcomes is the therapist's lack of understanding (Cooper, 2008).

In recent years insights from neuroscience have been brought to bear on the realm of psychotherapy. In particular, Allan Schore (1999, 2008) has articulated a convincing argument for affect regulation as being a key factor in the development of the self, and therefore a key factor in child counselling and psychotherapy.

Affect regulation

Affect regulation is the ability to regulate emotional arousal: it is a core factor in human development and a causal factor in psychopathology (Schore, 2003a, 2003b). Schore and Schore (2008) offer an interpenetrating and overarching theory, which integrates classical attachment theory, object-relations, self and relational psychology with their neurobiological underpinnings. Seen from this vantage point, the underlying cause of many personality, emotional and behavioural disorders is the inability to regulate affect or digest painful and unpleasant feelings. When these feelings are left undigested or unprocessed they leak out in the form of difficult and challenging behaviours, such as aggression, bullying, withdrawal, isolation, hyperactivity and separation anxiety, and even learning difficulties. Children struggling with their feelings may exhibit symptoms at home, such as sleeping and eating disturbances, soiling or bed-wetting, phobias, obsessions and nightmares. These troubled children, and indeed all children, need help to process their feelings. To process a feeling it needs to be experienced, expressed, and thought about in the presence of a safe adult. It is the containment and empathy of the adult and the adult's own ability to self-regulate that facilitate the development of self-regulation in the child. This is not something that can be learned by 'talking about', instead it must be experienced 'in relationship with'.

The implication of this work is that children need a relationship with an empathic adult in order to be able to learn to regulate their emotional states. A small child having a tantrum does not have the capacity to self soothe but needs the soothing presence/touch/words of an emotionally attuned adult to help them. There is nothing automatic about developing the ability to self-regulate our emotions. It is gained in and through relationships. Many of the children who find themselves in therapy will be dysregulated, and will require a therapist's active emotional involvement in order to begin to build the capacity to self-regulate. Affect regulation is therefore a central process in child therapy. The task is to transform unbearable feelings into thinkable thoughts (Geddes, 2006). From a Jungian perspective the child borrows the therapist's ego, or as Dan Hughes puts it, 'piggybacks on my regulation'.

Schore's theory of affect regulation, like Rogers' person-centred psychotherapy and Kohut's self-psychology, places empathy at the heart of the work.

We can conclude that empathy is essential and the key therapeutic factor in child therapy, and at this point we will now consider the various 'facets of the empathic frame' within which development and change are nurtured (Moursund and Erskine, 2003).

Presence

Empathy requires the therapeutic presence of a therapist. A therapeutic presence means being open and available to the other: it is being aware of the self and other, as well as flexible, creative and receptive; it means the therapist having enough space in their mind to be able to take in the child's feelings and to ponder those in their heart; it is a way of being rather than doing; it involves an ability to be still, to be comfortable in their own skin, and comfortable with silence.

Having a therapeutic presence is about being in the present moment (Stern, 2004), not dwelling on the past or worrying about the future. Siegel (2010) discusses how presence can be developed through mindfulness practice (discussed in Chapter 9) and how it is a significant factor in a therapist's ability to help others. Without presence, empathy does not seem likely. An implication, here, is that we need to take our own psychological wellbeing very seriously if we are to be able to care for the psychological needs of children. When a therapist is able to be fully present then they are available to tune into the child's emotional experience. This sense of affect attunement is a vital facet of empathy.

Affect attunement

Stern (1998) defines affect attunement as 'The performance of behaviours that express the quality of feeling of a shared affect state without imitating the exact behavioural expression of that inner state', or 'How you get inside other people's subjective experience and then let them know that you have arrived there, without words'. It is characterised by being non-verbal and cross modal. Communication between attuned people shares the same timing, shape and intensity.

Baby games such as 'Peepo' are good examples of attunement in action, where the adult's exclamation of 'Peepo' matches the dyad's sudden visual connection. There can be a sense of satisfaction and delight in moments of attunement.

> Ava plunges her hands into the sand so they are out of sight. She fixes me with her gaze. She begins to wiggle one finger and the sand trembles over that moving finger. I vocalise 'ooooOOOooooOOO', resonating with her movement. Then when the finger finally pops out of the sand, into view, I stop abruptly with a final whoop. Eye contact is held fast and we are both grinning. We are attuned, joined together in sharing an affective subjective experience without words. Then the next finger begins to tremble the sand ...

According to Stern (1998), this ability on the part of the mother (or primary caregiver) to provide affect attunement is key to the infant's healthy psychological development. It is an implicit relational communication and happens out of an awareness between infants and their carers. In therapy we focus on the child and purposely attempt to attune ourselves to their affective state. When we attune then each partner in the dyad resonates in the same fashion as when two strings of a violin resonate. In resonance there is the sense of the dynamic and interactive and communication flows in both directions. This relates to the concept of relational depth (Mearns and Cooper, 2005). There is a sense of communion, belonging and a deep understanding and this is the heart of empathy as a participative process. When this happens, the child will feel not only seen and heard but also felt.

Attunement is also the means by which a particular baby becomes a member of a particular family through the process of selective attunement. An example here is the mother who is quiet, shy and withdrawn, and finds it easier to attune to her baby's more quiet and gentle emotions: when her baby is loud and boisterous this mother is less engaged and the baby's emotional state gains less emotional validation. Over time, with repeated selective attunement of this nature, this baby may display more of the affective states that received attunement and fewer of the less validated states. As Alice Miller puts it, children learn to get their mother's smile and avoid her frown, and this applies to feelings as well as behaviours.

The implication for us as child therapists is that we need to have a wide emotional range in order to be able to attune ourselves to all the affective states that our child clients might present with. We need to be able to work with all the feelings a child experiences and have the fullest possible perceptual and intuitive awareness of that child. This is another argument for child therapists to engage in their own personal therapy.

However, no matter how competent and sensitive we are, there will be occasions when we misattune to children. We will then notice a change in the rapport. The child is likely to break eye contact with us, perhaps even turn away, and a sense of awkwardness will ensue. What is imperative is that we make an attempt at reparation and are able to re-attune and re-engage with the child's feelings. Ruptures in relationships will happen and repairing these is redemptive. Experiences of rupture and repair are also therapeutic.

Affect attunement between mothers and infants happens unconsciously and is a non-verbal communication. The mother acts as a mirror, reflecting back to the infant an image of itself in her eyes. In healthy relationships this is a beneficial and creative process. Tronick's still face experiment, which involves the mother keeping her face still and not responding normally to her infant, illustrates the profound influence of a mother's face. When a mother is not responsive then a baby quickly become distressed. (The still face experiment is available on YouTube.) Mirroring is a useful metaphor in child therapy and is used by both Kohut and Winnicott. A mirror offers a reflection and thus proves existence. Psychologically the confirmation and validation of a mirroring mother will contribute to a child's sense of self. The qualities and characteristics of the mirror are therefore important. As therapists we need to think about the image of the child they are mirroring back: what image of self is our child client seeing in our eyes and face?

We have seen that both the research evidence and the work of major theoreticians concur, and have established that the concepts gathered together here under the umbrella of the real relationship are of the utmost importance. The real relationship strand of the therapeutic relationship is absolutely at the heart of therapy with children, and therapists need to spend a great deal of time working to develop their thinking and their skills in this area. In therapy a therapist is the empathic adult who helps a child regulate emotion, by being present, attuning, resonating, and therefore facilitating the development of a healthy sense of self.

The next chapter explores the interventions available to therapists to build and sustain a therapeutic relationship. But first we will turn our attention to the ways the real relationship can be skewed and we will now explore the transferential relationship.

The transferential relationship

Transference and countertransference are significant concepts, about which much has been written, particularly in the area of psychoanalysis and psychodynamic counselling and psychotherapy. They were first articulated by Freud and are seen as central tenets of analytic work. This section explains these concepts and how to work with them in child therapy.

We all have a template or a central relationship pattern that serves as a prototype or a schema for shaping subsequent relationships. So, for example, a person with a very critical and punitive father is likely to expect men to be critical and punitive towards them, as this is the template they will have for relationships with men. This phenomenon is termed 'transference'. Past relational experiences are transferred onto the present. Transference is a form of projection: an aspect of a person's internal world is projected onto an external person, and then that external person is treated as though they are exhibiting the aspect.

Gelso and Hayes (1998) define transference as 'the client's experience of the therapist that is shaped by the client's own psychological structures and past, and involves displacement onto the therapist, of feelings, attitudes and behaviours belonging rightfully in earlier significant relationships'.

Transference occurs in all relationships in life and has its origins in childhood, a time when we were small and lacked autonomy over our own lives. It is no surprise then that authority figures such as teachers and therapists are likely candidates to be the recipients of transference projections. In addition, the deliberate focus on relationships in therapy intensifies such projections, as will the lack of knowledge of a therapist's personal life. This means that transference onto the therapist is likely to gather.

Transference is characterised by inappropriate or unrealistic feelings (Gelso and Hayes, 1998). When we become the recipient of a child's transference projection we may feel as though they are addressing someone standing behind us, as it doesn't feel like us. There is often a disproportionate intensity to transference, or an inexplicable absence of feeling, when emotion would normally be present. There might also be an illogical tenacity, namely the child might cling to the projection in the face of contrary evidence. This all happens out of awareness.

Occasionally, a child will tell us we are like Mummy or Daddy. More often, the transference is acted out behaviourally and/or communicated through image, story and play. Schaverien (1992) argues that transference and countertransference relationships are revealed in the images created in therapy. The image itself embodies the transference and this means that images, stories and play will contain significant relational information for the child therapist. This information can help us understand and think about how the child is feeling about us. If the child's image is of a giant bullying a little mouse then we need to be thinking and asking ourselves how we might be behaving (or feeling, or being perceived) like the giant, or how we might be behaving (or feeling, or being perceived) as the mouse.

This transference relationship runs alongside the real relationship and as the work progresses there will hopefully be a gradual experience that the past does not necessarily need to be repeated in the present. The therapist can provide a 'corrective emotional experience' (Kohut, 1984). In analytic psychotherapy the transference relationship has been seen to be central to the therapeutic process and interpreting the transference that will be key to the success of the work. Contemporary thinking, in child therapy, is that often it is more therapeutic to think about the transference and discuss it in supervision rather than directly refer to it with the child. This is known as working *with* the transference (Blake, 2008).

When we talk directly to a child about their feelings about us then this is known as working *in* the transference. It is similar to decoding the metaphor of an image or play and can therefore result in the child being shamed or humiliated. It can also prove exposing, confronting or just too personal. This is referred to as the transference interpretation being too 'hot' (Blake, 2008).

Transference phenomena are recognised by most schools of psycho-therapy and related concepts, and their theoretical frameworks include:

- stimulus generalisation (cognitive behavioural therapy);
- internal working model (attachment theory);
- scripts (transactional analysis);
- organising principle (intersubjectivity).

Kohut (Siegel, 1996) usefully identifies three particular types of transference that arise in therapy in relation to three areas of psychological need: the mirror, idealising, and twinship transferences. The mirror transference arises in relation to a child's need to be mirrored, which for Kohut means affirmed, validated and taken pleasure in. When this need is met then it becomes the foundation of ambition and a realistic sense of self. When there is a deficit in this area then a child will remain hungry for admiration in an attempt to nourish their impoverished sense of self. They will be attention seeking because they are attention needing. They will behave in grandiose ways, characterised by exhibitionism and omnipotence, seeking to ameliorate their lack of self worth and their excruciating sense of being unlovable.

The idealising transference relates to the infant's need to be calmed and reassured by a big, powerful, knowledgeable adult. These experiences become the basis of ideals and values in the mature self as well as leading to the ability to self-soothe. However, if these needs are not met then the ideal hungry child will seek out others, who are beautiful, powerful, and gifted in some way, they will need to admire and idealise someone in order to feel whole, and therefore they will yearn to attach themselves to an omnipotent, omniscient, big person in order to feel secure and safe.

The twinship transference appears in therapy in relation to the need to resonate with the similar qualities of others. If adequately met, this need becomes the root of identifications with others and kinship. It is also the origin of a sense of a separate self. Children with deficits in this area will seek out others who are like them, or seek to be like others by conforming to their dress, views, customs, hairstyles and music tastes, etc.

The closed conditions of therapy provide an environment that facilitates the emergence of transference phenomena, and these understandings will help us provide the emotional environment that is likely to repair developmental deficits.

Countertransference

There is much confusion in the literature regarding this concept and the word is used to describe a range of phenomena, from all the emotions experienced by the therapist to the therapist's transference to the child's transference.

Gelso and Hayes (2007) examined the concept of countertransference in great detail and offer a theory that is both 'meaningful in practice and scientifically generative'. It supports therapists' thinking and understanding as well as stimulating further research. Their theory pertains to work with adult clients but is also acutely pertinent to child therapy. It is rooted in systematic research and summarised as follows. Countertransference is a two-person phenomenon and is co-constructed. This chimes with the intersubjective view (Stolorow and Attwood, 1992), where in a relationship with two sets of organising principles in play then for one person to be understood both participants need to be considered. Gelso and Hayes (2007: 25) defined countertransference as 'the therapist's internal or external reactions that are shaped by the therapist's past or present emotional conflicts and vulnerabilities'. Countertransference, therefore, has its origins in a therapist's unresolved conflicts, vulnerabilities and deficits, which normally have their roots in childhood. Countertransference is triggered in therapy when the child client touches on or activates these aspects of the therapist. This manifests in a number of ways (i.e., emotionally, cognitively and behaviourally). Therapist withdrawal, avoidance or under-involvement with the child and their material could be a sign of countertransference. Conversely, so could over-involvement. In particular, a therapist who feels or behaves aggressively towards a child is highly likely to be experiencing countertransference. Cognitive distortion is also a result of countertransference. Studies by Gelso and Hayes, cited in their (2007) book on countertransference, found that therapists were likely to 'under or over-estimate the sheer frequency of client material when it touches on their own issues'. These distortions can then have a big impact on the work. The unambiguous implication here is that an uncomprehended and unmanaged countertransference will be detrimental and interfere with the therapist's ability to work effectively.

Gelso and Hayes (2007) also suggest a 'double helix of hindrance and potential benefit' that is brought into play by countertransference in the therapeutic relationship: when not understood and unmanaged this is likely to prove a hindrance; when understood, controlled, and used for the benefit of the child it can be positive. They identify five key factors that facilitate the management of countertransference:

self-insight, self-integration, empathy, anxiety management, and conceptualising skills.

Self-insight refers to a therapist's ability to be aware of their own internal vulnerabilities, difficulties and conflicts, to recognise when their responses might be off kilter and be able to reflect on this. The need for self-awareness and insight supports the argument that therapists need to engage in their own personal therapy.

Self-integration is about the character and qualities of a therapist. They need to be basically solid and sound, with a good sense of their own personal boundaries. Such a therapist will be able to offer a therapeutic presence as well as tune into children's emotions. The idea of the therapist as 'wounded healer' is much vaunted nowadays, with the implication here being that it is the therapist's wounds that need to be 'healed enough', and the therapist as a mirror needs to be clear enough.

Empathy was discussed in detail earlier in this chapter. It promotes a focus on the world of the child and therefore stops the therapist focusing on their own difficulties.

The fourth factor is anxiety management. This is about the therapist's ability to contain their anxiety (i.e., not to suppress it, but to feel it and think about it). This relates to the therapist's ability to self-regulate.

The last factor is conceptualising skills. These are the skills required to think about what is happening in the therapeutic relationship: they involve having a sound knowledge and understanding of theory, and the ability to link that theory with practice.

Managing countertransference is therefore a demanding business, requiring therapists to be open, honest and non-defensive in their self-examination. It requires both reflection and reflexivity: reflection involves thinking about the child after the session and in supervision; reflexivity is an on-the-spot reflection or reflection in action. It involves being aware of what is going on in ourselves and simultaneously being aware of what is happening in the child and of what is happening in the process of the interaction between us and them, and it is therefore more than the sum of its parts. It is purposeful, active and relational. It means our being both an observer to our interactions and experiencing the impact of ourselves on each child and them on us.

These understandings will support us in the demands of managing countertransference. Much of what a child will communicate in therapy is non-verbal, and thus we will find ourselves in a place of 'not knowing'. A sound grasp of theory will help and support our thinking by providing us with a map by which we can navigate unknown territory.

Defences

Painful feelings are a natural and normal part of life. From the very first day of life, even in the most emotionally healthy environment, we will experience necessary losses (Viorst, 1988) and optimum frustrations (Kohut, 1984). It is natural and normal to protect ourselves from psychic pain and to unconsciously develop mechanisms or strategies that will serve as barriers to that pain. These defences help us manage both intra-psychic conflicts and anxieties, as well as interpersonal relationships. They have an adaptive and useful function in human development. However, they can become unhelpful, even damaging, if they solidify into personal characteristics. They are ways of denying or distorting reality to make it more bearable.

The concept of defences is emphasised in the psychodynamic school of counselling and psychotherapy. It is also discussed in terms of barriers and resistances (Davy and Cross, 2004) and most theoretical frameworks are in accord with this idea. Anna Freud (1937) first comprehensively described and classified types of defences, and her ideas have been extended throughout the twentieth century.

Notably, Vaillant (1992) categorised defences into four hierarchical levels. The first level is referred to as pathological: these are the most severe manifestations of defences and serve to avoid the need to cope with reality. These are normal responses in children, but in older individuals they are considered pathological and can be seen in psychosis. This level of defences include:

- extreme denial – refusing to accept the external reality (e.g., refusing to believe a loved one has died);
- conversion – converting an unbearable feeling into a physical symptom such as paralysis or numbness;
- delusion – believing (often persecutory) untruths about reality;
- splitting – experiencing reality, people or events as all good or all bad;
- distortion – skewing the external world to agree with the internal world.

Level two defences serve to reduce anxiety and are described as immature defences although they manifest in people of all ages. This level of defence, when employed excessively, is associated with depression and personality disorders, and these can seriously impede adequate functioning in life. This level includes:

- projection – this is attributing one's own unacceptable feelings and thoughts to another (e.g., Liam behaves towards Jake as if Jake is angry, whereas Liam is actually angry but it is outside of his awareness);

- passive aggression – aggression is expressed indirectly;
- idealisation – attributing out of proportion positive qualities to another;
- acting out – taking action with no awareness of the emotion that is behind the behaviour.

The third level involves neurotic defences that are prevalent amongst most people. These can assist us in coping in the short term but become problematic with overuse. Examples of level three defences are:

- displacement – unwelcome feelings or impulses are redirected at a less threatening target (e.g., Amy is angry with her teacher but kicks Mary);
- dissociation – separating or distancing oneself from the experience of an emotion so that it is not felt;
- hypochondriasis – fixing anxiety onto worrying about having a serious illness;
- rationalisation – excusing behaviour through faulty logic;
- reaction formation – behaving in a way that is in direct opposition to what is actually felt.

The final category is that of the mature defences. These are ways of coping and integrating painful experiences into the personality that are healthier. These level four defences may have stemmed from previous less evolved mechanisms but have since developed to be adaptive and helpful. Examples of these are:

- altruism – serving other people as a way of looking after the self;
- anticipation – preparing for future difficulty;
- humour – expressing and acknowledging emotional pain in an amusing manner;
- sublimation – transforming painful feelings into beneficial activity (e.g., art or sport).

The examples given above are not exhaustive and many authors will identify numerous others. These Vaillantian ideas are useful to us however, and give us a language with which to think about what might be happening in our child clients. The issue now becomes one of how we can work with defences.

A Rogerian approach would be to conceptualise the results of defence mechanisms as incongruence and offer the core conditions discussed earlier in this chapter. Seen through the lens of self-psychology, defences are compensatory structures providing recompense when psychological needs were not met. The remedy is a reparative emotional experience that involves attuning with the underlying developmental need.

Contemporary thinking in psychodynamic work now chimes with these approaches (Howard, 2010). Directly interpreting a defence by verbally making it explicit can not only be shaming and exposing but can also lead to an intensifying of the defence rather than a loosening. The point is that the defence is there for a reason and it affords the psyche protection. Exposing the defence can feel like criticism or an attack and therefore feel persecutory.

In child therapy there will be occasions when a child will tell us about how they coped with difficult or traumatic experiences. This gives permission for you to also talk about defences. It is important to be affirming of their coping strategies even if these are now proving unhelpful. To validate that it was a very sensible thing to suppress all feelings of sadness when Grandma died because they were unbearable can be helpful, alongside introducing the idea that now perhaps those feelings can be borne and felt and thought about, that they do not have to do this on their own, and that always suppressing our feelings can be impoverishing.

Older children and adolescents who have good cognitive functioning might benefit from cognitive behavioural interventions that challenge distortions in thinking by reality testing. This way of working is discussed in the next chapter.

Attachment relationship

John Bowlby, who was a psychiatrist and a psychoanalyst working with maladapted children, pioneered attachment theory. Attachment theory has ascended to a prime position in therapists' thinking. It has both an explanatory and predictive power.

Bowlby drew a parallel between humans and other mammals and suggested that attachment behaviour, such as crying on being separated from parents, was a biological survival strategy (when mammalian young cry they elicit comfort from adults). He went on to develop a set of patterns of attachment between infants and caregivers, based on a close observation of the behaviour of mother and infant dyads. These attachment styles are:

- secure attachment;
- insecure attachment (avoidant);
- insecure attachment (ambivalent);
- disorganised attachment.

There is clear evidence from many robust research studies, both cross-sectional and longitudinal, that strongly associate secure attachment with good functioning across social, emotional and cognitive spheres (Prior and Glasser, 2006). Securely attached infants will most likely develop into confident, high functioning children and adults.

Insecure avoidant attachment is strongly associated with anti-social behaviour, aggression and negative affect. An insecure-ambivalent attachment is strongly associated with passivity, anxiety and with-drawn behaviour. The associations with disorganised attachments are dissociation, aggression, hostility and controlling behaviour.

Secure attachment occurs when the primary caregiver is consistent, emotionally sensitive and responsive, and able to think about the mind of the infant. In this way the carer becomes a secure base for the child from which the latter can go out and explore the world. In therapy the therapist's provision of a secure base, via contingent and sensitive emotional and mind-minded responses, can be a reparative experience.

The next two chapters will focus on the various interventions available to therapists.

EIGHT Working with Thinking, Feeling and the Importance of the Body

Carol Holliday

This chapter expands on the importance of taking a holistic view of the child. Recent scholarship in philosophy and neurobiology (e.g., Damasio, 2000, 2006, 2012; Johnson and Lakoff, 2006) has emphasised the connectedness of thinking and feeling and how 'the body provides the ground reference for the mind' (Damasio, 2006: 223).

In all interactions with the external environment the brain and the body participate in concert. Damasio (2006) tracks our understanding of the human mind from being located in the ether to its twentieth-century residence in the brain. He then goes on to suggest that the mind depends not only on the brain but also on brain-body interactions, and that a more appropriate location for the mind is the body. What we need to understand is that the brain does not equal the mind: they are clearly related but a biological reductionism of the mind to the brain is limiting. The mind includes the body proper, it is more the invisible manifestation of a nexus of, as yet, poorly understood interactions (Panksepp and Biven, 2012), while the mind is more than the sum of its parts.

Thinking, feeling and doing are interrelated and interpenetrate each other. Doing includes behaviour and is important, as children will act out what they experience in their bodies when they are not able to feel or think about their experiences. In this book we are following Damasio's (2012) understanding of emotion and feeling. In this view, although related, there is a distinction between emotions and feelings. Emotions are actions carried out by our bodies, such as facial expressions, gestures and postures, visceral changes, etc. They arise as emotion-triggering regions of the brain are activated. This results in chemicals being released into the bloodstream and the relevant actions ensue. Emotions are, therefore, a collection of observable responses.

Feelings are perceptions of what is happening when we experience an emotion. Feelings are images of actions: they are private under-standings of internal experiences. Damasio (2012: 110) emphasises that 'feelings are based on the unique relationship between body and brain that privileges *interoception*' (emphasis in original). This means privileg-ing stimuli that originate inside the body. Our feelings, therefore, offer us significant information about our internal milieu and ourselves. They tell us what matters to us.

Attending to the body, to breathing, posture, movement, musculature and skin tone, is therefore a key aspect of child therapy. A further implication of the web of interconnectedness of body, brain and mind is that it allows us to think about the idea of a *relational pharmacopeia*. A child in a warm, secure relationship, experiencing safe, positive, physical touch such as hugs and cuddles, will have a body flooded with feel-good chemicals such as oxytocin. Often, in therapy you will find a child will come close and lean against you whilst engaged in play. This can be hugely beneficial for them, helping them to feel calm and secure. Conversely, a child experiencing threat or hostility will have a body flooded with stress hormones such as cortisol, and they will feel miserable, anxious or aggressive.

The central argument here is that the body, emotions, behaviours, feelings and thinking are intimately entwined, and that any therapeutic approach must involve working with all these elements. Additionally, emotions and feelings are crucial as they offer information about the child's internal world and tell us what is important and significant to that child. Emotions and feelings matter: they are the currency and language of the therapeutic encounter. This puts emotions and feelings at the heart of the work.

Feelings are not positive or negative, they are all useful and mean-ingful. It is normal to experience feelings, although some might be difficult and painful. The stance we need to take is to be accepting and befriend our feelings and those of our child clients. We need to be open and gently curious, to empathise and understand and com-municate our understanding. In this way we can assist our child clients to express, experience and think about their feelings. They are then processed or digested and become integrated into the personality rather than denied, split off or neglected. This processing happens in and through a relationship using images and words. (We discuss working with images in the next chapter.) In the sections that follow we include a range of emotion words, as it is vital to have access to a nuanced, emotional vocabulary in order that we can wrap children's experiences in words. We can nurture this capacity in ourselves by reading good novels and poetry to expand our vocabulary. Lieberman et al. (2007) demonstrate how putting feelings into words helps process difficult emotions by disrupting amygdala activity and activating the prefrontal cortex. The amygdala is involved in emotional processing and lower activity correlates with lower arousal. The prefrontal cortex is associated with executive functioning, including moderating our social behaviour. Naming feelings is therefore therapeutic: those children who find their way to our therapy rooms are likely to lack this ability.

Panksepp (1998) employs the metaphor of emotional circuits to talk about distinct emotional systems that are common to mammals including humans. These are:

- fear and anxiety;
- rage and anger;
- panic (separation distress);
- seeking;
- play;
- care and nurture;
- lust.

These circuits are unlearned, predictable and universal: they are not claimed to be exclusive. Damasio (2012: 125) additionally discusses social emotions, such as compassion, embarrassment, shame, guilt, contempt, jealousy, envy, pride and admiration. These are triggered in social situations, as they are physiological in the same way as other emotions, but they are younger in evolutionary terms and some may be relevant only to humans.

The nature of, and ways of working with, particular feelings are explored in the next section. The most common presenting problems for children and young people in therapy are depression, anxiety disorders and conduct disorders. We therefore discuss sadness, fear and anxiety, and anger in particular. We also discuss shame as this has a crucial role in therapy and we look at the importance of promoting and amplifying joyful and peaceful states.

Shame

Shame is universal: we all know shame and it is a core emotional experience. We feel shame as children and throughout our lives. It is experienced as a profound sense of worthlessness and as an attack on one's very being. Shame is deeply painful and the self is experienced as inadequate, inferior, and basically unlovable. It is a social emotion, experienced in relation to others as well as in relation to an internal object.

Shame is distinct from guilt, which is a feeling about an action. We feel guilty when we have done something bad. We feel shame when we experience ourselves as being bad. Guilt is about doing, shame is about being.

The family of shame feelings include embarrassment, humiliation, ridicule, disgrace, indignity, dishonour, ignominy, and being discredited.

We feel shame when we experience failure, when insulted or rejected, when criticised or blamed. It is a social emotion and is experienced in relation to an external other as well as an internal judge. In childhood, a failure to achieve grades, being bullied, not gaining the approval of adults, and being rejected by peers are all sources of shame.

A characteristic of the experience of shame is the need to hide. Shame motivates us to move away from others, to avoid exposure, to defend against and deny vulnerabilities and inadequacies. This in turn leads to further shame. Shame makes us feel small and to want the earth to open and swallow us from view, to remove ourselves, or at the extreme, cease to exist.

In shame there is no eye contact, the head hangs down, the shoulders droop, there is a turning away, a contraction of the body. We shrink. There is also blushing and a sense of feeling hot. We might choose to bury our face in our hands.

On our initial education programme for child therapists I give a workshop on shame. A part of this workshop involves students in making an image of their experience of shame. No suggestions are made so some are abstract and some more literal. Over the years I have seen over a hundred such images and I have observed some common features: eyes are very common, often eyes in the sky; arrows are also common, pointing and sharp; some beaks and claws. Then there is the recipient of the eyes or arrows – small, sometimes a mere dot, often red contrasting with a pervasive black or grey. I have never had a student who was not able to evoke the experience although many have found the image work painful. The gallery produced by this exercise results in a powerfully felt understanding of shame.

This is hugely important, because the very fact of coming to therapy will be shame provoking and produce shame anxiety. As a result, therapists need to be alert to this, and able to recognise shame because the child will be working to hide it. We need to pay attention to building a working alliance and creating an environment in which a child will feel safe enough to reveal themselves. Above all we must be accepting of that child. Whereas the healing for guilt involves confession and an act or words of reparation, the healing for shame is an acceptance of the self despite weaknesses and failures. A child cannot achieve self-acceptance unless another person first accepts them .

Erikson (1951) identifies shame as being key in toddlerhood and this stage of development is discussed in Chapter 4. A healthy resolution at this stage of life is likely to result in a person who knows their own mind, who has a good self-image, is generous, able to negotiate and maintain self-control. For this to happen, the social environment must provide clear boundaries, affirm their developing autonomy, make a distinction between who a child is and what a child does, and model that it is acceptable to make mistakes. Otherwise, there is likely to be a lack of self-worth and experience of the self as intrinsically bad or unlovable, and thus the stage is set for the spreading of shame and the development of a shame-laden personality. This puts an onus on therapists to be very accepting when working with a child of this age, or a child of this emotional age, or a child whose troubles emanate from this stage of life.

Kohut's (1984) self psychology theory of development places parental empathy, in particular the primary caregiver, at the heart of healthy human development. He focuses on narcissistic traits and disorders that involve core feelings of inferiority, worthlessness and shame alternating with grandiosity, superiority and a contempt for others. He asserts that these painful self states stem from our experiences of primary psychological needs not being met in childhood, and that what is required in therapy is the corrective emotional experience of exquisite empathy.

The second key developmental stage of human development where shame comes to the fore is adolescence (Chapter 5) when there is a quantum leap in self-consciousness. How we are perceived in the eyes of our peers becomes highly important, and clothes, hair, shoes, and especially parents, can be sources of acute embarrassment. To make matters worse, skin erupts in acne and pubertal bodily changes advertise an agonising awkwardness.

In my twenty-plus years working as a therapist I have come to believe that a sense of worthlessness and the associated excruciating experience of shame, with its implication of being at core unlovable, is the bottom line for the children who find their way to therapy. It implies that what is required is no less than our love.

Fear and anxiety

'Fear is a genetically ingrained function of the nervous system' (Panksepp, 1998). It is a natural and intensely useful response to dangerous situations. The experience of fear alerts us to danger and moves us to take action to be safe. Typically the mammalian response is to fight, freeze or flee.

Fear feels absolutely horrible. When stricken with terror our blood runs cold, literally to our legs to facilitate running, leaving our faces white. We shake, and perhaps lose control of our bladder and bowel. Our heart will race and our rate of breathing increase. We will then replay the event in our dreams for several nights and need to talk to people about that event over and over again. Children will likewise feel compelled to play out the event over and over again.

A review of studies on children's fear shows a disagreement on the prevalence of fears (Muris and Field, 2008) but a consensus on what children do fear. The most common fears in children are a fear of danger and death (e.g., being in a car accident or getting run over), a fear of failure and criticism (e.g., academic failure), a fear of the unknown (e.g., the dark), a fear of animals (e.g., snakes), and medical fears (e.g., injections).

Whereas fear is associated with actual events, anxiety is our anticipation of danger or discomfort or fear, or of another horrid feeling (e.g., shame). Anxiety is a common experience and can be useful in that it can promote preparation (e.g., for an exam) or for due care to be taken (e.g., in crossing the road). The symptoms of anxiety include a shortness of breath, dizziness, palpitations, sweatiness, shakiness, a dry mouth, nausea, butterflies in the stomach, and blurred vision. Kohut's concept of optimal frustration is helpful in thinking about anxiety. If the level of a child's anxiety is kept within tolerable limits then they will learn how to cope and manage in anxiety-provoking situations. If, however, this anxiety is overwhelming then children will attempt to alleviate it by avoidance, as in social anxiety disorder, or control the anxiety, as in obsessive-compulsive disorder. These responses provide temporary relief but if they become entrenched then they become life limiting. Anxiety can prevent children and young people from participating in and enjoying life.

Silverman and Field (2011) estimated the prevalence of anxiety disorders in the UK and USA, amongst children aged between 2 and 18 years, as varying from 10 to 15% of the population. Anxiety disorders include:

- separation anxiety disorder;
- generalised anxiety disorder;

- social phobia;
- panic disorder;
- obsessive compulsive disorder (OCD);
- specific phobias;
- post traumatic stress disorder (PTSD);
- anxiety disorder not specified.

These are one of the most common categories of difficulty for children and young people. Anxiety disorders are often comorbid with other difficulties such as depression and/or behavioural difficulties. There is a sense of contagion around anxiety. Anxious parents beget anxious children, and anxious children promote anxiety in the adults around them.

Fear and anxiety belong to the tribe of fearful feelings, along with dread, terror, fright, qualm, wariness, scared, nervous, panic, concern and phobia.

Children who exhibit a fear of danger or death need reassurance from calm adults and age-appropriate information. It is highly unlikely that any of us will be hit by a bus or struck by lightning. They need to have a sense that the adults in charge are competent and will keep them safe.

Children who are exhibiting irrational fears of a 'monsters under the bed' variety also need to have their fears taken utterly seriously. These fears might not be so susceptible to reassurance because they are rooted in the realm of imagination. As such they are sometimes best addressed in that realm.

> Josh, aged 5, became afraid of the dark, and his bedtime rituals were becoming longer and longer. His harassed parents reasoned with him every night, explaining away his fears and reassuring him to no avail. When Josh was introduced to SuperTed who had a magic cloak that could protect both Josh and Ted, he was calmed, and as long as SuperTed was present, and the cloak had been activated, bedtime became less protracted and sleep came easier to Josh. In this example, Josh's worries were met and addressed in the realm of imagination.

Sadness

Sadness is the healthy response to loss and loss is a natural aspect of life. Indeed Judith Viorst (1988) goes as far as to suggest that life is a series of necessary losses from cradle to grave. Sadness, and its sibling disappointment, are regular experiences in the lives of children. There is the sadness of not sitting next to one's best friend on the school trip, or missing a party because of an illness. There is the major sadness of parental divorce or the death of a loved one, and the tragic sadness of being alone and lonely. Sadness is painful.

As with other emotions sadness is common and normal. It involves a lowering of energy and a tendency to withdraw from the hurly burly. Life becomes slower when sad. It is a time to reflect and a time for psychological recuperation and convalescence. This reflective stance allows us to come to terms with our loss. We need time to make new meanings and a new identity in the face of loss. Sadness allows grief and mourning.

Words for the feelings associated with sadness are sorrow, gloomy, glum, melancholy, grief, mourning, lonely, dejected, morose, misery, despair and depression. Images often associated with sadness are of low places such as valleys or swamps, or watery places such as lakes, pools, wells, springs and waterfalls, as well as raindrops and water rising.

Sadness is also adaptive: it elicits attachment behaviours in the adults around the child. The natural response to a sad child is compassion, care and concern. Sadness elicits social support and nurture. Contact with an understanding person is healing.

In therapy, as in life, if there is an attachment bond between people and that bond is severed for whatever reason, then there will be associated feelings of loss and sadness. This means that special attention needs to be given to how endings are managed in child therapy. Abrupt endings are to be avoided where this is at all possible.

Ideally, the ending of therapy is planned for with appropriate notice given and an opportunity to think about, and in particular feel, what it will be like. The ingredients of a good-enough ending are a reflection on the work together, perhaps remembering key images and significant events, a chance to express all the feelings involved in that ending, and an opportunity to think about and imagine the future when meetings will have finished.

Anger

Anger often gets a bad press. People fear that expressing anger will result in violence, and when anger is not well managed then this can be the case. Anger, therefore, is often suppressed and deemed unhealthy. However, as with all feelings it is useful and has its place. It is evoked when we experience injustice, see it perpetrated on others, are frustrated in our needs or desires, or when our boundaries have been violated. It is aroused when we feel we have been wronged and by physical or emotional pain. It is therefore often aroused by experiences of other emotions such as shame or sadness. Children are often referred to therapy for 'anger management'. In my experience as a therapist it is frequently the case that underneath the anger lie neglected feelings of hurt, loss or humiliation.

Anger involves emotional arousal, adrenaline and noradrenaline course through the bloodstream, and the heart rate increases. The fight reflex is activated and blood flow to the hands is increased. Our jaws clench and nostrils flare, our feet stamp, and our hands make fists. We mobilise and are ready for action.

The vocabulary of anger includes rage, hate, annoyance, irritation, wrath, fury, frustration, hostility, resentment and being cross. Our images of anger involve heat and explosion (e.g., volcanoes, fire, eruption, rockets or car crashes).

Children (and adults) need to learn appropriate ways of expressing anger, and there is a place for some psychoeducation in therapy when anger is a key issue. Anger can be expressed in a safe and healthy way that is not blaming of the other, by using what Gestalt therapists call the language of responsibility. This is where we make 'I statements' rather than 'You statements', thereby owning our own feelings rather than blaming (e.g., 'I feel angry ... ' rather than 'You make me feel angry ... ').

Angry children need to be taken seriously and listened to. It is important neither to retaliate nor to collapse in the face of anger. We need to be solid, calm and not escalate the angry feelings. Anger can be bottled up, swallowed, turned in on oneself, and is often underneath self-harming behaviours. Finding safe ways of expressing anger that do not hurt the self or others is an appropriate therapeutic activity. Examples are tearing newspapers or cardboard boxes, hitting soft cushions, bursting balloons, throwing soft balls, or shouting out loud. As therapists we are responsible for keeping the activity safe and ensuring no harm. Putting the expression of the emotion into words is also helpful.

Joy, happiness, and the more enjoyable affect states

Therapy is associated with mental ill health and painful, disrupting, emotional experiences. Therefore, it is easy for therapists to focus on the painful, sad, angry or frightening aspects of life. However, it is also important to promote and amplify the more joyful feelings a child might experience. Music (2011) draws on literature from neurobiology to argue that we have two separate systems for processing negative and positive affect. To be emotionally healthy it is vital to be able to process both kinds of emotion. Being able to enjoy joyful and exuberant affect states is associated with good physical health and longevity (Music, 2011).

We can defend against positive feelings just as much as the more painful feelings. This can happen for the same reasons: if our joy was not mirrored back to us then we are likely to split it off from our awareness. In this way some people learn to play up a miserable life, as opposed to a lovely life. Exuberance is noisy and messy and not easily tolerated by adults who are not in touch with their own joyful feelings. It is crucial to work with joy so that a child can assimilate this into their internal world. To possess a rich internal world is to have a most powerful resource for dealing with life.

Glad, joy, happy, contentment, serenity, satisfaction, thrilled, bliss, pleasure, amusement, delight, relief, ecstasy, wonder, awe and fascination are some useful words to describe the more enjoyable feelings.

The next section explores ways of promoting thinking and reflection, drawing on ideas from the psychoanalytic tradition and the cognitive behavioural approach, including mentalisation and mindfulness. This links with the next chapter as images and play can provide the distance required for reflection, as well as being used to allow emotional expression.

Working with thinking

We have established the importance of working with emotion and feeling and how the emotional sensitivity of the adults in children's lives is essential to their development. In tandem with emotional sensitivity adults need to be able to think about children, and in particular about what might be going on in their minds. The child therapy literature contains a number of related or overlapping concepts to describe this, which include mind-mindedness, reflective functioning and mentalisation.

Mind-mindedness is the ability of an infant's primary caregiver to make appropriate mind-related comments to that infant. Mothers who understand and verbalise their baby's internal state of mind are more likely to have securely attached babies (Meins et al., 2012).

Reflective functioning, similarly, refers to a parent's ability to understand, think about and hold in mind the infant's mental state.

Mentalisation is a term coined by Peter Fonagy that means the ability to think about and understand the mental states of another person. It is an imaginative act that involves perceiving and interpreting someone's behaviour, and involves an understanding that that behaviour is meaningful and purposive: it is about understanding the processes, thoughts, feelings, memories, needs, wishes and goals that exist in the mind of another. The mentalisation capacity of a parent predicts the attachment style of their children (Fonagy et al., 1991), and thus parents who can mentalise have more securely attached children. It is a concept linked to theory of mind.

Our task as therapists is to mentalise about our child clients in order that they can develop their own powers of mentalisation. As with affect regulation, it is not an ability that develops automatically but instead requires interaction with a more mature and sensitive mind. Children need to be mentalised with in order to acquire the proclivity to mentalise themselves.

Mentalisation is a significant concept that has achieved much traction, and it has explanatory, diagnostic and therapeutic powers. It is a concept that synthesises and reframes ideas from psychoanalysis and neurobiology, and provides a language for twenty-first-century therapists. The term does not include new ideas, rather it places an emphasis on bringing the internal mental states of the participants of therapy more explicitly into focus. In a recent paper widening the scope of the concept, Fonagy et al. (2011) discussed how this knits together with and illuminates existing perspectives and can be applied to a number of disorders. The Anna Freud Centre has developed a mentalisation-based approach called AMBIT for working with troubled young people and this is available on their website (www. annafreud.org).

Cognitive approaches to child therapy

Working with thinking is a key element of cognitive behavioural therapy. Classically, these approaches identify distress as stemming from distortions in thinking (for example, wearing negative glasses that only let us see the negative aspects in a situation). So Emily, who went to a fantastic party, when asked if she had a good time said that she hadn't because she didn't get the chocolate biscuit that she so badly wanted. Her negative glasses, or selective abstraction, caused her to select, remember and think about only the negative event, and to forget the many positive aspects of the party. The remedy for these distortions is to bring them to awareness and consider other possibilities. Emily needs to be helped to remember and think about the many positive things that happened at the party.

There are debates in the CBT community about the age at which children have sufficient capacity to participate successfully in CBT.

Stallard (2005: 105) states that certain core tasks must be achievable in order to engage in CBT. These are to be able to:

- monitor affective states;
- reflect on automatic thoughts;
- distinguish between and understand the difference between thoughts and feelings;
- engage in thought appraisal and cognitive restructuring.

These tasks imply a high level of cognitive functioning. Some suggest that children need to be at least 12 years of age before they can benefit from CBT, while others argue that if techniques are appropriately and creatively adapted then children as young as aged 7 can benefit (Stallard, 2005).

The research evidence suggests that CBT approaches are more beneficial with adolescents than younger children (McLaughlin et al., 2013). This is likely to be because cognitive capacity develops with age.

The evidence base suggests that CBT approaches are particularly helpful with anxiety disorders. There is less evidence for the success of other approaches, but this is because there has been less research in other therapeutic modalities and not because these are less successful.

The implication of the preceding section on emotion is that the most successful therapeutic interventions will be those that consider emotions, behaviour, thinking and the body together.

NINE Creative Therapeutic Interventions

Carol Holliday

Introduction

This chapter offers a range of practical skills for working with children. These strategies will foster the creation and maintenance of the therapeutic relationship. They include therapist self-care, the therapeutic skills of looking and listening, working with images, and interviewing toys or puppets. Working with sandplay, clay, music, movements and other art forms will be discussed. We believe that the natural language for the expression of emotion in children is through image, metaphor, story and play. Therefore, there is an emphasis on working creatively with a variety of arts media and play to offer hospitality to the psyche's multiplicity of manifestations (McNiff, 2004). The interventions aim to help children process their emotions through experiencing, expressing and thinking about these in the presence of an empathic adult, rather than discharging them in detrimental ways.

Personal development

It may seem a little odd to begin a chapter on interventions with personal development, but we believe that in a relational approach where as therapists we are the instrument of the work, and in this way our development, both personal and professional, must be taken utterly seriously. Working therapeutically with children is very demanding work, requiring good thinking skills, emotional robustness, self-awareness and an ability to play.

Self-care is an ethical principle that we must observe as therapists. Keeping fit, eating well, having a healthy social and relational life, are all aspects of this self-care. Doing things we enjoy and accepting ourselves are also important. There is a notion in Jungian psychology that to be good therapists we need to be wounded healers. This is an apt metaphor, but we would add that we have to be healed enough to engage in the work.

We need to be aware as therapists of our own vulnerabilities and recognise the idiosyncrasies of our own responses to feelings and emotional themes. We need to learn to be reflective and reflexive practitioners. Reflection happens when we retrospectively think about an event. Reflexivity is here-and-now reflection, or reflection-in-action, where we are simultaneously aware and thinking about what is going on in us, what is going on in the child, and what is going on in the relationship between ourselves and that child. A reflexive therapist is aware of and thinking about their own impact, in the here and now, both on the therapeutic relationship and the child. The following exercise is designed to help extend self-awareness.

Here is a list of some of the feelings and emotional themes that you will encounter and need to respond to:

- Anger.
- Feeling about to explode or burst.
- Fear and anxiety.
- Feeling wobbly or fluttery inside.
- Panic.
- Jealousy.
- Rejected, left out.
- Abandoned.
- Shame.
- Sadness and loss.
- Too much pain.
- Overloaded.
- Fragmented or in bits.
- Happiness, joy and exuberance.
- Calm and tranquil.
- Rubbished.
- Abused.

(Continued)

(Continued)

- Destructiveness.
- Hating.
- Stuck.
- Trapped or cornered or caged.
- Confused.
- Desperate.
- Horrified, revulsed or disgusted.
- Dirty, contaminated or polluted.

This list is not exhaustive but gives some idea of what might emerge. For each of these feelings or themes you can think of a time you experienced this feeling and consider:

- How did you feel?
- What images arose in relation to this feeling?
- How easy or difficult was it to express this, talk about it, think about it?
- Is this a familiar feeling for you?
- How do you feel now thinking back to then?
- Imagine being with someone who is experiencing this feeling.
- What happens to you – what is your emotional response?

This exercise will alert you to possible vulnerabilities you might have in relation to these emotional themes. You can then reflect on the action you need to take to ameliorate these vulnerabilities, such as working on them in your personal therapy.

Finally, in order to work in the ways we suggest below, it is important to have a rich and vibrant imaginal life and to be able to play. Go to the theatre, art galleries and read poetry. Make art, write stories, and have fun. It is useful to have in the back of our mind some of humanity's great myths and stories. The Greek myths, *A Thousand and One Arabian Nights*, Grimm's fairytales and Anansi are just some. These stories are often archetypal, and are tales about the psyche that move from a difficulty, through a task, to a resolution. They can shed light on difficulties and give clues for solutions.

A brief rationale for working with images in therapy with children and young people

The term 'image' here is used here to cover all arts media and therefore includes paintings/drawings, sculptures/models, story, play, music, dance, drama, puppets, poetry, etc., as well as mental imagery and lingual metaphors.

Using images as a means to understand children is clearly advantageous as story and play are often their natural and preferred modes of communication. Images offer a way to convey thoughts, feelings and memories that are non-verbal or pre-verbal and therefore beyond the reach of language. Stern (1998) discusses the development of the verbal self around the age of 2 years old, and describes language as a double-edged sword that cleaves a divide between subjective experience that can be talked about in words and subjective experience that cannot. When we learn to speak we also learn not to speak about those things that are unacceptable, thus working with the arts has the potential to facilitate the expression of a richer picture of lived experience than working with words alone. It can reach the parts other approaches can't reach. However, we must also bear in mind that words and language are also important. Very young children will have a limited vocabulary, and it is part of a therapist's remit to help them develop a language for their experience and wrap that experience in words.

In attempting to describe emotional experiences we naturally use metaphors. A metaphor describes something in terms of something else. We describe relationships as warm or cold (metaphors of temperature) or close or distant (spatial metaphors). We describe feelings as up or down (orientation metaphors) or in terms of images of place (such as in the pits, or on a rollercoaster).

Metaphors are symbolic when the association between the image and the emotional experience becomes more than the sum of its parts. In symbolism there is a joining of the image and the reality of the emotional experience it represents, so that working with the image has an impact on the emotional experience itself. A symbol is more than a mere representation, it includes unknown aspects in a meaningful way and can therefore be numinous. When working with troubled and troubling children there is often a sense of the unknown. Difficulties present in behaviours and symptoms rather than clearly defined logical and rational ideas.

Lakoff and Johnson (1980, 1999; Johnson and Lakoff, 2006), as a cognitive scientist and a linguist respectively, have developed a convincing theory of conceptual metaphor. This theory offers an explanatory account of the way images operate at a fundamental, embodied level to structure the way we think. This means that the images we have about ourselves, and our world, are inextricably entwined with, and symbolic of, the way we think and feel. We think feelingly. This chimes with Damasio's (2012) view, discussed in the last chapter, that feelings are images of emotions based on stimuli originating in the body, and that the mind privileges these stimuli. The implication of these ideas is that the images and metaphors that arise in us to describe our experiences can be trusted to be authentic and true.

Images can be used in therapy in a range of ways and for many purposes.

1 Mastery

To provide an opportunity for mastery over disturbing or potentially traumatising experiences. For example, a child who has been in a road traffic accident may need to enact the event in play over and over again. Each enactment is accompanied by a small reduction in the intensity of emotion as the experience becomes integrated into the personality. This is an analogous process to the adult's need to talk about a traumatic experience over and over again until it recedes in intensity.

2 Containment

The act of making an image on paper or in the sandtray can assist with containment. Relief is felt when intolerably painful or overwhelming and chaotic feelings are contained on paper or by the physical boundaries of a sandtray. Luke, a young man of 16, was freed from some of his inner world horror by painting a grotesque self-portrait. The relief he experienced reduced his suicidal thoughts. This links to the next point.

3 Externalisation

By externalising the feeling into an image a child can gain some distance from the feeling. This means that they might be able to see a new perspective or have an overview. In this way the child can move from an overwhelming feeling through image to cognition and insight. In the above example, Luke was able to create distance from the horror and see that although there was an aspect of his life that had been truly horrid, it was not the only thing in his life. He was able to move from despair to experience a small flicker of hope.

4 Epistemic sensing

This refers to the way in which art can be a way of knowing, understanding, learning and exploring. There is knowledge that is implicit and tacit, and therefore beyond words. For example, the knowledge of how to ride a bike or swim is sensory: there is no language for the experience. There can be a narrative of turning pedals or gripping handlebars, but that is of a different order.

This relates to ideas of two types of memory, explicit and implicit. Explicit memory is conscious, composed of facts, concepts, ideas and is lingual. It is concerned with information processing and reasoning. It is also termed 'declarative memory'.

Implicit memory is sensory and emotional. It includes the body memory. When riding a bike, the non-verbal body memory is implicit. The senses are the memory. The narrative of pedalling, turning the handlebars, etc. is explicit.

In traumatic situations language is less accessible and there are fewer words. This means explicit memories are less available. Trauma is stored in the body and sense memories. Images allow access to that which is implicit.

A task of therapy is to transform unbearable (unspeakable) feelings into thinkable thoughts. Images and play can therefore be used to express and communicate thoughts, feelings and memories, which have defied words but continue to crave recognition. These can assist in communicating the preverbal and nonverbal, to help communicate the 'unthought known'. The therapist uses themself to share a child's experience and verbalise the experience in a manner that is understandable, bearable and digestible.

5 Empathy

There is a sense in which an image reflects back to its maker a reflection of themselves or an aspect of the self or a feeling. This can enhance a stronger sense of the self and feel comforting. A friend of mine put it like this: 'Sad music listens to me'. Images can enhance the sense of being seen and being heard, and the image itself can be experienced as empathic.

6 Facilitation of emotional expression

Images can be used to surface feelings that have been denied, neglected or split off from awareness. Images have an affinity with feelings. They are both associated with the right hemisphere of the brain, whereas language and reason are more associated with the left. This means that working with images, and side-stepping verbal reasoning, are likely to elicit emotion that has been previously kept unconscious. In a music lesson, Emily, aged 6, was playing on claves. With each tap her face changed and she began to look sad. Soon her eyes filled with tears, and when her kindly teacher spoke to her Emily said that the tapping was like tears dropping. The image had facilitated the experience and expression of the feeling. The teacher then communicated her acknowledgment and understanding of Emily's experience.

9 Rehearsal of the possible

Images can provide opportunities to try out new ways of being. Risking attempting to make friends or being brave enough to approach a spider can be rehearsed in the sandtray or other medium to see what this feels like. This is especially powerful if the image has become symbolic.

10 Safety

Finally, remaining in the metaphor of the image can offer safety, and avoid exposure and shame. In the myth of Perseus, our hero is set the task of slaying the gorgon Medusa, but if he looks at her he will be turned to stone. In order to find her, hidden in her lair, he holds up his golden shield and uses it as a mirror to locate her. Looking directly at a gorgon is fatal but the task can be accomplished safely by looking at her indirectly. In therapy, metaphor can be the golden shield: it is often the case that looking directly at the issue is too shameful or painful or the issue is not explicitly known. Metaphors and images can allow an issue to be felt and thought about in an indirect way that is more manageable. It might be more possible to talk about or demonstrate teddy being left all alone, with no one to look after him, than to admit to feeling rejected and abandoned. In such cases it is important to remain in the metaphor of the image and not to decode it. If the child decodes the metaphor then that is a warrant for us to also speak directly. If there is a strong enough alliance then we might judge that it is beneficial to make gentle, respectful links between the metaphor and the external world, but the rule of thumb is that it is better not to.

A multiplicity of media

It is important to have available a range of arts media, clay or playdough, sandplay, puppets, musical instruments, and a doll's house with dolls, paint and crayons etc. This is because we have different sense preferences. Some people perceive and experience the world predominantly visually, and will tend to express themselves in visual images. Some will have an aural preference and others kinesthetic. Uninhibited children will choose the best medium for what they want to express and our intervention will not be required. With older children, or more inhibited children, we might need to assist them in choosing an appropriate medium for their presenting issue.

So if a child is telling us they feel warm and happy like a big yellow sun, then it is much more appropriate to suggest they show you with paint on paper than on the drums. Similarly, if their misery feels like a keening banshee then voice or instruments are likely to better express that feeling than paint. We are not suggesting that we must stick to a particular client's sense preference, but that we match our interventions to the material of the session. Sometimes it might be therapeutic for a client to work in a medium that is not their preferred one.

In the therapy room it is useful to have the materials and space available to facilitate drawing and painting, sandplay, clay work, puppets, music, drama, dance and movement, poetry and story.

Drawing and painting

Drawing and painting involve sight, shape, colour and form. It will be the medium of choice for some children and it will be familiar to all. It can be much easier to show on paper than to speak about troubling situations or feelings. Drawing in structured and semi-structured exercises and games can be useful both as assessment tools as well as ways to facilitate the therapeutic relationship. Examples include Winnicott's Squiggle game (Winnicott, 1958) where therapist and child take turns to draw a shape and invite the other to make something of it. A squiggly line can become a snake or a necklace or an animal etc.

Sandplay

Sandplay is a kinesthetic as well as a visual medium. To use sandplay we will need a sandtray, usually made of wood, with a base that is painted blue, measuring around 72x57x7 cms. With inhibited or older children we may need to facilitate their use of sandplay, putting our hands into the sandtray and moving the sand around, showing the blue base and explaining that it can be used to make mountains, lakes, buildings or whatever is desired. We must then invite our client to also experience the sand with their hands. (Have water available to keep the sand damp enough to mould.) In an ideal world we would have two sandtrays, one wet and one dry, but often there isn't the space and so one is fine. Then we can indicate the miniatures or toys, on shelves and in baskets, that can be used to make pictures and tell stories.

It is not necessary to have a huge array of items, as this could prove overwhelming, but most therapists who work in this way quickly build up a collection of suitable miniatures. Car boot sales are useful in this regard! It will be necessary to include the following:

- People.
- Phantasy/archetypal figures, such as witches, wizards, dragons, unicorns.
- Animals, jungle and farmyard.
- Vehicles (e.g., cars, lorries, planes, helicopters, tanks).
- Buildings.
- Domestic items such as doll's house furniture, toilet, sink, bath.
- Fences, cages, bridges.
- Natural materials (e.g. stones, feathers, shells, rocks, gems, blocks of wood).
- Vegetation such as cacti, palm trees, flowers.

Most children will now be able to make a picture in the sand. A simple prompt, 'Tell me about your picture', can be enough to elicit an account of the picture or the beginning of a story.

Clay

Clay is primal and of the earth, it can be moulded, squished, rolled, pounded, poked and pulled. It slips and slides, can be used for building and making. It can be a powerful medium for making what is elusive tangible and it can also be fun. Clay involves touch and skin contact. It is intimate, and if worked with eyes closed can lead to revelations beyond the visual. Most children enjoy clay, but there are some who find it difficult and don't like the sensation or look of clay on their hands. Clay can elicit the full range of feelings, including sexual feelings and feelings associated with poo.

Elbrecht (2012: 42) explains that the hands are 'extraordinarily complex sense organs', and argues that they contribute significantly to our perception of touch or haptic perception. She argues that our early basic physical and emotional development comes through touch and contact, through what she describes as the skin sense. Working with clay activates these early patterns, and therefore this potentially allows a therapist to work with very young non-verbal attachment or developmental issues.

Puppets

Puppets can be very useful, they can be held at arm's length, literally, and provide safety through the metaphor. They might be funny or absurd and this can add a layer of protection. They are smaller than the child and the child can feel in control. A puppet can be a useful third party to the therapy and become a confidant for the child. In my therapy room I have Sydney who is a squawking seagull, who occasionally swoops in to ask a question or whisper what he thinks into my ear. He is playful and friendly and sometimes it is easier for the child to talk to Sydney than to me. Puppets can be employed to heighten awareness and explore either intra- or interpersonal dynamics. They can also help with listening and negotiating, as well as working with conflict. Puppets can represent each side of a tension and the therapist can interview each puppet, being careful to give each equal airtime to each, and perhaps come to a resolution.

Music

We all have an innate musicality and some children find it particularly helpful to express themselves through music. It can be a very powerful medium to explore and communicate deeply held feelings. Therapists and children can listen to music together or make music together. A xylophone for melody, a small collection of percussion instruments and a drum are required. Most children will delight in having an attentive adult focused on attuning to them, and playing together can be a strong bonding experience for both parties.

Story

Each of the arts media we discuss in this chapter can lead to the telling of a story. A useful prompt in this is 'Tell me the story that goes with this image'. Sometimes it is therapeutic to read a relevant story to a child in a session and also useful to have a collection of stories that address key emotional themes. A few of these are listed below:

Burningham, J. (1999) *Simp.* London: Red Fox. This book addresses feeling unloved and finding a family.

Ironside, V. (1996) *The Huge Bag of Worries.* London: Hodder. This book is about sharing and dispelling worries.

Rosen, M. and Blake, Q. (2008) *Michael Rosen's Sad Book.* London:Walker. This is about sadness, loss and grief.

Sunderland, M. (n.d.) The *Storybooks for Troubled Children* series. London: Speechmark. These are a number of stories, each of which addresses a prevalent emotional theme.

Watt, M. (2007) *Scaredy Squirrel.* London: Happy Cat Books. This book is about acknowledging and overcoming anxiety.

It is also useful for us to have in mind a store of fairytales and myths. These are stories that have survived through the ages because they have something to say to us. They often have a structure that begins with a problem, and then there is a journey to undertake and tasks to complete. They end in a satisfactory resolution. They are replete with rich imagery that lends itself to a number of situations. It can be helpful to tell such a story when the child's issues prompt one to come to mind.

A lovely intervention is when you make up a story that resonates with the child's emotional theme, posing a difficulty then the means of healing. Sunderland (2000) explains in detail how to do this. Therapeutic stories can be powerful ways of indirect communication.

Drama, dance, movement and poetry require no special equipment; dramatic vignettes, gesture and pose, and verbal imagery can all be worked with in the ways we discuss below.

How we respond to what emerges in play and image work is fundamental and the next section focuses on the therapist's response.

Ways of working with children's images

Young children will most likely play spontaneously and use arts media freely, but children of secondary school age may be less spontaneous with the arts. Some younger children might have been discouraged and their natural spontaneity dampened. It is likely that these children will need your support and will have to be introduced to working creatively.

Beginning therapists sometimes assume that adolescents will refuse to work with images. I can honestly say that in twenty years of working with young people I have not found this to be the case. In the privacy of the therapy room, away from the eyes of peers and in the context of a relationship of trust, adolescents welcome the opportunity to play. I also work with images with adults. Confidence is the main issue here. If we are confident with the arts, and take a stance of assuming the process is beneficial, then our clients will receive the message that this is an okay activity. If we have doubts or feel embarrassed so will they. The best way forward here is to have multiple experiences of the arts and a positive attitude. Ideally taking a course in personal therapy using the arts would allow us to experience the benefits first hand.

Early in the therapy, when ways of working are being established, it is useful to couch introductions to the work as suggestions or experiments. In the examples below I am using the example of working with sandplay, but the possible interventions are also appropriate for other arts media such as painting, drawing, clay or playdoh, music, story, puppets and dance. In introducing the work we can use phrases such as, 'Let's try an experiment, how about you make a picture in the sand and we can work with it', or if something such as being told off by a teacher is being talked about you could say, 'I have a suggestion, show me in the sandtray what happened', or if sadness is being talked about, 'As an experiment, how about you show me your sadness in the sandtray'.

How to be and what to say when working with children's play, story and images

We have seen in Part 2 of this book that in order to develop in a healthy manner, children need to have their feelings understood and validated, to be seen, heard and felt. Therefore, we need to be able to look, listen and empathise. Unseen, unheard, and unfelt children will have no access to healing.

Active and empathic listening

In my early work as a therapist I met Ava who taught me a great deal, and here I pass on some of her wisdom.

Ava, aged 6, made an image with felt pens of a dolphin and a witch. She was very engaged with her image and was carefully colouring it in. I was tracking her and communicating that I was with her by making occasional comments. At one point I noticed out loud that the witch had a big smile on her face.

Ava: Yes. She was a nice girl really, but then she turned bad.

            [This was said in a matter of fact tone but with an emphasis on the word bad.]

Therapist: Gosh, she turned bad. I wonder what happened?

Ava: Well, nobody listened to her and so she turned bad. That's just what happens when nobody listens.

She was, of course, talking about herself as well as communicating to me that she really needed me to listen to her.

In order to really hear, we need to listen actively and empathically, and this means being able to bracket off our own thoughts and feelings, and clear our mind to make space available to a child. We need to be paying attention to and thinking about the tone of voice, the rhythm of speech, the pace and the volume, as well as the actual words a child uses. We must listen to the feelings underneath the words, to the bass line as well as the melody.

Active and empathic looking

When we look at a child's image or play, to really see what is going on, we need to imagine ourselves into the image and try to get a sense of what it feels like to be there. Margot Sunderland refers to this as 'imagining in'. This will give us clues as to what the child might be feeling inside. Do we feel scared in this image or do we feel safe? Our looking and seeing will also include noticing the child's visual cues, such as their facial expression and body language.

Responses

Our responses to children need to be understanding, accepting, permission giving, authentic, emotionally sensitive and thoughtful. In addition, these work best when they are brief. The focus of our response needs to be on the child and their emotional experience. Children are not going to be interested in a long-winded summary of what we have understood or are thinking.

The following types of responses are useful.

Tracking responses

These communicate our observations of what is happening, rather like a commentary. They include statements such as: 'there is a blue monkey in the corner', or 'the mermaid is buried in the sand' or 'the drums are fast and loud'. Responses of this nature show that we are involved, participating in the therapy and alongside the child. It is important to report the empirical facts by themselves and not to interpret by adding adjectives or adverbs. If a child has identified the elephant as angry then we can refer to the angry elephant, but otherwise we must desist lest we project our own material onto the child's image or play. Tracking statements also include reflecting back or paraphrasing a child's words. Putting them into our own words demonstrates our attentiveness and understanding.

Naming feelings

If we are certain that a child is feeling sad and that it is not our projection, then it is therapeutic to name that sadness. Wrapping the experience in words shows empathy and teaches a vocabulary of feelings. Children that find their way to our therapy rooms are not likely to have such a vocabulary.

Greek chorus responses (Sunderland, 2000)

These include the spontaneous Oooohs, Arrrghs, Zzzzzzzs and Kapows that empathically accompany the child's play. These need to be used intuitively to support the play and so we need to beware of taking over the play with our enthusiasm.

Questions

Questions need to be kept to a minimum as children can easily begin to feel interrogated. Generally, statements are better than questions as they are more likely to communicate understanding. Questions can be useful for clarifying if we do not understand. If we do ask questions then open questions (such as what, who, how, and when) are more useful than closed questions that only require yes or no answers. 'Why' questions are only useful if our intention is to promote thinking as these demand a cognitive answer.

Encouraging responses

These extend the work and include phrases such as:

- 'Tell me the [fairytale] story that goes with this picture.'
- 'If your picture had a title what would it be?' (This is useful to get at the focus of what is being communicated.)
- 'Tell me more.'
- 'What happened next?'

Identifying and dialoguing

Young children will often spontaneously engage in dialogue when playing, giving voice to the characters in their play. This dialogue is often laden with feeling and meaning, and can be a clear and direct communication of an important emotional theme. Some children will need more support to engage meaningfully with their images, particularly if there is little feeling evident in their play. In such cases it can be helpful to facilitate a dialogue with the image or some aspect of the image.

To do this we can invite a child to identify with an image, or an aspect of an image, to find out more about the character. For characters who are clearly in a relationship, such as those facing each other or on top of each other, when both have been introduced we can facilitate a dialogue. This is a particularly helpful intervention in cases of conflict, either interpersonal or intrapsychic, but we must be aware that the image can be about external people in the child's life, the child's relationship with an external person or they can be figures from their internal world. The example below illustrates this intervention in practice.

Alex, who is nearly 9 years old, was referred for being over anxious and becoming withdrawn. He has been for three sessions and often plays with the cars in the therapy room. Today he is lining them up in the sandtray to form an orderly row, side by side. He takes one blue car and brums it around the tray. Brmmmm brmmm. I join in with some brmming noises.

I say: Just for a minute, you be the blue car and I'm going to interview you. Hello blue car, I can see you brmming around, what are you up to?

Alex: 'Not much, just going round.'

Me: Not much, hmm. And I can see a big line of cars too. How do you feel about them?

Alex: I don't know, they speak a different language to me. I can't understand them and they can't understand me. We can't talk together.

Me: What's that like for you, to speak a different language and to not understand each other?

Alex: Well I want to understand them.

The emotional tone of the conversation has now changed dramatically. There is a poignant sense of isolation and alienation that was communicated through the image work. This was not previously accessible to Alex in words because of his normal immaturity of language and ability to communicate, and because it was not quite in his awareness.

I notice his blue t-shirt, like the car, but I do not verbalise this. I sense his acute need to understand and be understood, his experience of being different, feelings of perhaps rejection and inadequacy. I feel protective of him, not wanting to be too exposing. I also feel the need to tread lightly.

I say: It can be really horrid to not understand and to feel left out.

Alex looks at me for a long time in a way I think is thoughtful. Later in the session I return to the theme of understanding and I wonder if we understand each other. I ask him to tell me if ever he feels I do not understand him. In subsequent sessions we return to this theme and develop a warm bond as our understanding grows.

Rehearsal of the possible

After, and only after, we have explored the image and communicated our empathy for how things are, then it might be fruitful to facilitate an experiment where other possibilities are tried out. We remain in the metaphor of the image and enquire, 'Is there anything you want to change?' If there is, then we can invite the change to be made. It is then important to process the impact of the change: 'How do you feel now?' 'Has the title changed?' The danger with this intervention is that it can be used prematurely before the image has become truly symbolic and the change is then superficial rather than emotionally meaningful.

Use of a therapist's image

If an image occurs to us in the course of a session it is likely to have been evoked by the content of the session and it is sometimes therapeutic to voice this. This can be a lovely way of communicating our empathy. Similarly, if the feelings of the session remind us of a scene from a story or film that the child is likely to know, then this might be useful to share also.

Communicating empathy through image

There will be occasions when working with images to communicate our empathy can prove invaluable.

> Abi is 16. She has been separated from her siblings and mother for ten years and has little contact with them. She lives with her father. She was referred for depression and has now revealed self-harming behaviours. She is utterly self-reliant and comes reluctantly for therapy, but she does always come. One day she arrives abruptly, storming into the room. She sits on the floor, arms wrapped around herself tightly, and silent. She takes up hardly any space and remains mute. I sit with her and I speak sporadically, attempting to communicate that I am there, I am available, and I can see she is in distress. My words however seem ineffective, as if they are falling on deaf ears. Time passes and the sense of abandonment grows, despite my words and presence trying to initiate a connection. I pick up a piece of paper and box of crayons and put them in her reach. She picks up the pink crayon and makes a single dot in the middle of the huge sheet of white paper. To me this evokes an image of a naked abandoned baby. I say, 'Pink, tiny, alone.' I pick up another crayon, a darker pink one, and I draw a crescent around the dot. My intention is to convey care, compassion and containment, the possibility of being held, of not being alone. This provokes tears which then turn into sobs and then finally words as the story pours out.

This is an example of an instance when communicating empathy through an image was more possible than through words. In the same vein, it can be useful to sum up and encapsulate the emotional theme of a session in an image as part of the ritual of bringing that session to a close. Forms of words that are useful here are, 'So what I am hearing is, that it is like this for you … ?'. We can then depict an image (stick figures are fine). This needs to be brief and accompanied by a few precise words as in the example above. We also need to say words to the effect of, 'Is this how it is?' or 'Sometimes adults don't get it right, you tell me how it is', and offer an opportunity for the child to correct the image. It is also helpful to include our understanding of what might be therapeutic. Therefore, if the issue is feeling alone and abandoned then the empathic image can show this, and include an understanding of the need for connection with an empathic other.

Things to avoid

Common mistakes here are trying to talk a child out of their feelings (e.g., 'You don't need to feel sad'), missing the feeling by deflecting from it or simply not noticing it, leading rather than tracking, interpreting rather than tracking, asking too many questions, asking inappropriate questions, making judgments, invading with too many words, and abandoning with too few words.

Making facilitative responses is an art and a skill that will demand conscious effort, intuition and practice. Successful creative interventions have an elegance and poise. They also have a sense of flow. In the beginning we might feel clumsy, but it's a bit like learning to drive: with experience and practice these ways of working will come to feel natural.

Focusing

This is an intervention that is rooted in the person-centred tradition of counselling and psychotherapy. It was originally developed by Eugene Gendlin (1978) and has been articulated for use with children by Stapert and Verliefde (2008). Focusing integrates the body, image, feeling and thinking. It resonates compellingly with our argument from Damasio in the last chapter that feelings matter and carry meaning, as well as with the argument above for the value of image work. Focusing is a means of sensing and connecting with inner bodily felt processes. It employs the concept of 'felt sense', which means knowledge that communicates itself to us through our body. Focusing supports child development and the sense of a unique self. It also promotes the experiencing and expression of feelings in an authentic, accepting and empathic way. It is not about venting emotion, instead it is concerned with communicating with an inner knowledge. It depends on the therapist's or focusing companion's ability to offer the core conditions and be able to work in the ways discussed above.

Stapert and Verliefde (2008: 17) suggest that focusing teaches children the following:

- To make contact with a felt sense or bodily awareness.
- To trust that the inner sense knows something for them.
- To make contact with a bodily sense of specific problems or situations.
- To experience difficult, sad, angry feelings without either drowning in them or shutting them out.
- To know that it feels good to listen to the felt sense even when the sensations are painful.
- To learn how to express emotions in a useful way.
- To self-regulate feelings in each situation.
- To clear a space inside by placing the felt sense of a specific problem outside.
- To concentrate better on daily tasks.
- To remove emotional blocks to learning.
- To know themselves better.
- To know when to ask for help.
- To listen to other children and empathise with them, even in times of conflict.
- To accept other people and enjoy harmonious relationships with them.

Focusing, as originally conceived by Gendlin, is facilitated through a series of steps. In the first of these, a gap is cleared in time and space to allow room for the process, and then attention is directed to inside the body. Noticing breathing and/or feeling the contact of our body with the chair can help with this process. We must let our attention sink down into our torso, and we must not continue until we feel a connection with our body. The next step is discovering the felt sense. To do this we must stay tuned into our body until we feel a sensation emerging. We must then stay with this and allow it to unfold. (This is the felt sense.) Here we must try to use words to describe the sensation, and we need to be accepting whatever this is. The next step is to allow an image or symbol to emerge from the felt sense, and to acknowledge and greet this image as if it were a friend. After this comes resonating, the process of checking that the symbol matches the felt sense. We will need to go back and forth between the felt sense and the image until this feels exactly right. Another step involves welcoming and receiving what has been communicated. A further step can be used to ask questions and learn more about the symbol, such as, 'What is this about?' or 'What does this need?' or 'Is this familiar?' These steps overlap and there can be a sense of going backwards and forwards.

Focusing can be helpful for people of all ages. It is best practised with a focusing companion, and we are suggesting as child therapists we could be those companions. Once the technique has been learnt it can also be practised alone. It has resonance with the skill of identification and dialogue discussed earlier and with mindfulness practice.

Mindfulness practice

Mindfulness, like focusing, is a body-based practice that emphasises awareness and acceptance. It is the basis of mindfulness-based cognitive therapy (MCBT), developed by Mark Williams and others at the University of Oxford, and MCBT is now a NICE-recommended treatment for depression and in particular for depression prevention (Williams and Penman, 2011). Courses in mindfulness practice for children are currently offered at Bangor University. At its core, mindfulness practice involves daily meditation. Its practice interrupts negative automatic thoughts and encourages self-acceptance and compassion, and therefore this disrupts the two pillars of depression which are a bleak and persecutory inner world and critical self-talk. Mindfulness can be usefully introduced in child therapy to give opportunities to experience calm states, but because it is an experiential practice it really only works if the practitioner also engages in their own mindfulness practice. This in itself can be a powerful form of self-care.

TEN   Intervening to Work with Other Relationships

Fiona Peacock

Introduction

The practicalities of living and counselling in a community such as a school can lead us to reflect on how to respond to people outside of the counselling room. All students in a school/college are clients, some actual, some potential. The majority will never use the counselling service and wouldn't need to use the containment from the therapeutic frame of individual counselling. They are normal, ordinary, developing human beings in an ordinary dynamic community, in as much as any human is 'normal and ordinary' and any educational establishment is ordinary. However, they still have something to gain from the experience of a counsellor operating as part of the educational community.

Reflection and exploration about working with children and young people who are deeply embedded in a community, be it an educational, family or statutory such as being a child who is Looked After, can challenge counsellors trained in individual methods of therapy.

Individual training can give rise to a bias toward holding the therapeutic frame (Gray, 1994) more strongly in the face of challenges from the community to 'keep them informed'. Views can be held about one person, and one person only, being the 'client'. Working with children in challenging systems, such as Children Looked After (CLA), can provide opportunities to learn new ways of providing therapy that could enhance work with other children and young people. CLA can present with a significant impairment to their attachments, may often be difficult to engage, and might also have resisted the positive adult figures that now form their new community. Such experiences lead us to reflect on how the therapeutic frame can be adapted to work with the system around the child, for the benefit of that child.

In this chapter we will explore some ideas and models that can inform our practice in this area, broadly shaped around the following questions:

- What do we do?
- Why work with others in the child's system?
- When in the treatment process is it helpful to intervene with other relationships?
- Who would benefit from this approach and who to include?
- How do we do this?

Why intervene to work with other relationships?

Part 2 of this book looked at the developmental tasks of childhood and adolescence. Underpinning these developmental tasks there lies the whole issue of how, in infancy, the blueprints necessary in order to manage the challenges of emotional life are laid down via the dyadic relationship between infant and primary caregiver. We are creatures of relationship, and where the attachment process has happened in a good enough way, we are also herd creatures.

This however can sit uncomfortably in our westernised culture of individualism and it is worth testing this out for ourselves. With a group of friends, starting to speak in a much quieter tone of voice will provoke a response. What happens? Do they get quieter too? Or we can go into an early years or Year 1 classroom and see how a teacher gains the attention of the whole class by clapping a rhythm or tapping their shoulders. The majority of the class will soon join in and in this way the teacher has sufficient quiet and attention to move on to the next activity.

If we are essentially herd animals, then it becomes necessary to consider the wider system and how this impacts on an individual's capacity to fulfil their potential or how it may lock them into an unhelpful position.

Foulkes (1983), father of the Group Analytic Psychotherapy approach, quotes Erik Erikson of *Childhood and Society* fame, saying:

... the growing child must derive a vitalizing sense of reality from the aware-ness that his individual way of mastering experience (his ego synthesis) is a successful variant of group identity and is in accord with its space-time and life plan. A child who has just found himself able to walk seems not only driven to repeat and to perfect the act of walking by libidinal pleasure in the sense of Freud's locomotor erotism; or by the need for mastery in the sense of Ives Hendrick's work principle; he also becomes aware of the new status and stature of 'he who can walk' with whatever connotation this hap-pens to have in the co-ordinates of his cultures' life plan. (1983: 11)

The developmental tasks that occur throughout childhood and adoles-cence are a revolving and evolving process of psychologically connect-ing up to others to enable growth and development, and then to disconnect from one relationship (partly or wholly), followed by recon-necting in a different way or to different people or groups. In this way issues of independence versus dependence, identity, intimacy versus isolation, faith and responsibility, are worked through. Nitsun (1996) suggests that groups frustrate narcissistic and individualistic needs by not providing an empathic mirror for the individual.

Central to the narcissistic myth is the role of the 'mirror'. Pines (in Lear, 1984) identifies two mirroring processes that can occur in groups: 'one is primitive confrontational and destructive, indicating a fixation to a dyadic model of relationship. The other is exploratory, negotiable and dialogical, where both persons, or more than two persons can share the same psychological space, one in which differing points of view are accepted and understood' (Pines, in Lear, 1984: 128). Hence the group environment of the school itself can bring to the surface the attachment deficits (or indeed strengths) that a child may be carrying with them.

Wright (1991) suggests that in the dyadic relationship/primary attachment the father role can act as positive pull on a child, drawing them away from the potential of becoming fixated on the mother/ infant symbiosis. We could suggest that this drawing away from the dyadic relationship can be significant in ameliorating rage that could result from the primary attachment relationship feeling ruptured or impoverished. Such experiences could come from a child experiencing caregiver illness such as postnatal depression, loss through death or divorce, or removal into care. The community in which a child func-tions can offer a reparative opportunity for such children by balancing the paternal (primarily cognitive and left-brained functions) with the maternal (primarily affective and right-brained functions). This can potentially enable children to move from the primitive experience of mirroring to the more helpful (in terms of classroom learning) position of Pines' second form of mirroring.

A Year 1 boy regressed in his behaviour following the birth of a sibling. He would cling to the classroom teaching assistant (TA). The more the class teacher tried to encourage him to join in with class learning the more he would cling to the TA. The TA felt that given time he'd naturally move on as he settled in to having the new sibling at home. The class teacher felt angry that 'her authority was being undermined'. She found herself wanting to 'make' the boy leave the TA. She had the insight to recognise that was not like her, and the reflexivity to want to understand this rather than act on it. Together they sought a consultation with the school counsellor to ask her to see the child. The counsellor felt the child was processing a normal transition, and that it would be more helpful for the child to do this in the community to which he belonged.

In discussion the teacher was able to discharge some of her frustration and recognise that she felt 'left out' of the close relationship that the boy and TA were having. The TA was able to acknowledge that she felt overwhelmed by the boy's needs and anxious that the good working relationship she had with the teacher might be impaired. The TA was the mother of three children, something she often talked about in the staffroom. The teacher had not yet had any children. The counsellor recognised a potential dynamic pattern so asked the TA about how she had managed when her children had been born. The TA didn't talk about how she managed the relationships between siblings, but recalled how she and her partner had struggled to adjust to the relationship becoming a triad. She recalled that she had enjoyed the baby so much her partner felt excluded, but things had improved when she had been able to see this and let her partner take more of a part in the baby's care.

This prompted a discussion between the TA and teacher about how they could 'share the baby care'. In class they verbally acknowledged what each other was doing and appreciated this in the other. This shifted the process into the verbal realm and seemed to interest both the boy and others in the class. Spontaneous discussions emerged about 'when my little brother/sister was born ...' between other class members, and there was a real energy in the room. The TA stopped taking the boy to one side to 'protect him' from others seeing his emotion, but sat with him in the body of the class. Other children commented on how hard it was for him 'now Mummy has another baby'. Games about baby care started to be played out in the home corner by other children. The next day the boy was less clingy and connected up with some girls in the home corner, not joining in but watching their play. The day after that, a Friday, he was seen very roughly near drowning the baby doll in a bath. Following their discussion with the counsellor the teacher and TA didn't intervene, but observed and monitored. They said nothing to the boy, trying not to trigger a shame reaction in him, but felt anxious themselves. After that weekend the boy showed no more clingy behaviour, and a few weeks later proudly brought in a picture of him holding his new sibling.

In this case the intervention was very similar to the clinical supervision a counsellor may receive. It enabled the teaching professionals to liberate their own resourcefulness in managing a situation supported by the counsellor's deeper understanding of how countertransference responses may influence practitioners from many professional training backgrounds. This gave educationally trained staff the confidence to let this child express his feelings of anger at the loss of his exclusive relationship with his mother through his rough treatment of the doll, rather than intervening to 'teach' more socially appropriate behaviour. The intervention, therefore, facilitated the child's natural developmental process within a supportive community that could respond to his needs.

Gerda Hanko (2002) discusses how by creating a climate of exploration between teaching professionals using psychodynamic understanding, childrens' learning experiences can be enhanced through the expression of their social and emotional difficulties. These difficulties may first be expressed through behaviour that impedes classroom learning. She feels that by liberating each teacher's insight, and raising awareness of the psychodynamic drivers of children's behaviours through work discussion groups with staff, these staff also provide each other with supports and mutual affirmations of professionalism.

There may be times when a child's community is unable to respond to that child's needs. To intervene purely with the child to facilitate their development, while not enabling their system to change, can be counterproductive.

A Year 4 girl was referred to the counsellor for aggressive and angry outbursts in the classroom. Other pupils were afraid of her. Her parents gave consent for her to attend counselling but refused to come in to meet with the counsellor themselves. Although reluctant to engage with the girl due to the lack of contact with the parents, the counsellor did accept the referral in light of the level of anxiety her behaviour was causing her peers and teachers. The girl attended four sessions using play and art work to express some of her aggression which seemed to be directed at her mother. There was nothing in the work that could be taken forward as a child protection issue, although the counsellor's countertransference left her concerned that there were potential issues. These were discussed in supervision and with the school head in the context of whether the work should continue beyond the assessment stage. There was some improvement in the girl's behaviour in the classroom.

Before a final decision could be made the girl was accommodated. Her mother took her to social services offices, saying she was out of control. The girl refused to see the counsellor again and had to change schools as her foster placement was some distance away. The school head encouraged the girl's class teacher to go and visit her. The story came back, via the teacher, that the girl had for the first time shown aggression to her mother. She had been too scared to do this in the past and now she felt this was a total loss of the relationship with her mother. Unable to voice her anger at the counsellor, she rejected that relationship just as her mother rejected her. The counsellor happened to hear of the girl a few years later: she had had several foster placements, was self-harming by cutting, and refusing to engage with mental health professionals.

Such experiences come along with hard lessons about identifying where the main difficulty lies in a system, who or what the client is, and having the courage as a counsellor to refuse to take on a case before the system has been sufficiently engaged. In the above example an underlying difficulty in a system was uncovered while there was no framework in place to enable that systemic difficulty to be contained or addressed in therapeutic work.

By setting a consideration of the system at the heart of the work, systemic psychotherapy sets the boundary and frame for therapy in a different place from that of psychodynamic work. Consideration is given to the meaning of the interaction between members of the system rather than the focus being placed purely on the behaviour of one member of that system (Jones, 1993).

With the benefit of hindsight a very different approach could have been taken to the above case. Even if the family system could not engage with a therapeutic process, the classroom system may have. This might then have supported the child without challenging the balance of power so directly as to destabilise the situation altogether.

The above case represents a failure in basic counselling practice. The counsellor responded to the anxieties of the system by not addressing those anxieties with the presenting clients (i.e., staff and other students) and by a failure to form an appropriate working contract and therapeutic frame with the person who came into the counselling room. Perhaps by first engaging with the anxiety of the people in the system we might have been able to reach a point where this child could have engaged with therapeutic interventions. Alternatively, she might have been able to confide to her class teacher something of what was happening at home, rather than acting it out, so that a more positive response could have been offered via Social Care rather than the child feeling rejected by the mother.

It is often the failures in practice that highlight the issues that need to be addressed in forming a theoretical position to support the counsellor in future encounters. The above 'failure' highlights the need to be

clear on the contract we negotiate with the organisation we are working within. This includes a discussion of who the client may be. The
assumption with many non-counselling professionals is that we will
work individually with children and in doing so this will 'solve the
problem'. It may take some time and careful dialogue with a key contact in the school to help them think about the role of the counsellor
being not only to work with individuals but also to work with the system of the school itself.

There are many challenges in this integrated form of work, and it
becomes vital to build trust by being seen as a member of the community while at the same time enabling pupils to have faith that the
personal content of their sessions will remain confidential. Being part
of the community can also enable counsellors to pick up issues early:
sitting in on assemblies, being on the playground, sitting in the staffroom, can give us a massive insight into not only how individual
children are managing the interpersonal relationships but also about
the entire school's 'emotional healthiness'.

The younger the child, the more directly their ego strength is bound
up in the community that is raising them. Working with the community around a child to maximise that child's potential means a counsellor who is embedded in a community like a school will benefit from
having a theoretical orientation that enables them to set appropriate
therapeutic frames and boundaries around work, as well as a wide
range of clinical skills and modalities that can be used to address a
spectrum of presenting issues and severities.

When and who

As a general rule, the younger the child the more likely it is that we
will need to, want to, or have to, include others in the work.
Winnicott famously said 'There is no such thing as a baby – meaning
that if you set out to describe a baby, you will find you are describing
a baby and someone. A baby cannot exist alone, but is essentially
part of a relationship' (Davis and Wallbridge, 1981: 30).

Models of work such as Theraplay® are founded on working with
this dependence to relative dependence to an independence trajectory
as described in Winnicott's 'The Theory of Parent-Infant Relationship'
(see Winnicott, 1965). The frame around such work would always
need to include the parent or primary caregiver usually participating
in the Theraplay itself, or if that were not possible, that the idea of
the parent is held firmly in the midst of the playing and thinking with
the child.

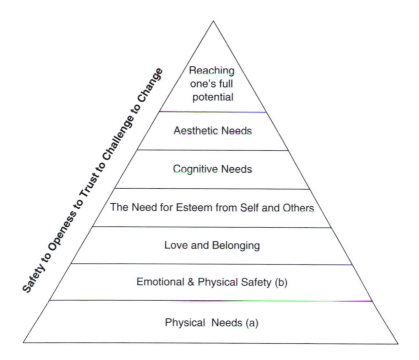

Adapted from Maslow's Hierarchy of Needs.

a includes the need for food, drink, not too hot, not too cold, enough sleep, sex, action

b includes the need for familiar routines, protection from perceived as well as 'real' dangers, physical and emotional

Figure 10.1

When children may have suffered interpersonal trauma in infancy and this has not been addressed, chronologically and physically they will continue to grow and develop but emotionally and psychologically their development may be stuck or impaired at various points along the developmental path. The age of the child may therefore not be the best pointer from which to judge the emotional developmental stage they have reached.

Maslow (1943) proposed a theory of personal motivation which he termed a 'Hierarchy of Needs'. Without being entirely faithful to the way he intended it to be used, this model can be very helpful in helping assess where a child is in terms of development and reflecting on the kind of intervention that may be most helpful.

Maslow proposed that in order to progress through the hierarchy, the needs of each stage had to be met in a good-enough way so that an individual was intrinsically motivated to progress to the next level of the hierarchy.

If a child is presenting with physical needs it will be necessary to include others and address those needs. It may not be a counsellor's direct role to discuss with the parents whether a child is being given enough to eat or whether their clothing is adequate. It is, however, the counsellor's professional duty to pass this information on to appropriate people to ensure that that child's physical needs are being met, and to determine what may be happening to create the situation where such needs are not being met. Depending on the contract with the school, it may be appropriate for the counsellor to support staff in having these conversations with parents and in helping those staff make decisions about where the information needs to go.

As a school counsellor it may not be uncommon for a young person to present with issues that are located around their need to feel safe. Where there are issues relating to physical safety, again there is clear expectation that the responsibility is on the counsellor to pass these concerns on via the organisation's child protection processes. As an employee of an organisation there is no question that as a counsellor we have to work within the organisational protocols. It can be more challenging though when we are self-employed and the contract with a school is solely to provide a counselling input.

A Year 8 girl (aged 13) disclosed in the course of counselling that her father had slapped her face. Although the girl hadn't made any other allegations of physical chastisement she had presented a picture of her father as authoritarian and prone to verbal aggression. The girl had been referred for disruptive behaviour in class (talking, non-participation, being rude to teachers when challenged). The counsellor discussed with the girl what action might be taken about her disclosure, reminding the girl of their contract which was that 'if you tell me about anyone being hurt I will have to pass that information on, but I would discuss that with you first'. The girl didn't want the counsellor to tell anyone and started minimising the event, saying she deserved the slap as she had been 'lippy'.

The counsellor was then presented with a dilemma, because as an independent counsellor she realised that her contract with the school was unclear about what her responsibilities were if such a disclosure was made. The school had a general agreement with parents that counselling was available to all students if students wanted it. The counsellor felt the girl was Gillick competent, and although she had been encouraged to tell her parents that she was coming for counselling she had chosen not to.

Having discussed the case in supervision, where she reflected on not only the disclosure but also the general presentation of the girl, the counsellor phoned the local Social Care Duty Team to run the case past them as a 'what if' scenario, giving no names at this stage. This enabled her to have some idea of what could happen if a case was reported to Social Care. The Duty Social suggested it would be better for the school to make any referral rather than the counsellor as an independent practitioner. This seemed wise to the counsellor, as she was only on site one day per week.

The counsellor talked to the girl again, saying that as she had been hit and the counsellor was concerned for her safety that she felt she did need to tell the school Child Protection Officer.

The counsellor told the school's Child Protection Officer who then met the girl. She denied that her father had hit her and the matter was taken no further.

The girl continued in counselling and seemed to find it helpful in terms of managing her behaviour better in class. However, she didn't talk spontaneously about her family again and was evasive when the counsellor raised the matter. The girl decided not to carry on with the work when the agreed number of sessions came to an end.

The girl re-presented for counselling with 'stress' in Year 11, just before her GCSEs. Having done some basic stress management work the counsellor reminded the girl about the work three years previously, and asked her what it had been like for her when the counsellor had involved others. The girl said that it was the first time she had told anyone that her father could be physically as well as verbally aggressive. After the school's Child Protection Person had talked to her she realised that people were taking what was happening seriously. She had talked to her Mum about it for the first time and her father had never hit her again. Her parents separated 18 months after the first counselling sessions ended. She felt more comfortable at home now and was hoping she would be able to stay on and do A-levels. The counsellor asked if the girl would have preferred the counsellor to have done nothing. The girl said yes, it would have been more helpful to have spent time thinking about how she, the girl, could have told someone what was going on.

Knowing how to involve others where children present with issues of emotional safety requires a good assessment of what the nature of the emotional safety issue may be. We all regress to some degree when under stress, and a sense of emotional safety can be compromised by life events such as school changes, the arrival or departure of parents/partners, the arrival or departure of step/siblings, exam pressures, illness or injury.

If, on having made an assessment, it appears that a young person has experienced sufficient emotional safety in the past in order to display the capacity to retain a sense of self-esteem, then depending on the chronological age of the child and the severity of the presenting issue, as counsellors we could consider either short-term individual work for the child or enabling the system around that child to provide support so the child's natural healing process could happen. The example of the Year 1 boy earlier in this chapter is such a case: his behaviour was not unsafe or truly problematic for those around him, it was a natural life transition, one that many of his peers had already lived through; his class team were very keen to support him; and taking him out of class for sessions might have confirmed that there was 'something wrong' with the way he was coping.

The younger the child, the more likely it is that they are still in the normal process of developing their attachment patterns and internal working models. They are more likely to still be driven by right-brain processes so are also more likely to gain most from treatment methods that enhance and embed good attachment behaviours in their natural environment or relational system. Supporting the school to provide training sessions to parents or parental support groups can be valuable. Watch, Wait and Wonder can be a useful model to adapt for this kind of input, enabling parents to learn just to enjoy non-judgmentally and to mindfully observe their children. Groups could be for parents only or could be run for parents and children together. Both Theraplay and Watch, Wait and Wonder are excellent models for such work.

For a young person who is in latency or adolescence, individual non-directive therapy could offer some space to enable some balance to be restored.

A Year 6 boy (aged 10 years old), who generally was a high academic performer and confident in class, became very tearful and lost interest in his work. Staff felt he was very anxious about transferring to secondary school, but to them this seemed at odds with his usual confident presentation. Given the age of the boy and the nature of the contract with the school, the usual policy was that both parents and child would be invited to a first appointment together. At this appointment it emerged that there was a very high level of stress at home due to an older sibling having ongoing treatment for a serious illness. Generally the boy seemed to cope with the sibling's frequent emergency admissions and parental absences, but it seemed the thought of losing the stability of his school environment meant that his usual coping mechanisms were impaired. We agreed that the counsellor would offer the boy 4 sessions (which was all that could be fitted in before the end of term) plus a final meeting with his parents.

During the sessions the boy drew but also used playdoh. The counsellor felt it was hard for him to let himself be 'messy' and so process the 'messiness' of his home life. In session 2 she asked the boy if he would like to use some clay during session 3. The boy said yes. Unfortunately the school was very short of space to enable a 'messy clay session' so this took place on the playing field under some trees at a time when no one was due to come out to play. The boy became totally absorbed in making pots and was able to sink into this creative mess. The Early Years pupils then came out for an unplanned runaround and were of course immediately fascinated by what was happening. The boy remained absorbed in his work, and after a brief exchange with the Early Years teacher, the counsellor broke off a large lump of clay and gave it to the other children who were then also soon absorbed in pot making, thus guarding the client's boundary albeit it in an unusual way.

Session 4 was spent looking back at what he had created and thinking about what this meant in terms of his feelings about his sibling, family and moving school. He decided on what he wanted to show his parents at the next meeting and also decided that he would like the counsellor to keep one of the most messy creations which he felt was something about her sibling but didn't know what. The boy was very eloquent at describing his art work to his parents while not talking about the meanings these had to his inner world. His parents felt included in the work, but the boy felt that the privacy of the content of his session had been respected.

Engaging parents in this way can have many advantages. Guishard-Pine et al. (2007) talk about a 'protective shield' that a multi-agency team around CLA can supply. This concept can equally apply to children in their birth families. Engaging with and supporting this protective shield can provide containment for the child beyond the therapy room, enable the work of therapy to continue after sessions have stopped, provide children with a sense of safety in the counselling process, knowing it is endorsed by their parents, and contain adult anxieties about the therapeutic process. It can also model unconditional positive regard to adults so that parents/carers feel able to entrust their children to the counsellor.

If it seems that the attachment deficiencies of the child or young person are so severe and entrenched that emotional safety is significantly compromised, then it could be more appropriate to use a specific attachment-based way of working such as Theraplay or Dan Hughes' (2006) model of Dyadic Developmental Psychotherapy (DDP). Both these models have work with the primary caregiver as a central part of their methodology.

Once Maslow's Hierarchy of Needs has been used to identify the 'point of stuckness' for a child, we need to therapeutically target the level below in order to try to enable that child's intrinsic motivation for growth to be released. So for the child with a lack of a sense of emotional safety, stemming from longstanding attachment difficulties, we could try to offer a therapy that had a high level of tactile or sensory input, thereby ensuring that the physical needs of that child were met. In this way the child could experience how having their physical needs met would give rise to the experience of emotional safety in the same way as an infant starts to internalise a sense of safety through their daily care. Models of work such as Theraplay meet the needs of the developmental age of the child while still respecting the chronological age of that child. Using Maslow in this way also shows why it is beneficial to enable a carer to continue this kind of input between therapy sessions, thus continuing the child's daily experience of therapeutic care.

With children and young people who appear to have reached the Maslow stages of love and belonging and the need for esteem, generally we would work first with individuals whilst keeping in mind the systems they inhabit. Hedges (2005) presents useful ideas on how to work with systemic ideas even where working with an individual. Once the work is established we can ask, if it seems appropriate, if there is anyone the young person would like to bring 'for real'. With an older age group it is not uncommon for them to bring along individuals who they would like in the session anyway. Friends, boyfriends and girlfriends, can all turn up unexpectedly to sessions, and in doing so can provide valuable insights for the counsellor by which they can assess how a young person is perceived by friends: this can also provide a client with a safe opportunity to reflect on how their peers see them.

Children who are Looked After, or who have significant input from other statutory services, can create some challenges in terms of engaging with the network of relationships around them. As the primary caregiver may not necessarily be the person who is exercising parental responsibility, determining who does hold this responsibility and seeking appropriate consent to see the child are vital. This can be equally valid in thinking about children who are living with a birth parent. Where birth parents are no longer together it may be necessary to seek out the other parent and gain consent for work, clarify the boundary, and contract for work in order to protect the integrity of that work.

As well as formal consent from the person exercising parental responsibility, the primary caregiver, if they are a different person, also needs to feel in a positive relationship with any therapeutic work so they are able to support the child. For a CLA or other children who may be reluctant to engage in direct work, working with a foster carer or parent can change the dynamic of the family environment enough to start a process of change for a child. A child who may be experiencing issues around poor self-esteem, who might see coming for counselling as another sign of their failing, may be significantly helped by working with parents/carers around how they can enhance their sense of love and belonging, with the result that the child can find the internal motivation to experience esteem from self and others.

What and how

The counsellor as a consultant to the system

The theory underpinning this idea is discussed in more detail in Chapter 13 where the challenges of working in a multi-agency or multi-professional setting are considered. The role of consultancy can be similar in some ways to supervision, enabling staff to step outside of the situation and view things in a way that can re-resource them to manage the emotional challenges of pupils within the classroom context. As with supervision, consultation with staff members can provide restorative, formative and normative experiences.

As well as this one-to-one consultation about specific children, the counsellor may offer staff development groups, thereby enabling staff to move to a more reflective position when it comes to considering children's emotional needs while still remaining in their primary role as teachers.

The counsellor may also need to act as a consultant in Team Around the Child (TAC) meetings, being mindful of the process that could be going on in the meeting that might reflect something of the inner dilemma a child could be facing. Using Foulkes' (1990) ideas of mirroring and the group matrix, TAC meetings can be viewed as a therapeutic encounter in themselves. In an ideal world as counsellors we wouldn't have to act in a consultative role in a TAC meeting while being the counsellor individually to the child. However, as we don't live in an ideal world, it is important that as the child's individual counsellor our preparation for this meeting should be thorough, and where possible, that the child is consulted on what we as their counsellor intends to feed back to the TAC.

A 14 year old CLA had engaged with the counsellor. She seemed to be starting to trust her and to talk in more depth about the experience of living in foster care. After a six-session assessment a multi-agency meeting gathered to review whether the work should continue. The child had agreed the counsellor could feed back that she wanted to continue to come for counselling and that she was finding it helpful, but didn't give consent for any

(Continued)

(Continued)

details about her feelings on being in a foster placement to be discussed. During the course of the meeting a heated discussion arose between the social worker and foster carers, with the social worker suggesting the foster carers were being too controlling of the young person and the carers saying that the social worker didn't understand how vulnerable the young person was. The counsellor posed the same question to each: 'What do you think the child thinks of the placement?' Neither the carers nor the social worker could give a solid-sounding answer to this. Each agreed to ask the young person what she thought was helpful or unhelpful about the placement. The counsellor returned to the work with the young person with the question 'If you could really say anything to your carers about the placement what would it be?' She followed this with 'What might get in the way of saying that?' This led on to some role play, and two weeks later the young person asked if her carers could come in at the end of the session 'to see her play'. The carers were able to respond to the young person's 'telling' that she both liked and disliked the containment they were offering. She reflected back this insight in words and felt that the carers had really heard this ambivalence she was struggling with. It seemed that both the social worker and the carers had been correct in the review meeting.

Model of intervention

Theraplay bases an intervention on the healthy attachment behaviours displayed between caregivers and infants. It uses games to support children in engaging with adults or peers, managing challenges, accepting appropriate nurturing and managing structure. It is an adult-led therapeutic approach usually involving the child's primary caregiver, where the focus is specifically on the needs of one child. It is lively and fun-filled, focusing on the child's here-and-now engagement rather than consciously raising and dealing with the content of past difficulties.

Very recently The Theraplay Institute have started a programme called Sunshine Groups, which is not specifically a therapeutic programme but aimed at supporting a nurturing and positive right-brained learning culture in classrooms. Group Theraplay can also be used to begin to engage with children who are displaying attachment-based difficulties and to work with small groups of children who may be having difficulties in managing relationships with peers or self-regulating. Rockingham Primary School in Northamptonshire uses the model significantly in its school culture (Radwan, 2010).

The example that follows is a real case which the mother very kindly gave her consent to share. Any identifying details have been changed.

Mark was a Year 1 child referred to a Theraplay group consisting of four children. He had a diagnosis of Asperger's and ADHD. In the Theraplay group he found it hard to join in despite other children trying to encourage him. He also found it difficult to take turns (a structure-based issue) or accept/give appropriate nurture. By the end of the six sessions he was spending most of his time in the group hiding under a table and withdrawing more when I or his peers tried to encourage him. In the end I felt the safest thing was to leave him and let him watch the activities, but in reality I felt I had failed both Mark and the other children by not making a proper assessment for the group.

Mark continued to cause concern for staff and his mother and so I agreed to offer Mark and his mother a Marschak Interaction Method (MIM) assessment for Theraplay. The recording of this was played back to mum as part of the assessment and treatment planning process. This enabled her to see that, although she wanted to engage with Mark, often they were 'miscuing' their non-verbal communication and she was sometimes relating to Mark as someone who was more her peer than a young boy.

Instead of offering a direct Theraplay intervention which was logistically difficult for mum, together we devised a mini Theraplay plan that she could enjoy with him at home. This included eye contact games ('How long can you stare into my eyes without smiling?', mirroring games ('I'm going to make a shape with my body, I want you to make the same shape, I bet you can! Now you make one for me to copy'), nurture-based games such as 'making a pizza' on the child's back (kneading the dough, spreading the tomato paste and sprinkling the cheese give opportunities for mother and child to play with different tactile sensations), and structure games such as getting the child to punch through a sheet of newspaper (but only when Mum says 'go').

I met with Mark's mother a couple of times over the following six weeks or so. She reported back on which games were working and what was difficult and in this way we adapted the programme. I was also very touched when she said something along the lines of 'I'd never learnt to play with him before'.

After the six weeks she was reporting significant improvements in his relationships at home and with peers. The Goodman's Strengths and Difficulties Questionnaire (www.sdqinfo.com/) was used before and after the input but didn't show much change either on the parent or teacher forms. The parent-rated HoNOSCA (www.liv.ac.uk/honosca/) scores had fallen from 30 (very, very high), before the home Theraplay programme, to 3 (well within the normal range) after six weeks, suggesting the mother was feeling things were much improved. The teacher's descriptive report indicated no specific behavioural changes in class from Mark, but she commented that he had made the biggest academic progress in the class over the course of Year 1.

Hughes' (1997, 2006) DDP model of work refers to the games used in Theraplay and sees these as suitable for his model of work. The significant difference in his way of working is to actively bring in past interpersonal trauma. His model is very intensive and challenging. Like Theraplay it is therapist-led while still being child-centred. It also involves carers in the process.

Watch, Wait and Wonder (WWW) (Cohen at al., 1999), like Theraplay, seeks to enhance the attachment relationship between child and caregiver. Unlike Theraplay it is child-led, with the carer/parent being encouraged to not intervene in the child's activity but to minutely observe and reflect on that activity.

First devised in 1980 by Jerome Dowling and David Wesner in the USA, WWW recommends the primary caregiver gets down on the floor with the child, does not intervene, but is interested in their every play so that child's world becomes mutually explored and understood. The original concept was developed for families experiencing difficulties and aimed at infants and children up to 4 years old. It may require parents to take a very different approach to their usual childcare practice because it asks them to not intervene but to be mindful of the meaning of the child's play and can therefore increase their sensitivity to the child's needs.

These models can be adapted to safely involve relevant others from the child's system in the therapeutic work.

Notes

Theraplay® is a registered service mark of The Theraplay Institute, Evanston, IL, USA. See www.theraplay.org for more information.

All the examples in this chapter are fictionalised, drawing on the many children I have worked with and the many schools I have worked in over the years. No individual should be able to recognise themselves from these examples, and if any of my former clients wish to discuss the examples with me I would be delighted to hear from them. They have all taught me so much and I thank them.

PART 4

Professional Issues in Counselling with Children and Adolescents

ELEVEN Professional and Ethical Issues in the Beginning and Ongoing Phases of Therapy in Schools

Tracey Fuller

Introduction

Ethical dilemmas in working in the opening stages of therapy with children are very common. The majority of these orbit the professional and legal tensions that exist in attempting to provide confidential space for children (McGinnis, 2008). According to the BACP's Ethical Framework 'Working with young people requires specific ethical awareness and competence' (2010: 6). Much also depends on individual circumstances, developmental needs, levels of risk, and therapeutic and other relationships (Bond, 2010). What may be the best course of action in one situation in one setting with one client may be wholly inappropriate in another. Ways of working ethically alongside teachers, other professionals and parents also require active consideration.

Dilemmas in working therapeutically with children and young people often result in a potential conflict between the principles of autonomy, fidelity (trust) and that of beneficence (Daniels and Jenkins, 2010). This tension can also exist in adult work where risk is involved, however, with children it becomes a major feature of the work: this is because their younger developmental stage inevitably means that children are more powerless and vulnerable to abuse and harm. Our requirement to protect and act in young people's best interest can conflict with children's right to trusted confidential space and autonomy (McGinnis and Jenkins, 2011). Child counsellors perhaps work uniquely at the intersection of these rights. The opening (and ongoing) stages of therapeutic work include assessment and review meetings and initial contracting with young clients. The initial setting-up of the school counselling service is also strongly implicated here, as this will often determine a counsellor's level of success in maintaining the therapeutic relationship, no matter when an ethical dilemma arises.

We would argue that three factors seem important in maintaining helpful relationships with children through ethical challenges:

- Careful and explicit contracting with young people, parents and the school, in terms of confidentiality and its limits in the face of safeguarding concerns (McGinnis and Jenkins, 2011).
- Appropriate and clear service level agreements and protocols that underpin the school counselling, combined with ongoing communication about these in practice (Pattison et al., 2009).
- Developing an approach that puts transparency at the forefront of therapeutic practice with young people, in order that information sharing is based routinely on informed consent, wherever immediate safety allows (McGinnis, 2008).

These elements, alongside the reflective use of regular supervision, form a helpful basis for ethical counselling practice in schools.

In order to develop a justification for the above approach to ethical dilemmas in the opening and ongoing stages of therapy, we will start by briefly outlining some of the debates, legal frameworks and dilemmas as regards confidentiality in schools. This will be followed by a discussion of beneficial communication with teachers and children's networks, and some reflections on initiating a counselling service in a school. First, sessions with children and the setting-up of transparent contracts will be explored, as will managing assessment and review meetings. This will be followed by a case example of using a transparency and reflective supervision to help face the ethical challenges provoked by a child protection disclosure. The chapter will conclude with some reflections on the importance of school counsellor self-care.

Confidentiality and ethical dilemmas: balancing trust and safety

'Confidentiality especially with regard to children and young people ... perpetually demands thought and dialogue ... there is very little that is universally agreed, other than it provokes strong feelings' (McGinnis, 2008: 126). McGinnis points to the depth of the debate as regards confidentiality with children. The BACP Ethical Framework states that confidentiality is an 'obligation arising from the client's trust' (BACP, 2010: 3), while Baginsky (2004) argues that school counsellors are in a paradoxical position: confidentiality is upheld as being vital to children but counsellors equally have a role to 'liaise with pastoral management staff, special needs co-ordinators, year tutors, class teachers, governors, parents and support agencies' (McGinnis and Jenkins, 2011: 12). The Welsh Government's School Counselling 'Toolkit' suggests counsellors are required to 'work with, and alongside other services and agencies in a collegial manner, whilst maintaining appropriate levels of confidentiality' (Hill et al., 2011: 6), yet some studies have highlighted that the culture within schools does not necessarily respect children's right to a confidential space (Jenkins and Palmer, 2012).

Young people's views on confidentiality

There is much evidence that an expectation of confidentiality is a key consideration for young people in seeking therapeutic help (LeSurf and Lynch, 1999; Boulton, 2007; Fox and Butler, 2007). Confidentiality is attractive to young people contemplating using a school counselling service, whilst the fear that it may not really be confidential may inhibit some others (Burnison, 2003; Fox and Butler, 2007). This factor may have a developmental aspect with older adolescents in particular having the greatest concern about the confidentiality of the service they received.

Confidentiality: three approaches in law

A basic understanding of the three legal approaches to children's rights supported in law provides a supportive framework for school counsellors in seeking to reflect on ethical dilemmas in schools. This is a complex and continually evolving area that can seem far removed from the relationship with an individual young person. (For a comprehensive exploration of confidentiality with children and children's rights we would recommend Baginsky, 2007; Fox and Butler, 2007; Daniels and Jenkins, 2010; McGinnis and Jenkins, 2011; Jenkins and Palmer, 2012.) Three models of children's rights that are supported by different legal statutes and case law are briefly outlined in Figure 11.1.

Despite this breadth of legally supported positions to children's rights, within schools there is a tendency to over-emphasise the primacy of the welfare approach (Friel, 1998; Daniels and Jenkins, 2010).

Confidentiality: Three approaches in law

The 'Welfare Model'

This pre-supposes that adults are best placed to make decisions affecting the welfare of children and young people. In terms of ethical values it prioritises beneficence over principles of autonomy. Pastoral systems in schools tend to be run according to this principle. Daniels and Jenkins suggest that this approach is essentially 'adult-centred' and regards parents as the main consumer of education despite moves to the contrary in actual legislation such as The Children's Act 2004 (2010).

Participatory Approach

This model suggests that children and young people have the right to be involved in decisions that affect their lives and wellbeing in accordance with their age and level of maturity. This principle is supported by a variety of legislation to varying degrees, including Article 12 of the United Nations' Convention on the Rights of the Child 1989 and the Children's Act 1989. This model is often found to be acting in decisions about residence and parenting where the court will actively seek young people's views. In ethical terms this balances autonomy and other ethical principles such as beneficence.

Independence Model: The 'Gillick principle'

This is based on the 'Gillick principle' where children under the age of 16 can be provided with confidential treatment (including counselling) provided they demonstrate 'sufficient understanding' of the nature of the issue (*Gillick v West Norfolk Area Health Authority*, 1985). The Children's Legal Centre suggests that mature children/young people have a right to seek independent advice and counselling without parental consent (Children's Legal Centre, 1989: 12). The 'Fraser guidelines' further elucidated this area by setting out further criteria to justify such intervention, importantly that:

1. The young person had refused to have their parents informed.
2. The provision of counselling was seen as being in the young person's best interest.

A helpful checklist of the application of Fraser guidelines to counselling situations can be found in Daniels and Jenkins, 2010: 70. The concept of 'Gillick competence' has been applied to maturing adolescents, often over 14 and under 16, who are deemed of sufficient maturity to assent to counselling without parental consent.

Figure 11.1   Three models of children's rights (adapted from Daniels and Jenkins, 2010)

A national survey found that 41% of schools required evidence of parental permission in order for young people to gain access to school counselling services (Jenkins and Polat, 2006). In many secondary schools parents are informed about the existence of the school counselling service and are given an opportunity to 'opt-out' for their son or daughter if they actively object (Jenkins, 2010). The position in primary schools however is different as parental permission is nearly always required (Jenkins and Palmer, 2012). The misrepresentation of the concept of *in loco parentis* has been criticised by some workers (McLaughlin, 1996; Jenkins, 2010) as it has been erroneously interpreted to suggest that schools must exercise a 'duty of care' in substitution for a parent's. This may then have been used to over-ride the rights of children and deny access to counselling for some students who do not have parental consent.

How confidentiality is practised by school counsellors may vary greatly according to the nature of the agency that provides it (McGinnis, 2008; Daniels and Jenkins, 2010). Counsellors directly employed by schools in particular may be subject to the same employment conditions that apply to teachers (i.e., to work under the reasonable direction of the head teacher; see Daniels and Jenkins, 2010). Counsellors may also feel vulnerable to embedded tensions between ethical practice and their employment expectations. This suggests that it may be easier to practise ethically in schools with the support of an external agency or commissioning authority, where counsellors may be more protected from sudden changes to their contracts and are able to ensure a greater continuity of service for children (Harris, 2009).

Having briefly explored some of the debates about confidentiality we will now investigate information sharing in schools, its evolution as well as its potential benefits.

Schools and information sharing

Children's networks greatly impact on their well-being and helpful communication with that network can affect meaningful change and be powerfully therapeutic (Hoffman, 1993; McGinnis and Jenkins, 2011). Teachers are the professionals who have the greatest daily contact with children and as such they are often very concerned for their wellbeing and will seek to work together to support and protect them (McGinnis, 2008; McGinnis and Jenkins, 2011). Schools will routinely share information formally and informally in order to do this (McGinnis and Jenkins, 2011; Lamb, 2012). A counsellor arriving in a school, with a clinical model about the necessity of providing confidential space in order to create the therapeutic frame and maintain the ethical principles of fidelity and trust (BACP, 2010), may experience a professional 'culture clash'. They will have to adapt to an environment where the practice of sharing information is regarded as good practice (Lamb, 2012).

It is perhaps helpful for counsellors working in schools to understand something of the evolution of school's approaches to information sharing.

The Children's Act 1989 set down that local authorities have the responsibility to 'safeguard and promote the welfare' of children (Part 3, Section 17). This act gave local authorities the legal responsibility to investigate whether children are suffering or are likely to suffer 'significant harm' (Section 47). In the wake of the Laming Inquiry (2003) into the repeated failure of professionals to protect Victoria Climbié, followed by the 'Every Child Matters' Green Paper (DfES, 2003) and the resulting Children's Act 2004, the culture of sharing information in order to safeguard children has become deeply embedded in cultural practice within and between statutory agencies, including schools (McGinnis and Jenkins, 2011; Jenkins and Palmer, 2012). There are complex arguments as to whether this 'culture of mandatory reporting' of suspected child abuse is legally valid, and whether it should extend to include counsellors based in schools, with perhaps those employed directly by schools having the greatest requirement to disclose safeguarding information (Brown, 2006; Daniels and Jenkins, 2010; Jenkins, 2010; Jenkins and Palmer, 2012).

A further extension of the sharing of information between professionals has been developed by the coalition government (HMG, 2010), despite some workers' misgivings about evidence of a positive impact for the children themselves (Baginsky, 2007; Daniels and Jenkins, 2010; Jenkins, 2010). For children who are considered as perhaps not 'at risk' but 'in need', multi-disciplinary CAF (Common Assessment Framework) plans are implemented (Department of Health/Department of Education and Employment/Home Office, 2000). CAFs require the sharing of much personal information about children, including their needs, behaviour, learning and family background, amongst a wide variety of professionals including teachers, social workers, CAMHs (Child and Adolescent Mental Health Service) workers, educational psychologists, etc. CAF plans then become part of young people's records in schools and other statutory settings (HMG, 2010). TAC (Team around the Child) and multi-professional meetings are also widely used in schools to support children (Bomber, 2009).

The practice of sharing information about children has been driven by the need to prevent further tragedies and failures in safeguarding as happened with Victoria Climbie. It is within this professional, legal, political and socio-cultural context that a school counsellor will have to work. We have sympathy with Daniels and Jenkins' powerful (2010) argument for the value of providing truly confidential space as a practice that empowers young people and prevents a later retraction of safeguarding disclosures. However, in practice this requires counsellors to manage and assess high levels of risk, which may only be tenable and safe where individual counsellors' work is supported (and held as confidential) within multi-disciplinary teams that include social workers. School counsellors often work as lone mental health professionals amongst teams of educators. Undoubtedly, ethical and safe school counselling work does require an understanding and active assessment of clients' developmental level and degree of vulnerability. For example, it may be helpful for a 15 year old to have more autonomy to determine the timing and manner of their disclosure about *past* sexual abuse by a non-resident adult in a way that empowers them rather than increases their experience of powerlessness. In contrast, to keep confidential concerns about an 8 year old who has said that they are regularly hit with a belt would be dangerous and unethical. How school counsellors make such assessments and apply ethical principles in practice requires much further research (Jenkins and Palmer, 2012). School counsellors need to work alongside their teaching colleagues in a way that carefully balances young clients' rights to a trusted space with managing the transparent flow of information to best support and protect them. They also need to make an effort to understand and respect the professional culture of education of professionals working together.

For these reasons we believe a polarised position with regard to confidentiality is essentially unhelpful in schools. Learning to practise with transparency with young people is an appropriate and practical route through these perceived professional tensions. We argue that a 'specific competence with ethical matters' as regards counselling students in schools requires a nuanced practice that encompasses all of the following (BACP, 2010).

- Children have the right to trusted confidential therapeutic relationships (where their immediate safety allows).
- Young people and children become attached to adults who will greatly affect their wellbeing. School counsellors need to communicate with the people and systems around the child as they can be a powerful resource and act to affect change.
- As young people's developmental stage progresses towards mid-late adolescence greater individuation often results in a desire, and a greater capacity, to make their own decisions and to have 'private-non-parental space' (Frankel, 1998).
- 'Informed consent' (where their immediate safety allows) and transparency should be at the heart of the sharing of information from counselling sessions (McGinnis, 2008).

- Information sharing by the counsellor should be determined by the potential benefits for the child, their developmental age/stage, and whether there are safety issues at stake (McGinnis and Jenkins, 2011).

We will go on to explore transparency and informed consent in the following section and in the case example of Sophie on p. 185.

Working transparently with children, young people and teachers

McGinnis (2008) argues for a transparent practice that puts 'informed consent' by the young person at the heart of most information sharing. Allowing young people to retain a degree of control over disclosures is crucial (McLaughlin, 1996; Dogra, 2005; Jenkins and Palmer, 2012). Much has been written elsewhere about what constitutes 'informed consent' which is beyond the scope of this chapter to explore (see Pearce, 1994; BMAED, 2004; NSPCC, 2009; Daniels and Jenkins, 2010), however, in this context we are describing negotiating consent with each young client for the sharing of material from their counselling sessions with other named adults.

In working alongside teachers it is also helpful to understand their professional expertise and the pressures they experience. Children who are referred to counselling may provoke strong feelings in the adults around them of powerlessness, rage, fear and hurting, and these can potentially lead to a culture of blaming and psychological splitting (Heyno, 2009; Music, 2009). School counsellors can helpfully disrupt this cycle by providing a more integrated position that offers hope to the student and hence to their teachers (Music, 2009). Containing and listening to teachers' anger and anxiety about clients can be a key part of our daily role. Delaney (2009b) describes the importance of reframing discussions with teachers about pupils to focus on their underlying (often attachment) needs. Others emphasise the necessity of 'translating' pupil behaviour and the anxiety that often underpins it (Bomber, 2009). There is a lack of reflective space for teachers and generally an absence of professional supervision despite the support they may provide for students (Lloyd, 1999; Hanko, 2002; Geddes, 2006; Bomber, 2009). It may be hard for a teacher to tolerate a pupil who is causing them to feel powerless, to be listened to when they are not supported or listened to themselves. Counsellors need to avoid getting drawn into psychological splitting themselves by blaming teachers. We strongly believe that working ethically in a school context requires empathy for school staff as well as pupils. Acknowledging the difficulties and remaining non-defensively curious are often helpful responses in conversations with teachers. Such dialogue also provides an opportunity to model transparent working with children and respect for their right to make choices about the decisions that affect them.

Service level agreements

Establishing a therapeutic frame with one individual client is dependent on the outer structures that support the overall school counselling service. Issues such as rooms, referral routes and numbers, record keeping, understandings about confidentiality, timetabling and managing communications with staff, all greatly impact upon a counsellor's ability to practise effectively and ethically. Service level agreements between the school and the counselling service potentially provide the most helpful structures in order to offer containment for the counselling (Pattison et al., 2009). Developing a shared understanding about the nature of the counselling, matters of confidentiality and safeguarding is ultimately the best foundation for ethical practice in schools (Cromarty and Richards, 2009). These agreements also need to predate face-to-face work with children.

School counselling has been widely found to be beneficial to young people in schools (Cooper, 2004, 2006; Hill et al., 2011). However, many schools are unaware of the ethical intricacies of setting up such a service, and there are often unrealistic expectations with regard to time and referral rates (Baginsky, 2004). McGinnis (2008) argues that counsellors should be able to present their legal and ethical responsibilities clearly so that others understand that they are not being 'precious' or 'secretive'. Equally, counsellors need to be aware of schools' and local authorities' responsibility to safeguard children and the protocols involved.

Time spent making relationships with teaching staff at school, and with external agencies such as local CAMHs teams and children's services and in jointly planning a service, has been linked to positive outcomes (Cromarty and Richards, 2009). School inset and staff meetings can be used to inform and educate staff about the counselling service. It is also equally vital to find ways of introducing the role of the counsellor to the students such as special assemblies and visits to classes. The role of a counselling service link person in a school may be vital in this process (Armstrong, 2011). This aspect will be explored in the following chapter. Harris (2009) highlights the importance of the attitude of the school leadership if counselling is to become an integrated service in school.

Rooms and timetables

Finding a safe space to carry out counselling can be a sensitive issue in school environments, and especially in primary schools where space is often at a premium. It is common for many spaces to have multiple and competing purposes: for example, a small group room may also be a first aid room. It is vital to find a comfortable room that does not have an association for children with 'being in trouble'. Further, as spaces are often shared it is common practice for adults and children to enter rooms unannounced. It is necessary to consider the siting of such rooms in order to consider the privacy of young clients attending counselling sessions both within their sessions and en route to and from them. Establishing the necessity of an uninterrupted safe space and the concept of therapeutic boundaries requires discussion and information for staff. Matters of timetabling the counselling appointments also demand forward discussion, with some schools preferring a rotation of counselling slots so that students do not continually miss the same lesson.

Recent reviews of school counselling services such as Pattison et al. (2009) outline a number of recognised key ingredients (as listed below), although further research is required to establish shared understandings of the meaning of each of these factors.

Important recognised ingredients for a school counselling service

- Sustainable funding.
- Employing professionally qualified counsellors with experience of working with children and young people who are in regular clinical supervision. (*Counsellor's should be members of professional bodies such as the BACP and UKCP who have clear ethical frameworks.*)
- Providing a safe and private space in school for the counselling to take place.
- Service should be viewed as a non-stigmatising and integrated part of school provision.
- Specialist evaluation and monitoring of the service should be in place.
- The service should operate in a way that meets the requirements of current legislation and offers confidentiality within the limits required by safeguarding.
- Counsellors must work in a way that is flexible and respects and values diversity.

- Counsellors must work in a 'collegial' manner with other agencies and professionals whilst maintaining appropriate confidentiality.
- The service must employ counsellors who are approachable and have the personal qualities to create trusting therapeutic relationships (adapted from Pattison et al., 2009:170–72).

Meetings can be very difficult to arrange given the restraints of school counsellor working contracts and teacher workloads and priorities. It can be difficult finding time to liaise with school staff when most counsellors are employed on a part-time basis, with their hours often being linked to numbers of students to be seen rather than the time to set up and manage the service (Cromarty and Richards, 2009; Harris, 2009). Ways of ensuring opportunities for such communication are perhaps a very pertinent focus for commissioners of school counselling services (Cromarty and Richards, 2009).

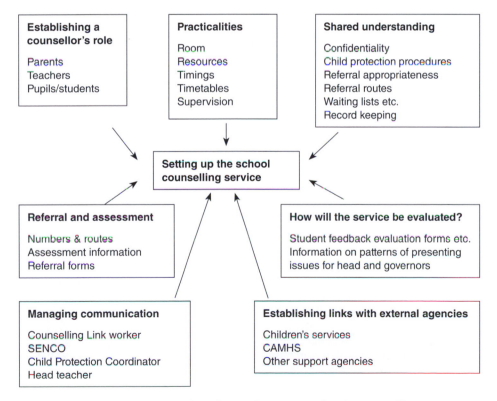

Figure 11.2   Factors to consider in setting up a school counselling service

Figure 11.2 shows a suggested network of factors that may require consideration when setting up a school counselling service. We believe that developing a clear understanding and ongoing dialogue around the factors listed above is essential to support the school counsellor (and hence their clients) when ethical dilemmas do emerge (McGinnis, 2008).

Encounters: initiating a transparent therapeutic contract

The first assessment session with a child or young person is a vital platform for ensuring future ethical practice (procedures for running assessment and review meetings that involve parents/ staff are outlined later in the chapter). Initiating a respectful relationship with a young client includes outlining (in a developmentally appropriate way) the confidentiality of the sessions and its limits. This is not a 'once and only' procedure as it is often helpful to return to this contract and further discuss its implication, for example where a counsellor believes that a client is about to disclose safeguarding information (NSPCC, 2009; Jenkins and Palmer, 2012). In secondary schools it can also help to have a simply written confidentiality statement displayed in the counselling space, such as can be seen in Figure 11.3.

Counselling agencies will often have protocols and assessment forms for evaluating a service and assessing risk, such as Goodman's (1997) Strengths and Difficulties Questionnaire, that need to be completed in first sessions. Counsellors have a duty to further assess for themselves whether they are best placed to support a young person. Where there is a high level of risk, such as in the case of suicidal clients, or where the counsellor believes there may be highly complex

---

What you say to your counsellor is confidential. They will not share what you tell them unless:

- You want them to because it would be helpful for somebody else to know.
- You (or another young person) are in serious danger.

It can be helpful to encourage clients to ask questions and to test out hypothetical scenarios around this. With older clients it is also important to discuss explicitly that this contract includes 'seriously hurting' themselves.

Figure 11.3   Example of a counselling agreement

needs, or an underlying undiagnosed disorder or mental illness, it may be best for the client to be referred on to (or work in tandem with) a service where they can be supported by a multi-professional team, such as the local CAMHs. This is commensurate with the counsellor working within the bounds of professional competency and in the best interests of the client (BACP, 2010; Bond, 2010). Young people (and parents) need to be included in the onward referral process. Clients' consent should be sought, and where age appropriate, young people can contribute and have access to any written onward referral information (NSPCC, 2009). Offering such opportunities can work against clients feeling disempowered or rejected by an onward referral. Pre-existing relationships with local CAMHs teams can be very helpful at this point in easing such referrals.

Engaging with the network around the child

We learn from systemic theory that children do not live in isolation and their relationships are a key part of how they learn about themselves (Wilson, 1998). Boundaries are formed and tested against other people to help children develop a sense of self and their place in the world. Meeting with the wider network, or 'system of concern', can enhance the relationship with the child, and (with consent) the wider system can be given information about the therapy, increasing the opportunities for understanding for everyone (McAdam and Lang, 1994). Communication with parents can offer the possibility of significant therapeutic movement and affect change for the child. This can also be a resource for the counsellor, providing stories of hope and courage, different perspectives, new solutions and unexpected information that can enhance that counsellor's thinking and practice (White and Epston, 1987; Hoffman, 1993).

How to engage with the wider network

Initial assessment meetings often involve parents, especially in the primary phase. Later counselling review meetings usefully may involve parents and other family members, and sometimes teachers. Maintaining the assumption that everyone in the child's network wants the best for that child contributes towards the co-creation of a respectful and quietly optimistic environment (Smart, 2012). The counsellor may take a position of curiosity and humility. The function

---

1. What would it be helpful for your parents to understand?
2. What are they happy to share?
3. What material (if any) do they want to keep confidential?
4. Who do they want to do the sharing? *Some clients want to share their experience of counselling themselves, while others prefer the counsellor to 'translate' their feelings for them.*
5. Do they want to be present? *Some clients may fear criticism or embarrassment in such meetings.*

Figure 11.4 Transparent preparation for a review meeting with a client

of meeting the wider network is less about giving answers or guiding others to a pre-meditated point, and more about joining with others in a common concern for the child, with a wish that together new communications and ways of thinking might emerge (Smart, 2012). It is also a demonstration to the young person that they are being held in mind by so many people, in a way that is orientated towards an appreciation of their qualities and abilities (Bomber, 2009). Review and assessment meetings require preparation and reflection. Review meetings demand specific preparation with the child, including asking them who they feel it would be helpful to be present.

Such preparation may include a developmentally appropriate discussion with clients (see Figure 11.4).

Review and assessment meeting process

When meeting with a family or professional team, the counsellor is responsible for holding a safe enough space (Smart, 2012), so a clear description of the context of the meeting enables a contract to be negotiated that includes an exploration of concerns and a common purpose of mutually finding the best way forward. McAdam and Lang (1994) use four context markers for the counsellor to set the scene (see Figure 11.5).

Confidentiality may also be outlined, included a marker between the public and the private domains of a conversation. It is helpful for the counsellor to connect with everyone in the room, including absent members such as other siblings (Smart, 2012). The counsellor might say, 'I would like to start by asking each of you in turn what your concerns are about Jane. What might her older sister say if we were able to ask her?' After spending time on hearing people's concerns, they may then ask about the strategies already tried or resources perceived.

Definition of relationship (*'Hello, I am Jane's school counsellor, and I have invited you all to this meeting today. I shall be leading this meeting.'*)

Marking the time (*'We have about an hour ... '*)
Place (*'Thank you for coming to the school ... '*)
Content (*'I understand the goals of this meeting are to find a way forward for Jane, but perhaps you have some ideas about today's meeting as well?'*)

Figure 11.5   Ways of marking the context in assessment and review meetings

A counsellor's preparation with a young client will support that person to feel confident to share any communication that the client has given consent for (such as 'When I am very angry on the surface I often feel very worried inside and I don't know what to do about it'). The counsellor may be able to give a positive re-framing to blaming or hopeless comments. There is also an opportunity to hear about resources and exceptions to the problem. New stories may emerge that are free of the concerns that contribute to a single perspective of the child as a problem bearer (White and Epston, 1987).

At the end of a meeting with the wider network, it may be helpful to make time to review the conversation, consider how it may or may not have been helpful, and think together about themes or ideas that people might carry forward. It is important to value the communication and the event of the meeting in itself as a recognition of care for the young person, and to model this to all involved.

Working ethically with situations involving risk with young people

There are many situations involving risk that will raise ethical dilemmas in the opening and ongoing stages of counselling. This is increasingly the case perhaps as children mature towards adolescence, where risk taking is a feature of young people's development (Cozolino, 2006). For example, underage sexual activity can be a particular cause of ethical tension (Jenkins, 2010). The introduction of the Sexual Offences Act 2003 and the Bichard Inquiry 2004 (Home Office, 2004) recommended the routine reporting of underage sexual activity in order to protect young people from sexual exploitation, with all sexual activity under 13 to be regarded as 'statutory rape'. This approach has been robustly criticised by the BMA as access to sexual health and family planning services is crucially dependent on offering young people high degrees of confidentiality (Department of Health, 2004).

Equally, working alongside young people who are self-harming is ethically challenging for school counsellors. Best (2005) highlights how school pastoral systems routinely contact parents where self-harm is disclosed, arguing that where abuse underlies the cause of the self-harm this may not be in the best interests of the young person. NSPCC (2009) guidelines for counsellors suggest working to de-stigmatise self-harm, explore its underlying feelings and causes, minimise risk, and negotiate onward referrals where possible.

It is beyond the scope of this chapter to review all the possible sources of dilemmas that counsellors will face in this area. The following section focuses on working with safeguarding concerns as possibly the most common ethical dilemma that characterises school counselling work.

Maintaining therapeutic alliances through child protection disclosures

The worry that our clients may be unsafe or being harmed necessitates us as counsellors to weigh three conflicting ethical principles against each other: beneficence in the form of the child's welfare; the fidelity and trust in the therapeutic relationship; and their autonomy in their right to confidentiality. The BACP Guidelines on Good Practice in Counselling in Schools suggest that where a conflict exists between a child's right to confidentiality and their right to be protected, the latter must take precedence (McGinnis and Jenkins, 2011). However, the simplicity of this statement can belie the intricacy of working to maintain a therapeutic relationship with a young person in the event of child protection disclosures, designated child protection teacher involvement, children services' referrals, and police investigations. As counsellors we need to keep the young person and their feelings in constant focus. Opportunities need to be maximised to maintain or repair trust in therapeutic relationship, and simultaneously encourage a sense of personal agency, whilst working with others, to promote a client's safety. The reality of traversing this territory where competing ethical principles are at variance with a fearful, angry or traumatised young client is stressful for school counsellors. Regular, accessible and reflective supervision can give an opportunity for counsellor anxiety to be managed in order to reflect on the demands of these competing ethical principles, and find a way of maintaining a trusting and helpful relationship with clients.

The case example below is used to describe how supervision was utilised to reflect on the risks Sophie faced, and the challenge of assessing competing ethical principles. Due to the sensitivity of this material this case study is a composite constructed from real clinical situations with several young people.

Working with Sophie: a commentary on a school counsellor's ethical reflections

Sophie (aged 14) referred herself to counselling by putting a note in my counselling post-box, and initially did not want her parents to be informed. I outlined a contract with her that let her know that what she shared would be confidential unless she was in danger. Sophie's father had split from her mum and she now lived with her mum and step-dad. She also has an older step-brother (aged 20) who was the son of her step-dad. Towards the end of the initial assessment session she cried as she related that she didn't like spending time with her step-brother because she found him scary and he 'gave her the creeps', especially if he had been drinking which she said he did a lot. She said he looked at her in a 'funny' way but she was unable to elaborate on this, although clearly upset.

In supervision I reflected on my initial tentative concerns and 'gut-suspicion' that Sophie might be being sexually abused by her step-brother based on the fearful, shameful and powerless counter-transference reaction I was left with when Sophie exited. I agreed that the best course of action was to work on developing the relationship but to continue discussing any concerns in supervision. We discussed how at this stage I believed that it was in Sophie's best interests to access counselling and that she was developmentally competent to make that decision (Gillick competent), but that I would continue to discuss with her the possibility of letting her mother know about the counselling when it felt appropriate. We also agreed that I would ask the counselling link worker for any known information about the family and how Sophie was managing at school.

At this point, when the situation was unclear, Sophie's right to autonomy and need to develop trust (fidelity) in the relationship were taking precedence.

Sophie returned the following week agitated and flushed. Five minutes from the end of the session she disclosed in fractured tears that her step-brother came into the bathroom drunk when her mum had been out and touched her breasts and asked to have sex with her. She was very scared that he would do this again or worse.

At this stage I believed that Sophie had suffered *significant harm*. Sophie clearly needed to be protected and kept safe (*beneficence*) and I wanted her to retain as much trust in the therapeutic relationship as possible (*fidelity*). I hoped that it would be possible to persuade her that having taken the courageous step of telling me she would consent to me sharing this disclosure so she could be protected from a further assault. I also wanted to be respectful of my client's right to *autonomy* commensurate with her age and developmental stage.

I reassured Sophie that she had done the right thing in telling me. I also let her know that I was very worried about her. I actively sought her permission to share the information so that she could be protected (informed consent). Initially, Sophie was unhappy about anyone else being told. She was worried about the impact of this disclosure on her mother and whether she would believe her. She also feared that her step-brother would 'take it out on her'. Because of the timing of this disclosure at the end of the session, I asked Sophie to come back after break so we could speak some more. I then checked with Sophie that she had somebody to support her over break-time.

Break-time gave me an opportunity to reflect and make an 'emergency' phone call to my supervisor. Together we shared our concern for Sophie and her need to be protected from further harm from the step-brother (*beneficence*). I discussed my anxiety that Sophie might retract her disclosure if I shared the information without her consent. My supervisor further encouraged me to give Sophie as much autonomy as possible within the situation and to be as transparent with her as possible in order to maintain trust in the relationship or at least give a better opportunity to repair the therapeutic alliance later (*fidelity*).

When Sophie returned I reminded her of our initial contracting about limits of confidentiality. I let her know that I was too worried about her safety and that others needed to be told so she could be protected. I listened to and acknowledged her angry and panicky feelings about this. I asked her what she would want to happen if this were happening to her best friend rather than her, whereupon Sophie admitted that she would want the guy stopped and her friend safe. This gave me some leverage to help her reflect on how others who cared about her would feel. Reluctantly she agreed that it might be the only way of stopping him and she admitted that same hope had made her come along to counselling in the first place. I let her know that initially the Designated Child Protection Teacher, who was the deputy head, would need to be told, and I asked her if she wanted me to tell her, or whether she wanted to tell her herself with my support. I reassured Sophie that the material she had talked about that was not to do with the assault could stay confidential. I discussed what was likely to happen next (i.e., that a social worker might come and talk to her about her experiences in school, and that at some point they would go and talk to her mum and interview her step-brother).

Sophie was given an opportunity to contribute to and see the content of the written referral that was faxed off that afternoon to children's services. In the days that followed a social worker came and spoke to Sophie at school and interviewed her parents and step-brother at home. I kept in communication with the Designated Child Protection Teacher and with children's services so as to understand what was happening in the investigation for my client. Initially Sophie's step-brother moved out pending further investigation, although he moved back in several weeks later with continued children's services involvement and monitoring. I was able to support Sophie throughout this process and worked towards repairing the trust in the therapeutic relationship. This involved re-contracting with her and making clear what could remain confidential. There was no police prosecution. Sophie, although fearful, upset and angry at various points, did feel generally believed and supported and ultimately safer and less isolated. She continued in counselling for a further ten months.

In the period of time that followed this disclosure I sought to prioritise *transparent* working with Sophie. This helped her to feel more included and powerful in the process and helped ultimately to restore *trust* and *fidelity* in the counselling relationship.

This brief case example concurs with what has been initially explored in a recent study by Jenkins and Palmer, that in reality 'School counsellors, and others working therapeutically with young people, are likely to be involved in a complex process of balancing confidentiality with maintaining the therapeutic alliance and applying risk management policies' (2012: 557). As previously stated, how counsellors in schools in general work through these situations involving risk, and how they manage the ethical dilemmas involved, is a subject that requires much further investigation. In these ethically challenging situations it is helpful to find a route that is both transparent for the client, and respects their stage of development and right to make choices, with their need to feel protected (NSPCC, 2009). As previously stated, in any ethical challenge, the individual context and circumstance are key determinates of eventual practice. However, the following counsellor checklist is tentatively suggested as helpful. It is based on professional experience and a reading of literature in the field, including the NSPCC's Procedures and Core Standards (2009), the BACP's Ethical Framework (2010), McGinnis and Jenkins (2011), Daniels and Jenkins (2010), and *Working Together to Safeguard Children* (HMG, 2010).

Reassure the client that they have done the right thing in letting you know.

1. Tell the young person that you are concerned about them.
2. Seek informed consent for the sharing of information (wherever safety allows).
3. Where consent cannot be gained work in a transparent way through the referral process. Seek to repair and maintain the therapeutic alliance.
4. Discuss who you are going to talk to and the likely consequences. *This is most often the Designated Child Protection Teacher in the school.*
5. Be mindful to limit the disclosure of counselling material to matters that affect the client's safety.
6. Try to give the client options: listen to their feelings and opinions.
7. If possible share with the client, or compose together, any written communication about the situation (as is developmentally appropriate).
8. Continue to listen and acknowledge the client's feelings throughout the process.
9. Continue to seek the support of a supervisor.
10. Try to discuss or repair any loss of trust in the counselling relationship. Re-contract.
11. If unsure about the level of risk of 'significant harm', it can be helpful to contact the local **children's services** and discuss *anonymously* your concerns.

Figure 11.6   Checklist for working with Safeguarding Disclosures with young people

Counsellor self-care

Working with risk and child protection concerns can be highly stressful for school counsellors. Uniquely amongst other professionals in schools, counsellors are seeking active contact with young people's powerful feelings that may underpin the trauma of abuse for example. Equally uniquely, counsellors have theoretical frameworks and support structures such as supervision (and or personal therapy) that allow them to reflect on the emotional impact of this work on them. Taking seriously the BACP (2012) guidance on our responsibility as counsellors to ensure that our work does not become detrimental to our health is vital. We recommend the authentic use of supervision both to support us with our ethical dilemmas and explore the impact of this challenging work on our wellbeing. Ultimately, it can be very comforting that, as children are embedded within networks, we are usually not alone in seeking to support our clients.

Conclusion

As cautioned in the final phrases of the BACP's (2010) Ethical Framework, there are no easy answers to meeting the challenges of competing ethical principles in the initial and ongoing phases of therapeutic working in schools. We have outlined how a working knowledge of some of the legal basis for children's rights to confidentiality is helpful, as is an understanding of the potential resource of working together with parents, teachers and other professionals to affect change, and support and protect young people. We have highlighted the importance of clear initial contracting with young clients, and the value of embedding school counselling services within service agreements that support ethical practice. Through exploring working with safeguarding concerns we have highlighted the value of working transparently with young people, keeping them in focus and negotiating onward referrals (wherever safety allows). We suggest that an ethical approach in the initial stages of counselling needs to be mirrored by an ethical understanding of teaching pressures, the emotional experience of working with young people and education contexts, as well as the impact on counsellors themselves. How school counsellors practically work through such ethical dilemmas is a subject that still requires much research and we look forward to further developments in this area.

Notes

I would like to thank Tanya Smart for her contribution and support with this section.

TWELVE 'Just because we can't talk about the sessions, doesn't mean we can't talk': Professional and Ethical Issues in the Ongoing and Ending Phases of Therapy

Eileen Armstrong

This chapter will examine the professional and ethical issues that can emerge in a school setting during ongoing therapy and at the stage of ending therapy with a young client. Ethical and professional issues appear particularly within the area of confidentiality and communication between the counsellor and other people around the client. The BACP (2006) guidelines for counselling in schools outline the importance of confidentiality for young clients within a school setting, and also stress the need for communication between the counsellor and other professionals in both the school and wider setting. McGinnis (2008) suggested such communication was possible whilst keeping within the confidential frame of sessions, a view supported by Pattison et al. (2009) and the Welsh Toolkit (BACP/Welsh Government, 2009) and Counselling Strategy Review (Welsh Government, 2011). Achieving this balance can be difficult. The confidential frame of the counselling session is important for the young client to feel safe within, to enable an exploration of feelings and thoughts about their situation. It can be threatened or broken in the ongoing counselling relationship by the school setting and safeguarding issues, and through communication with parents, teachers and other agencies.

The case material for this chapter is drawn from practice within a peripatetic counselling service, and from a small-scale research project carried out in 2011 within five neighbouring primary schools, examining confidentiality and communication through the experiences of counselling link people.

Link people are members of staff identified at the start of counselling delivery in a particular school, who will act as a point of contact for the counsellor in ongoing work. The quotations from individual link people and a counselling service manager are all taken from the research project interviews. All the names of participants and schools have been changed to protect confidentiality. Case material linked to children is based on composite experiences, again protecting individual identities.

The school setting

The school setting itself can have ethical implications for a counsellor. One primary link person in the research project commented that 'Providing a space and everyone in school knowing that space has to be provided and you cannot be disturbed', can prove difficult. It can also be a challenge to keep private, who actually comes for counselling:

> And for a child to go out of a lesson to go for counselling and people know it's happening … maybe sometimes … some of the children that have been before would know when you're walking in the class who you are and what you're getting them for. (Anne, Primary counselling link person, April 2011)

It could be argued that it is easier to maintain some anonymity within a busy secondary school setting, where young people are moving around more. However, research has also shown secondary-aged young people questioning how confidential and private counselling can be within their daily school life (Fox and Butler, 2007; Pattison et al., 2009). The location of the counselling room, which can often be shared with other activities, is crucial in maintaining some feeling of privacy for young clients. There may also be dilemmas when the room is being used by other professionals, and about how a counsellor deals with this to protect the confidential space in ongoing counselling. In spite of such difficulties, it was felt by participants in the research project to be important for the young clients to have the counselling take place within the familiar school environment.

Safeguarding issues, examined in Chapter 12, may also impact on the ongoing counselling relationship. A counsellor who is contracted to work in the school setting is often required to disclose safeguarding and child protection concerns to the designated senior member of staff in school. The development of a confidential space for young people to determine how and when disclosures could take place alongside trusted professionals in organisations such as Children First in Scotland and ChildLine, and argued for by Jenkins (2010), may not currently be possible to offer within ongoing therapy in schools. One staff member commented:

> My understanding is that you will keep that private between you unless something is said that would indicate a cause for concern that might be child protection related, and just the same as I would never promise the child never to tell something and never to repeat something, that you operate on exactly the same principle because that's our duty of care. (Emma, Primary counselling link person, April 2011)

The following case material gives an example of the impact of the school setting as the counselling develops.

Karen is a qualified counsellor, working for an agency service in a number of schools. She is coming into Fern Primary School to see two young children referred to the service. The school is funding the provision, and there has been an agreement to provide a confidential space for the work to take place within. The counsellor works to the same child protection policies as the school, in that if a disclosure takes place in the session, it needs to be reported to the senior member of school staff designated as the safeguarding officer. Both sets of parents have met with the counsellor briefly, and have agreed to the work going ahead, signing the referral forms. Karen attended a staff meeting for teachers to briefly outline how the service works in schools and the confidentiality policy being followed. The space given to the counsellor to use is a multi-purpose small room, used for other one-to-one work, group work, and for teachers during their preparation time. In spite of the 'Please do not disturb' sign on the door, members of staff come into the room during the first few sessions to collect materials. A child also knocks on the door, looking for a teacher. The confidential space is threatened by such interruptions, the first client in particular reacting warily to people coming in and out as she plays and talks with the counsellor. Following this experience, the counsellor speaks with the link person in the school, who reminds staff in a whole school meeting about the commitment to provide a confidential space for this work. The school suggests an in-service training session to build further understanding about the counselling work.

At a later date, a child protection disclosure takes place within one of the sessions. Karen reminds the child of their initial contract that she needs to tell someone in school if one of the young people she sees is in danger or is being hurt. She writes down what has been said, her young client agrees to her seeing the link person who is also the designated safeguarding officer, and the concern is passed on to the school to be dealt with in their safeguarding system. Karen logs this with her service and supervisor. She is given feedback by the school about what has happened with the disclosure in the following weeks.

The quality of and information provided in set-up meetings is important for the ongoing work, with an understanding built in of the nature of the counselling sessions and the need for a physical confidential space. A counsellor permanently based within a school may build up this understanding over time. For those coming in from external organisations, the link person can assist with this, as can clear information and in-service training relating to the work (Welsh Government, 2011). The initial contract with the client may need to be referred to in ongoing work, especially when a disclosure is made. Within the school setting there are also specific dilemmas linked to communication with parents, teachers and other professionals.

Communicating with parents

Communication during ongoing sessions with parents will build on how the counselling was set up, and whether it could include an element of feedback. The Fraser Guidelines linked to the Gillick case in the UK courts (in 1985) protect the rights of young people to confidential medical advice. Currently, if a child is assessed as 'Gillick competent' to make decisions for themselves, the parent would not necessarily be involved in a therapeutic situation, and certainly by secondary school age (Bond, 2002; Daniels and Jenkins, 2010). This applies to ongoing and ending therapy as well as the beginning stage. Counselling in primary schools usually requires parental agreement. Ethical dilemmas may appear in remembering who the sessions are for and the conflict this may present for parents wanting information about how their child is getting on. A common question may be, 'How do I know this is helping my child if I don't get any feedback?' As the young person moves towards individuation from the parents, an element of keeping secrets from their carers becomes key (Finkenauer et al., 2002). Daniels and Jenkins (2010) suggest the counsellor can be a mediator with parents. This in itself may present issues for the counsellor to work with. Small-scale research referred to in this chapter (Armstrong, 2011, unpublished) suggests a role in managing this ongoing communication for counsellors coming into schools through a school link person. The following case material illustrates this.

Max is 7 years old and was referred following family break-up. His mother found out about the service through the link person and talked with her about setting up the sessions. She declined an initial meeting with the counsellor, which was offered as part of the counselling service to all parents, giving further information about the counselling sessions and offering the parent the opportunity to share some of the background for the child's presenting issues. As the counselling progressed, the mother came into school wanting to know the content of the sessions and expressed surprise that there was no feedback. She spent time with the school counselling link person, who acted to protect the confidentiality of the sessions. Confidentiality was more thoroughly explained and the counselling service information leaflet shared again to answer some of the concerns. The emphasis was on 'it's for your son to be able to spend his time sharing his thoughts and feelings' (Beth, counselling link person, April, 2011). The link person made herself available to the parent, and no meeting was sought with the counsellor. The frame of the ongoing sessions was protected, and the child given space away from the parent to discuss his concerns.

Amy is 6 years old and received play-based counselling sessions for a term, linked to behaviour in class and the need to develop relationships. Her parents were reluctant at first, due to their daughter's young age, but after meeting the counsellor felt this was an opportunity which could support their daughter and their own family relationships. In response to these parental concerns, the counsellor offered to give general feedback via a telephone call at least twice during the term. Before this happened the counsellor talked with Amy about ringing her parents, and about what the counsellor could say about the sessions. Feedback was in general terms and as agreed with the child client. It kept the parents on board with the sessions, and they observed changes at home in relationships during the course of the counselling.

Communicating with teachers

Class-teachers, form tutors and classroom assistants are often the people in schools who know young clients best, and who are used to having feedback during ongoing interventions from external professionals. On the one hand they can see the importance of the young person having someone external to home and school to talk to, but on the other hand they want information to best help the child move forward in their lives. This conflict has been illustrated in research from Scotland (Cooper et al., 2005; Cooper, 2006) where some class-teachers, whilst recognising the importance of confidential relationships within counselling, also wanted more feedback to support young people in the wider school context. Burnison (2003) also suggested better communication was needed to support the counselling work within the NSPCC Northern Ireland setting. Within the primary-based counselling research project, counselling was seen by the participants in the context of the whole support offered in school, the schools asking for ongoing communication. One staff member commented:

> I suppose it [confidential counselling] is quite erm ... alien in some ways to the culture of primary school, because normally within primary school the parents come in and tell you lots of things that are happening in the family, and it's normally shared with the people who are involved with the child. (Beth, Primary Counselling Link Person, April 2011)

This was different from the counsellor keeping the content of sessions confidential from those involved in the client's wider life. Another link person, Emma, stressed how difficult it was for the person coordinating support, if there was little or no feedback from the counsellor.

One way of managing this is through meetings with staff during ongoing therapy (Music, 2008), although there are ethical dilemmas present in this linked to keeping confidentiality. Involving the young client in agreeing on what should be fed back can help (McGinnis, 2008). Another way is through the link person, using them as a buffer between the counsellor and teacher, so that general information can be fed back through this link. A service manager within the research project commented:

You can feedback information that ... that isn't breaking confidentiality but is helping them help the child while you're not there for the rest of the week. We've learnt as a service that if we're going to successfully work with schools we have to give a little, and if we give a little very often they are more than happy to take that. (Fiona, April 2011)

However, some primary schools reported that when using a link person the class teacher can be left out of the loop and an opportunity is lost to move things forward. Hamblin (1993) placed the school counselling relationship within a 'Chinese Box' concept, i.e., the confidential space surrounded by layers of teachers, peers, the wider school community and the young person's external environment. These layers all input information into the counselling space, and in turn the student and counsellor need to decide together what moves out of the space and who it should be shared with. It may well be for some young people, the class-teacher or form tutor is the trusted adult in school with whom they want to share insights from the sessions, or strategies which may help them in class. This communication dilemma is illustrated in practice through Hannah's and Tom's experiences.

Hannah is 8 years old. She was referred due to peer relationship problems and behaviour within school and at home. Positive progress was observed by the counsellor in terms of developments in creative play, naming and expressing emotions, and building a relationship. However, as the therapy progressed her behaviour in class became more extreme. The teacher needed support and the ethical dilemma presented of how to go about this without breaking the confidential frame. General feedback was given by the counsellor and some theoretical feedback in terms of behaviour due to possible attachment difficulties being acted out in the classroom (Geddes, 2006; Delaney, 2008, 2009a). The school accepted the importance of maintaining the confidential framework for the child and support was put in for the class-teacher by the link person and head teacher, protecting the frame of the confidential space, whilst allowing both input and output in terms of communication about Hannah's reactions in school.

Tom is 9 years old. He was referred because his complex family background appeared to be affecting his life and learning in school. The confidential frame was maintained by the counsellor, and general feedback as agreed with Tom was given via the link person. It was observed toward the end of the therapy that the class-teacher had been a 'missing link'. The timing of the peripatetic counsellor coming into the school was such that the teacher was always busy with her class. Feedback had been given but she had felt excluded. To address this, the school and counsellor agreed that, with the next child, an initial meeting would take place including the class-teacher to set up the boundaries for feedback. Feedback through the link person had protected the confidential frame, but something more was needed to work with the child in the whole context of his life.

A similar dilemma becomes apparent as a counsellor works alongside other agencies involved in a young person's life.

Communicating with other agencies

In the UK, following inquiries into serious child abuse cases such as that of Victoria Climbié (Laming, 2003), the then Labour government set up the Every Child Matters Programme (DfES, 2003), aiming to better protect children's rights and meet their needs, and encouraging amongst other strategies multi-agency cooperation when working with individual young people. Jenkins and Polat (2006) examined the multi-agency context that could result from this for counselling in schools and other agencies when working with young people. Mary Baginsky (2007) argued multi-agency working had developed without solid research evidence that this was the best way forward for children's services. Since then, the Coalition government has moved the emphasis via the Department for Education to helping children achieve more, whilst appearing to maintain a commitment to the assessment of the underlying causes of need. Integrated working practices have been continued (HMG, 2010), although with a shift to more local arrangements, more commissioning, and a new child-centred approach to Child Protection (Munro, 2011). The reality is that counselling with children and young people is impacted on by background policies, and counsellors are currently working within situations where they are often part of a team of professionals around the young client. Instead of offering one-to-one counselling and an individual confidential contract with the young client, some will work in ongoing situations where there is an agency view of confidentiality being shared within the team of professionals involved with the child or young person. Professional and ethical dilemmas can be seen as this is put into practice within the UK context of the Common Assessment Framework (CAF), stemming from Every Child Matters in assessing need and planning support. Regular review meetings of the Team

Around the Child (TAC), Team Around the Family (TAF), or Team Around the School (TES), support ongoing work in this context with children, young people and their wider environment by involving all the professionals around a child and their family or carers. A similar approach has been adopted with children in care in the UK (Looked After Children).

In practice, different views of confidentiality may emerge between agencies. The counsellor may, for example, present a brief report rather than attending the TAC/TAF meeting. If attending, limited verbal feedback may be given, working within the individual contract of the confidential frame with the child. The school link person may be in a difficult position with other professionals not understanding why the counsellor gives such limited feedback. One link person in the study, Emma, suggested the counselling service could provide more information about their confidentiality policies to other agencies providing children's services, enabling better understanding from the other professionals involved in such meetings. She felt strongly that at times confidentiality made a 'nonsense' of working together to support the child: 'That's the danger isn't it … do you know things that could help?' and 'When does that confidentiality get overridden because actually it would be better if I did say something?' This conflict is explored in Abi's situation.

Abi is 10 years old. She is a 'looked after child' and as such there are regular meetings about her involving all the professionals monitoring her situation and carers. She was referred to counselling with problems relating in the school situation with peers and at home with her carers. The counsellor was asked to present a report at a meeting. Abi knew this meeting was coming up: the counsellor decided together with her what information could be shared that had come from the counselling situation, using informed consent to prepare the report. Information was limited to statements such as 'enjoying the sessions' and 'using creative activities to think about things'. It was reported back by the link person that the other professionals would have liked more information, and the counsellor was asked to attend the next meeting. The ethical dimension was discussed at supervision and with a manager, and again Abi was involved with deciding what feedback to present. The meeting was difficult for the counsellor, hearing detailed information from the other professionals, whilst sticking to the agreed limited feedback. A brief outline of the service policy was given in the meeting to explain the reasons for feedback of this nature. The other professionals appreciated the counsellor's presence as part of the professional team around Abi, and were able to ask questions about the confidentiality policy.

Bridges between confidentiality and communication

In presenting these case examples of practice when ethical and professional issues arise linked to protecting the confidential space, some bridges are suggested which could help in the specific situation.

The young client

The young client acts as a bridge in communication through the notion of informed consent. It is possible to build into ongoing therapy an agreement between the counsellor and young client about what can be shared with others (McGinnis, 2008; Music, 2008; Daniels and Jenkins, 2010). Dawn, a link person in the primary school research study, commented:

> If they have the power really and the control of informed consent that doesn't break any trust they're building with the counsellor or any trust they place in the process and agreeing to it. And it ... it provides a bridge where something really would be better being known by the school and better being known by the right adults.

This can prove helpful when feeding back to parents, teachers and other agencies. Power relationships must be taken into account to enable informed consent to take place in a meaningful way, ensuring a young client is not conforming to adult authority with the counsellor in a similar way to other school relationships. A manager in the research project described the process as giving the young client 'a voice', with the confidential space becoming a vehicle to share some of the concerns, thoughts and feelings with other people in their wider world. The child or young person may become confident to speak for themselves, or ask the counsellor to speak on their behalf. At other times, the sessions will remain private: in the growth towards individuation from parents and caregivers, this is perhaps what is required.

In Amy's situation, decisions were made together about what to share with Mum about the sessions. This was on a simple level, working to involve Amy in the decision-making process. In a similar way, feedback about Hannah was shared with the class-teacher without breaking the confidential space. Abi's involvement in preparing what the counsellor fed back to the multi-agency meeting also highlights the principle of working with the client's consent to bridge the confidential space and the wider communication with school staff and other professionals.

The counsellor

The counsellor offers a bridge in terms of protecting the confidential space with the child and being able to assist the flow of information. The situation they work in will determine how the bridge is constructed within ongoing work. Daniels and Jenkins (2010) describe three approaches to children's rights which may impact on therapy and confidentiality in school and other settings, namely the welfare, participatory and independent approaches. Working in situations where there is a welfare approach to confidentiality, more feedback to schools and parents may be expected. The counsellor working to a participatory or independent view of children's rights will be more likely to work with the foundation of informed consent to decide with the young client what goes outside the confidential space to the wider Chinese Box (Hamblin, 1993).

It is also important for the counsellor in a professional situation to adapt to the ethos of the different schools they go into, enabling communication to be suited to the specific situation. Dawn commented that in her school 'I think the thing is you [the counsellor] don't approach it like you're a closed book – you will talk to us and you will have a conversation but you're quite clear about where the conversation begins and ends'. This meant that 'just because we can't talk about the sessions, it doesn't mean we can't talk'. She felt communication should be 'informal and when it is needed' (April, 2011). A manager in the study also commented:

> I really do feel flexibility is so so important because we are not working with adults ... we are working with children, and we have to keep their best interests at the forefront. And sometimes that may mean erm ... that we need to pass on information. (Fiona, April 2011)

When giving feedback to teachers, it is partly about being available if there are queries, something which can be difficult to manage within the peripatetic situation, as with Tom, but which in Hannah's situation worked in a balanced manner. All link people in the research commented that the external nature of the counsellor was important in giving the child confidentiality and a new start with someone outside the family and school situation: 'It's somebody who's got no knowledge of the background so a clean sheet of paper to be able to say and do what they want' (Emma, April 2011).

The link person

A bridge which is highlighted as good practice within the Welsh Toolkit (2009), and referred to in William Baginsky's (2004) survey, is that of using a link person in schools for the peripatetic counsellor to receive information from and channel general feedback through. In research on multi-agency working (Baruch, 2001; Salmon and Kirby, 2008) having such a link is key in referrals, ongoing feedback, and at the end of the counselling. Link people in the study commented on their role as being 'in liaison', 'as a buffer' and a 'point of contact' (April, 2011). They can also be important in having knowledge of the young people being referred in the wider context of the school. In Max's situation, the link person acted as the protector for the confidential space away from the parents. Hannah's situation likewise showed the link person and counsellor working in different ways to support the teacher, with the link person helping to manage the situation during the whole week when the counsellor was not in school, and the counsellor providing theoretical background. The situation with Tom also illustrates that when working in this way care must be taken not to exclude the class-teachers and make them feel like a missing link.

In schools where a counsellor works full-time within the staff team, a link person may be identified within the pastoral system, enabling similar school roles to develop, and protecting confidentiality whilst communicating with the wider staff. In situations where there might be a team of counsellors within a school, one of the team could act in a more managerial liaison role, linking with the wider school and departments as in the Place2Be model.

Endings

One ethical dilemma linked to ending counselling, is who makes the decisions about this stage of counselling? In an ideal world the young client and counsellor should be able to do this within the confidential space. Within the reality of school-based counselling, there are pressures linked to funding, the waiting list of other possible clients, and sometimes parents hoping for counselling to continue longer than agreed with the client. This dilemma may be managed through a link person, who can organise the waiting list and liaise effectively with parents about the decision to end. Funding can also cause a difficulty, and links back to the contract with the young client. If it is clear, for example, that the counselling will be for a time-limited period such as a term, this needs to be set up in the initial contract with the young person: if it can be extended beyond that, a review and decision making about the ending need to be built in. It is vital to have time to work towards an ending, so that a young client can review their progress, identify any concerns that are remaining, and work with the counsellor to check out support systems in the wider context of their life. For young people who may have had experience of sudden bereavement, family splits or changes in schooling, a positive experience of working towards a planned ending can help in their future life experience.

The flow of information gives rise to another professional and ethical dilemma. Reports are often prepared with anonymous information such as clients' initials or codes, rather than full names. However, these will be stored alongside other school information in each young client's personal file. Schools see this as a positive process: 'In terms of record keeping for the SENCO that that provision has been given and has completed and stopped, so it's kind of clear in that way, in terms of audit trails' (Dawn, research interview, April 2011). The paperwork therefore becomes part of a young client's audit trail of interventions, to be with their records between different classes and different schools. Consideration needs to be given about the impact this may have upon the child, and the whole issue of their right to privacy and confidentiality (Daniels and Jenkins, 2010). Adults may access counselling often with their GP informed but no other information being passed on. A young person receiving counselling in school could be labelled by this.

One positive suggestion in managing a client's ending is of a link back into the schools' pastoral system through a trusted adult (Beth, research interview, April 2011). In schools where there are already mentoring schemes and a positive pastoral ethos, it may be possible whilst working towards an ending for the counsellor and young client to identify within the confidential space a trusted adult with whom that young person is familiar and comfortable talking to, thereby enabling the counsellor to feed the work back into the pastoral system.

Any ending within the school context will involve some preparation for the next child, highlighting the importance of communication with the school to enable a smooth transition out of and into counselling.

Case material – working to an ending

Max and his counsellor decided upon an ending time to the sessions, communicating this with the school link person. Mum asked for the sessions to continue, feeling there were still issues to resolve. The link person again managed this relationship, working with Mum to explain the work had reached a stage that the client and counsellor felt they could end, and that there would be a named person in school that Max could go to following counselling to speak with if issues came up for him. In the background for the school was the pressure of the waiting list and some needy children who the school wanted to refer. However, the commitment to Max remained, and he was able to work towards a planned ending with his counsellor.

Amy's counselling was set up to be funded initially as a term's work. This was made clear in the initial contract, and pictures were used to aid her understanding of when the ending would take place (in her case at Christmas). A tick list was made together in the sessions when there were a few left, to keep the ending in mind. Her parents were also clear at the outset that this would happen. With clear boundaries set, Amy used her play-based counselling time to the full, engaging well with the counsellor and the issues she came with. Towards the end, there was a marked change with Amy, in beginning to take responsibility for the structure of play in the sessions and choosing to finish a few minutes early. Role play initiated by her involved Amy in the adult role and the counsellor as the child. This was taken to supervision and it was commented that, at a simple level, Amy was managing the time and the ending herself with support from the counsellor.

With Hannah, as her counselling progressed it became clear to the school that she needed additional support. The positive progress in the therapy room was not carrying over into the classroom, although changes were commented upon at home. Whilst the counsellor could give ideas or strategies which could help, further intervention was needed. The Behaviour and Education Support team became involved, and as the counselling drew to an end, in-class support was set up. It was agreed to keep the ending separate from school holiday times, finishing a few weeks after the Easter break, as celebratory times were particularly difficult for this child within the family context. Once the date had been set, the boundary was kept to, and the counsellor and child reviewed the work together, revisited favourite activities, and made a positive ending to the therapeutic relationship.

Tom's ending was managed with support from the link person. Outcome scales developed by the service gave evidence of improved emotional wellbeing from the point of view of the child, parent and school. It also gave some concrete feedback to the school about the input of the counselling intervention. The ending here led into changes to the beginning of counselling for the next child in that school, in offering a meeting with the class-teacher as well as the carers so that everyone was aware of the nature of confidentiality and limits to communication which would be given.

It was important to manage the ending carefully with Abi, as a Looked After Child who had experienced many difficult and sudden endings in her life. This was supported by the link person, and put at an early stage to the team of professionals involved with Abi. The counselling had been extended through service funding. The other professionals wanted a further extension, but were unable to fund this. Decisions were influenced in the background by what was available, but were made in time for the counsellor to be able to set a clear finishing date with Abi, giving her an experience of a planned, contained ending.

Conclusion

In ongoing and ending therapeutic work with children and young people, account must be taken of the individual needs of clients, the therapeutic stance of the counsellor, and the specific school setting or other setting in which the counselling takes place. All these complex relationships weave into the pattern of relationships each young client has with their family and wider society, making the ethical and professional issues emerging complex for a counsellor to navigate through. Dilemmas in this area are a normal part of the therapeutic process and there are no rules about how to solve them. The case material presented here gives examples: other counsellors and schools may have approached these ethical dilemmas in different ways. Professional bodies such as BACP (2006; 2011) offer guidelines and an ethical framework which counsellors will need to apply within specific situations, keeping the needs of the individual client paramount whilst negotiating and using bridges such as the link person, the informed consent of the young person and their own communication skills to navigate the path between protecting the confidential space for a young client, and communicating effectively with the other professionals and carers involved.

Note

The project referred to in this chapter was a qualitative study for a Master's course, using semi-structured interviews and detailed analysis to identify major themes linked to confidentiality and communication in primary school counselling.

THIRTEEN
Psychotherapeutic Counselling in a Multi-Disciplinary, Multi-Agency Environment

Fiona Peacock

This chapter will look at the common issues, professional dilemmas and challenges that occur when working as a psychotherapeutic counsellor in a variety of working environments. A counsellor may have to engage with the multi-agency, multi-professional system surrounding a child with complex needs, so we will consider conceptual and theoretical frameworks that could support that counsellor in this environment.

Wherever we work; in a school, in Child and Adolescent Mental Health Services (CAMHS), in a voluntary agency, or in private practice, as counsellors we are likely to find ourselves facing the dilemmas and challenges of being the sole practitioner (i.e., the only psychotherapeutic counsellor) in that system while at the same time being part of the far wider system that surrounds a child. This system could contain people who are trained as therapists but come from other orientations or have had a wholly different professional training. Developing a robust theoretical model to think about the challenges that can arise in such situations can help keep the focus of the work on the needs of the child.

Is counselling a vocation or a job?

As with many things in counselling, it is the asking of the question that is most important as there can't be one straightforward answer. However, in any working setting there may be times when our professional commitment to our client, our adherence to the BACP Ethical Framework, and our obligation as an employee can present painful professional and personal dilemmas.

A child of 13 was on the cusp of school exclusion. They were recognised as a Child in Need and consideration was being given to whether they should be Looked After. The child's resident parent, the mother, said that if they were excluded from school then they would have to leave the family home. A multi-agency meeting had been called by the lead therapist in the CAMHS team to discuss with the social worker and mother the therapeutic plan.

The lead therapist had been trying to engage the mother in supportive therapeutic work as well as trying to engage with the multi-agency team around the child. The child's therapist, in this case a psychotherapeutic counsellor, was providing weekly individual sessions.

As the mother was saying the placement would not continue if the child was at home the whole day, the social worker was anxious about the potential school exclusion and feeling pressured by her manager not to accommodate the child. Without consulting the lead therapist she invited school to the meeting. At the meeting the school demanded that the child be seen by a psychiatrist as 'the therapy obviously wasn't working'. The social worker nodded in agreement and demanded to know the content of the sessions from the counsellor, with the unspoken message being that the therapy being provided wasn't 'good enough'.

Developing a theoretical model to help us think when under stress in groups

In counselling training Group Analytic theory is often overlooked as a valuable source of support in managing these multi-agency, multi-agenda and multi-stressor situations.

It is often said that a child's psychopathology becomes enacted in the family or professional system surrounding that child. What might be going on that a group of professionals might end up enacting some of the internal dilemmas that a child or young person can't articulate? Foulkes argued:

I believe, however, that there is quite specific resistance against accepting mental processes and multi-personal phenomenon, a resistance based on the very personal and as well as general consequences if we accept this truth, any change in any individual part of such network upsets the whole balance of it ... there exists a built in interest against it being uncovered, for this would entail taking far greater notice of what happens in their patients' networks as well as the doctor's own. Ultimately, it would mean that the whole community must take far greater responsibility for outbreaks of disturbing psychopathology generally. There is a very specific defensive interest at play identifying the fact of the inter-dependence which is here claimed: the cry 'but each is an individual'; and 'surely the mind is a matter for the individual' means, in this case, 'each for himself, I am not to blame for what happens to the other person, whether his is obviously near me, or whether I am involved in concealed ways, or even quite unconsciously'. (1990: 225)

De Mare (Lear, 1984), in talking about working with large groups from a Group Analytic perspective, states 'the problem for the rudimentary large group is its mindlessness, not how to feel, but how to think'. Such a process is evident in the vignette presented. The social worker 'knew' at some level that a 'minimum sufficient network' needed to be convened. Skynner (in Pines, 1983) proposes the idea of 'minimum sufficient networks', i.e., who exactly needs to be present to make working with the family 'group' viable? In our example there was heightened feeling in the group and they were unable to think. This led to scapegoating/projection of the unbearable feeling onto the person most connected to the 'symptom bearer' (i.e., the child) who in this case was the counsellor. As a psychotherapeutic counsellor the ability to reflect on the meaning of the whole while potentially being 'under attack' is a hugely beneficial skill.

Foulkes and Anthony (1984) talk about 'conducting groups' rather than leading them. Think about the roles of a conductor (lightning, musical, or bus). One of the roles in a multi-agency, multi-professional group could be to act as a lightning conductor, taking the emotional heat out of the situation. 'Meaning attribution' is seen by Yalom (1995) as a significant part of conductor efficacy. An intervention in the professionals' meeting that acknowledged huge anxiety on the part of everyone present may have 'taken the heat out of the situation'. A bus conductor function may likewise involve some kind of education to help other professionals know 'when to get on and when to get off' (e.g., by supportively clarifying the need for the boundary around the individual work, and giving some information about the way in which individual work helps to promote anxiety containment in the network). Enabling the whole group to find a way towards working together to hold the needs of the child in mind could also be seen as conducting an orchestra, drawing together the various professional talents and knowledge represented in the room along with the unique unconscious understandings each adult will bring as a result of their own connection with the child and the material.

Counsellors in statutory services

Professionals in statutory services will often talk about 'tiers' of service. The Children's National Service Framework (NSF) (DoH/DES, 2004) outlines this model: Tier 1 professionals provide primary care services, often universal services, and would seek to address the minor 'blips' in ordinary development; Tier 2 services are delivered, according to the NSF, by professionals related to Tier 1 provision (generally at Tier 2 something will have been identified as a 'problem' that is causing some level of difficulty to the child, family or other networks the child belongs to such as school); Tier 3 often refers to specialist services including local CAMHS teams for problems that are more 'severe or complex; Tier 4 covers highly specialised work such as day units, inpatient units and specialised outpatient teams. Counsellors are not mentioned anywhere in this four-tier model. One of the unspoken undercurrents that can lead to a therapist designated as a 'counsellor' becoming the scapegoated member of a multi-agency group is the status of 'counselling' in professional hierarchies.

While the therapeutic relationship offered by a psychotherapeutic counsellor may be in many ways the same as that provided by a child psychotherapist, a play therapist, art psychotherapist, etc., non-therapeutically trained colleagues from other agencies, when highly anxious, may fail to see the value of the non-directive listening space but would comfortably place their trust in professional hierarchies. In our example, therefore, surely a psychiatrist must be better than a counsellor? Developing an attitude of professional confidence is thus necessary. A practised, readily accessible description of what we do and why we do it, along with a developed capacity for engaging with, containing and processing anxiety, is a valuable tool in a counsellor's 'kit bag' that can be easily put to good use when under pressure. Using the language of the other professionals (e.g., articulating whether we feel we are working at Tier 1, 2 or 3) can smooth the process of communication. Responding to both the emotional content that other professionals bring and their general questions about what a counsellor does (however those questions are framed) requires a capacity to respond without defensiveness, without jargon, and without ego.

Developing a range of personal positions or core beliefs as a counsellor in relation to the multi-agency, multi-professional arena can help here. One core belief could be that everyone is doing their best for the child. Holding such a position of unconditional positive regard for the child *and* the network surrounding them can be challenging, particularly if we find ourselves in the scapegoat position. It is equally hard not just to breathe a sigh of relief if another professional, such as a social worker, is in that same position. Challenging such primitive processes in groups is a legitimate function of the psychotherapeutic counsellor trying to keep a focus on the needs of the child. The 'how to challenge' decision is often the one that calls upon us to use the insights gained from an understanding of group functioning and our learning from experience and clinical supervision. Painfully, we will learn most from the times when we get things wrong.

Anning et al. (2006) looked at the practical challenges of working in multi-professional teams, examining the real and difficult issues of sharing knowledge, coming from different perspectives on childhood drawn from different professional trainings, and the organisation and management of multi-professional teams.

Outcome measures and effective practice

With the pressure of audit, inspection and reduced funding on statutory services, there is a greater drive to have a quantitative method of demonstrating outcomes and systems to show that children are receiving appropriate intervention. It is worth developing a familiarity with the widely used outcome measure Goodman's (1997) Strengths and Difficulties Questionnaire.

Other ways in which CAMHS or other multi-disciplinary teams may seek streamline referral and assessment systems to ensure the most effective, efficient and appropriate treatment for children are via the Choice and Partnership Approach (CAPA). The latest model for CAMHS is OOCAMHS (the outcome orientated CAMHS; see Timimi, 2012) and the range of assessment and outcome measures that are in the CYP IAPT programme.

Some organisations will have obligatory outcome measures and traditionally counsellors have struggled with these, feeling they can interfere with the formation of the therapeutic relationship. However, these do have a value in terms of finding a common way of evaluating and communicating the level of difficulty a child is experiencing. A counsellor in a school, private practice or other smaller organisation can have the freedom to make decisions about which measures or tools to use based on their own professional judgment of the usefulness of the material for a client at that time in that particular context.

Dynamic administration and the Framework for Ethical Practice

Dynamic administration is a term drawn from Group Analytic psychotherapy, and refers to the wide range of activities and communications that a group conductor undertakes to create an environment that is as good as possible for the work of the analytic group to take place. As Behr and Hearst (2005) suggest, even such mundane tasks as setting out chairs has a dynamic significance in developing the network of communication in a group setting.

A consideration of dynamic administration seems pertinent to counsellors working in a range of organisational setting and in independent practice. It is connected to how the BACP Ethical Framework for Good Practice becomes 'lived out' in every aspect of counsellors' practice. The Ethical Framework, if integrated into the entire way a counsellor embodies their practice, is a powerful tool to enhance the professionalism of psychotherapeutic counselling: protecting clients; promoting understanding in those clients' supporting networks; and protecting the practitioner across a range of organisational settings. This view of the counsellor being fully committed to something beyond the functioning of the organisation is closely linked to the question of whether counselling is a vocation that may sometimes mean having to prioritise ideals and principles above the expectations of an employer.

So how much is counselling worth?

Within the NHS there is a salary structure for counsellors in the Agenda for Change framework. The Agenda for Change programme that was introduced in 2005 sought to bring parity of pay over a range of different professional trainings. Band 5 entry level and profiles up to Band 8 consultant counsellors can be found online. While there are bandings for counsellors it seems that within the NHS counsellors are being employed as different professions (e.g., primary child mental health workers, or other core professionals such as Community Mental Health Nurses, are obtaining therapeutic trainings but are still defined by their core profession). The level of salary for psychotherapeutic counsellors in other organisations is likely to vary widely. A strong argument can be made that posts requiring training to a professional standard and that require accredited status should be remunerated in line with the Agenda for Change bandings. However imperfect it may be, the Agenda for Change did attempt to look at various professions, the training that was needed to undertake those roles, and the responsibilities that come with those roles, and then find some parity of pay. Whether we like it or not, status is often judged by financial remuneration. Where counsellors can have some say in setting the levels of remuneration for psychotherapeutic counselling, this can be thought about in terms of upholding the status of the profession. There are, of course, very powerful counter arguments about the accessibility of services and whether the professionalisation of counselling does limit accessibility.

There is no 'answer' to such questions, but engaging with issues of remuneration for professional counselling services is, I would suggest, part of a counsellor's dynamic administration and ethical decision making in choosing whether or not to work in a specific organisational structure or how to set and explain their fees in private practice.

Supervision and CPD

Managing the boundary between individual work with a child and engaging in that child's network, requires a great deal of ability to be reflexive about a wide range of the unconscious material and to move that which is unconscious into the realm of the conscious when the child and the network are ready to receive this. Supervision is essential in this complex task, and the place where we can allow ourselves to be politically incorrect as part of its restorative function. Counter-transference has to be held and explored somewhere to enable us to process the complexity of material that may be projected onto us.

As discussed previously, the extent of counselling in the NHS may be obscured by those delivering psychotherapeutic counselling being designated as other kinds of professional. This can make it harder to access high quality *counselling* supervision in house in CAMHS and in some other larger organisations. As counsellors in a CAMHS service, or indeed in many organisations, we may find that in order to fulfil our own professional sense of development and personal accountability we may end up purchasing our own external supervision to supplement any internal supervision. There may be a need to educate line managers about the difference between management supervision and clinical supervision.

Some organisations may make the argument that if we are employed on the basis of being accredited counsellors then it is our responsibility to fulfil the requirements of ongoing accreditation, and hence supervision and CPD would fall to us to fund. This does reflect what happens in private practice and as such may be a valid position. However, the level of remuneration should then reflect this financial cost on ourselves as practitioners for maintaining our fitness to practice. This is in essence a facet of dynamic administration, in that the way in which we as practitioners address such issues will have a significant impact on our working relationships with both clients and colleagues.

On the surface, working in different settings may appear to present different challenges to psychotherapeutic counsellors. There may be differences in how children and families are assessed as suitable for a service, or in how the therapeutic outcomes might be measured. There may also be different languages used to describe the level of difficulty a child is having or the depth of work that is being provided. However, beyond these differences many of the dilemmas around supervision, CPD, managing multi-agency and multi-disciplinary work, forming and sustaining working relationships with non-counselling colleagues within, as well as outside, will be very similar.

As well as having sound practice skills, it will assist counsellors to have a sound theoretical model to help them think about and manage the dynamics of working in organisations. Choices and decisions made about things that initially may not seem directly related to the therapeutic work need to be carefully considered in order to ensure the clinical work is protected. The specifics of working in different environments (such as the NHS, voluntary organisations or private practice) may be different, but being able to reflect on counselling as an emerging profession as a whole across various organisational structures may help raise the professional profile of psychotherapeutic counselling as a professional activity in its own right.

Note

The example in this chapter is fictionalised. However, it draws on the many children I have worked with, and the many schools I have worked in, over the years. No individual should be able to recognise themselves from this example and if any of my former clients wish to discuss the example with me I would be delighted to hear from them. They have all taught me so much and I thank them.

References

Abramovitch, H. (2002) Temenos regained: reflections on the absence of the analyst, *Journal of Analytical Psychology*, 47 (4): 583–98.

Adamson, P. (2007) *Child Poverty in Context: An Overview of Child Well Being in Rich Countries*. Geneva: UNICEF.

Ainsworth, M., Blehar, M., Waters, E. and Wall, S. (1978) *Patterns of Attachment: A Psychological Study of the Strange Situation*. New York: Academic Press.

Aldgate, J., Jones, D., Rose, W. and Jeffrey, C. (2006) *The Developing World of the Child*. London: Jessica Kingsley.

American Psychiatric Association (2001) *Diagnostic and Statistical Manual of Mental Disorders* (4th edition). Washington, DC: American Psychiatric Association.

Armstrong, E. (2011) Confidentiality and communication: a study of the experinces of the counselling link person in primary schools. M.Ed. Thesis, Cambridge University Faculty of Education.

Anning, A., Cottrell, D., Frost, N., Green, J. and Robinson, M. (2006) *Developing Multiprofessional Teamwork for Integrated Children's Services*. Maidenhead: Open University Press.

Asay, T. P. and Lambert, M. J. (1999) The empirical case for the common factors in therapy: quantitative findings. In M. Hubble, B. Duncan and S. D. Miller (eds), *The Heart and Soul of Change: What Works in Therapy*. Washington, D.C.: American Psychological Association Press. pp. 23–55.

Axline, V. M. (1989) *Play Therapy*. New York: Churchill Livingstone.

BACP (2006) *Good Practice for Counselling in Schools* (4th edition). Lutterworth: BACP.

BACP (2012) *Ethical Framework for Good Practice in Counselling*. Lutterworth: BACP. Available online at www.bacp.co.uk/ethical_framework/

BACP and Welsh Assembly Government (2009) *School-based Counselling Operating Toolkit*. Lutterworth: BACP.

Baginsky, W. (2004) *School Counselling in England, Wales and Northern Ireland: A review*. NSPCC/Keele University. Available online at www.nspcc.org.uk/Inform/.../SchoolCounselling_wdf48931.p

Baginsky, M. (2007) *Schools, Social Services and Safeguarding Children: Past Practice and Future Challenges*. London: NSPCC.

Bannister, A. (2003) *Creative Therapies with Traumatised Children*. London: Jessica Kingsley.

Barker, D. J. P. (1998) In utero programming of chronic disease, *Clinical Science*, 95: 115–28.

Barness, L. A., Opitz, J. M. and Gilbert-Barness, E. (2007) Obesity: genetic, molecular, and environmental aspects, *American Journal of Medical Genetics*, 143A (24): 3016–34.

Barrett, M. and Trevitt, J. (1991) *Attachment Behaviour and the School Child*. London: Routledge.

Baruch, G. (2001) Mental health services in schools: the challenge of locating a psychotherapy service for troubled adolescent pupils in mainstream and special schools, *Journal of Adolescence*, 24: 549–70.

Behr, H. and Hearst, L. (2005) *Group-Analytic Psychotherapy: A Meeting of Minds*. London: Whurr.

Best, R. (2005) Self-harm: a challenge for pastoral care, *Pastoral Care in Education*, 23, (3): 3–11.

Bion, W. (1962) *Learning from Experience* (8th edn). London: Karnac.

Bion, W. (1970) *Container and Contained: Attention and Interpretation*. London: Tavistock.

Bishop, B. (2013) *Unexpected Lessons in Love*. London: John Murray.

Blake, P. (2008) *Child and Adolescent Psychotherapy*. London: Karnac.

Blos, P. (1967) *The Second Individuation Process of Adolescence: The Psychoanalytic Study of the Child*, 22: 162–86.

Bomber, L. (2005) *Survival of the Fittest: Teenagers and Attachment* (edited by A. Perry). London: Worth.

Bomber, L. (2007) *Inside I'm Hurting*. London: Worth.

Bomber, L. (2009) Survival of the fittest. In A. Perry, *Teenagers and Attachment*. London: Worth.

Bond, T. (2002) *The law of confidentiality – a solution or part of the problem*, P. Jenkins (ed.), Legal Issues in Counselling and Psychotherapy. London: SAGE Publications.

Bond, T. (2010) *Standards and Ethics in Counselling in Action*. London: Sage.

Booth, P. and Jernberg, A. (2010) *Theraplay: Helping Parents and Children Build Better Relationships through Attachment-Based Play* (3rd edn). San Francisco, CA: Jossey-Bass.

Bordin, E. S. (1979) The generalizability of the psychoanalytic concept of the working alliance, *Psychotherapy: Theory, Research and Practice*, 16 (3): 252–60.

Boscolo, L. and Bertrando, P. (1996) *An Introduction to Systemic Therapy with Individuals*. London: Karnac.

Boulton, L. (2007) Secondary school pupils' views on their school peer counselling for bullying service, *Counselling and Psychotherapy Research*, 7 (3): 188–95.

Bowlby, E. J. (1988) *Secure Base: Clinical Applications of Attachment Theory*. London: Routledge.

Bowlby, J. (1969, 1973, 1980) *Attachment and Loss*. London: Hogarth Press and Institute of Psychoanalysis (since republished and reprinted many times by Penguin).

Bradford-Brown, B., Larson, R. and Saraswathi, T. (2002) *The World's Youth*. Cambridge: CUP.

Braten, S. (ed.) (1998) *Intersubjective Communication and Emotion in Early Ontogeny*. Cambridge: Cambridge University Press.

Brazelton, T. B. (1982) Pre-birth memories appear to have lasting effect, *Brain/Mind Bulletin*, 7 (5): 2.

British Medical Association (June 2006). *Child and Adolescent Mental Health: A Guide for Healthcare Professionals*. London: BMA.

Bronfenbrenner, U. (1970) The psychological costs of quality and equality in education, *Psychological Factors in Poverty* (edited by V. Allen). Chicago, IL: Markham.

Bronfenbrenner, U. (1974) Developmental research, public policy, and the ecology of childhood, *Child Development*, 45 (1): 1–5.

Bronfenbrenner, U. (1979) *The Ecology of Human Development: Experiments by Nature and Design*. Cambridge, MA: Harvard University Press.

Bronfenbrenner, U. (2005) *Making Human Beings Human: Bioecological Perspectives on Human Development*. London: Sage.

Brooks-Gunn, J. and Graber, J. (1996) Transitions and turning points: navigating the passage from childhood to adolescence, *Developmental Psychology*, 32: 768–76.

Brown, A. (2006) In my agency it's very clear, but I can't tell you what it is: work settings and ethical challenges, *Counselling and Psychotherapy Research*, 6 (2): 100–7.

Buckroyd, J. (1992) 'I was sick and you visited me: facilitating mourning with hospital patients and their relatives', in E. Noonan and L. Spurling (eds), *The Making of a Counsellor*. London: Routledge.

Buckroyd, J. and Rother, S. (2008) *Psychological Responses to Eating Disorders and Obesity: Recent Innovative Work*. London: Wiley.

Burnison, B. (2003) *It's OK to See the Counsellor*. Northern Ireland: NSPCC.

Cairns, K. (2002) *Attachment, Trauma and Resilience: Therapeutic Caring for Children*. London: British Association for Adoption and Fostering.

Carey, L. (2006) *Expressive and Creative Arts Methods for Trauma Survivors*. London: Jessica Kingsley.

Cattanach, A. (2008) *Play Therapy with Abused Children* (2nd edn). London: Jessica Kingsley.

Chiron, C., Jambaque, I., Nabbout, R., Lounes, R., Syrota, A. and Dulac, O. (1997) The right brain hemisphere is dominant in human infants, *Brain*, 120 (6): 1057–65 (doi: 10.1093/brain/120.6.1057).

Chugani, H., Behen, M., Muzik, O., Juhasz, C., Nagy, F. and Chugany, D. (2001) Local brain functional activity following early deprivation: a study of post institutionalized Romanian orphans, *Neuroimage*, 14: 1290–1301.

Church, E. (1994) The role of autonomy in adolescent psychotherapy, *Psychotherapy,* 31: 101–8.

Clarkson, P. (2004) *The Therapeutic Relationship.* London: Whurr.

Cohen, N. J., Muir, E., Lojkasek, M., Muir, R., Parker, C. J., Barwick, M. and Brown, M. (1999) Watch, wait, and wonder: testing the effectiveness of a new approach to mother-infant psychotherapy, *Infant Mental Health Journal,* 20 (4): 429–51.

Coleman, J. (2011) *The Nature of Adolescence.* Hove: Routledge.

Collishaw, S., Goodman, R., Pickles, A. and Maughan, B. (2007) Modelling the contribution of changes in family life to time trends in adolescent conduct problems, *Social Science and Medicine,* 65: 2576–87.

Collishaw, S., Maughan, B., Goodman, R. and Pickles, A. (2004) Time trends in adolescent mental health, *Journal of Child Psychology and Psychiatry,* 45: 1350–62.

Collishaw, S., Maughan, B., Natarajan, L. and Pickles, A. (2010) Trends in adolescent emotional problems in England: a comparison of two national cohorts twenty years apart, *Journal of Child Psychology and Psychiatry,* 51 (8): 885–94.

Cooper, M. (2004) *Counselling in Schools Project: Evaluation Report.* Glasgow: University of Strathclyde.

Cooper, M. (2006) *Counselling in Schools Project Phase II: Evaluation Report.* Glasgow: Counselling Unit, University of Strathclyde. Available online at www.strath.ac.uk/Departments/counsunit/research/cis.html

Cooper, M. (2008) *Essential Research Findings: In Counselling and Psychotherapy.* London: Sage.

Cooper, M. (2009) Counselling in UK secondary schools: a comprehensive review of audit and evaluation data, *Counselling and Psychotherapy Research,* 9 (3): 137–50.

Cooper, M. (2013) *School-based Counselling in UK Secondary Schools: A Review and Critical Evaluation.* Glasgow: University of Strathclyde.

Cooper, M., Hough, M. and Loynd, C. (2005) Scottish secondary school teachers' attitudes towards, and conceptualisations of counselling, *British Journal of Guidance and Counselling,* 33 (2): 199–211.

Cooper, M. and McLeod, J. (2011) *Pluralistic Counselling and Psychotherapy.* London: Sage.

Cozolino, L. (2006) *The Neuroscience of Human Relationships.* London: Norton.

Creed, T. A. and Kendall, P. C. (2005) Therapist alliance-building behaviour within a CBT treatment for anxiety in youth, *Journal of Consulting and Clinical Psychology,* 73 (3): 498–505.

Crenshaw, D. (2006) Neuroscience and trauma treatment: implications for creative arts therapists. In L. Carey (ed.), *Expressive and Creative Arts Methods for Trauma Survivors.* London: Jessica Kingsley. pp. 21–38.

Cromarty, K. and Richards, K. (2009) How do secondary school counsellors work with other professionals?, *BACP Counselling and Psychotherapy Research,* 9 (3): 182–6.

Dacey, J. and Kenny, M. (1997) *Adolescent Development*. Chicago, IL: Brown and Benchmark.

Damasio, A. (2000) *The Feeling of What Happens: Body and Emotion in the Making of Consciousness*. New York: Harvest.

Damasio, A. (2006) *Descartes' Error: Emotion, Reason and the Human Brain*. London: Vintage.

Damasio, A. (2012) *Self Comes to Mind: Constructing the Conscious Brain*. London: Vintage.

Daniels, D. and Jenkins, P. (2010) *Therapy with Children: Children's Rights, Confidentiality and the Law* (2nd edn). London: Sage.

Davis, M. and Wallbridge, D. (1981) *Boundary and Space: An Introduction to the Work of D.W. Winnicott*. London: Karnac.

Davy, J. and Cross, M. (2004) *Barriers, Defences and Resistance*. Maidenhead: Open University Press.

Delaney, M. (2008) *Teaching the Unteachable*. London: Worth.

Delaney, M. (2009a) *Classroom Link1: Counselling Children and Young People*. Lutterworth: BACP.

Delaney, M. (2009b) How teachers can use a knowledge of attachment theory to work with difficult to reach teenagers, in A. Perry (ed.), *Teenagers and Attachment*. London: Worth.

Department for Education (DFE) *Education Reform Act 1988*. London: HMSO.

Department for Education and Skills (DfES) (2003) *Every Child Matters*. London: HMSO.

Department for Education and Skills (DfES) (2005) *Excellence and Enjoyment: The Social and Emotional Aspects of Learning*. London: HMSO.

Department of Health (DoH) (2004) *National Service Framework for Children, Young People and Maternity Services: The Mental Health and Psychological Wellbeing of Young People*. London: HMSO.

Department of Health/Department of Education and Employment/Home Office (2000) *Framework for the Assessment of Children in Need and their Families*. London: The Stationery Office.

Di Giuseppe, R., Llinscott, J. and Jilton, R. (1996) Developing the therapeutic alliance in child adolescent psychotherapy, *Applied and Preventative Psychology*, 5: 85–100.

Diamond, D., Liddle, H., Hogue, A. and Dakof, G. (1999) Alliance building adolescents in family therapy: a process study, *Psychotherapy*, 36: 355–67.

Dogra, N. (2005) What do children and young people want from mental health services?, *Current Opinion in Psychiatry*, 18 (4): 370–3.

Dumont, M. and Provost, M. (1999) Resilience in adolescents: protective role of social support, coping strategies, self esteem and social activities on experience of stress and depression, *Journal of Youth and Adolescence*, 28 (3): 343–63.

Dunn, J. (2004) *Children's Friendships*. Oxford: Blackwell.

Dweck, C. (2000) *Self Theories: Their Role in Motivation, Personality and Development*. New York: Taylor and Francis.

Dweck, C. (2006) Is maths a gift?, in S. J. Ceci and W. Williams (eds), *Why Aren't More Women in Science? Top Researchers Debate the Evidence*. Washington, DC: American Psychological Association.

Dybdahl, R. (2001) Children and mothers in war: an outcome study of a psychosocial intervention program, *Child Development*, 72 (4): 1214–30.

Ecclestone, K. and Hayes, D. (2009) *The Dangerous Rise of Therapeutic Education*. London: Routledge.

Edwards, J. (1999) Kings, queens and factors: the latency period revisited, in D. Hindle and M. Vaciago-Smith (eds), *Personality Development: A Psychoanalytic Approach*. London: Karnac. pp. 71–91.

Egger, G., Liang, G., Aparicio, A. and Jones, P. A. (2004) Epigenetics in human disease and prospects for epigenetic therapy, *Nature*, 429: 457–63.

Elbrecht, C. (2012) *Trauma Healing at the Clay Field: A Sensorimotor Art Therapy Approach*. London: Jessica Kingsley.

Erikson, E. H. (1951) *The Eight Ages of Man: In Childhood and Society* (2nd edn). London: Vintage.

Erikson, E. H. (1967) *Identity, Youth and Crisis*. New York: Norton.

Erikson, E. H. (1994) *Identity and the Life Cycle*. London: W. W. Norton.

Erikson, E. H. (1995) *Childhood and Society*. London: Vintage.

Everall, R. and Paulson, L. (2002) The therapeutic alliance: adolescent perspectives. *Counselling and Psychotherapy Research*, 2 (2): 78–87.

Finkenauer, C., Engels, R.C.M.E. and Meeus, W. (2002) Keeping secrets from parents: advantages and disadvantages of secrecy in adolescence, *Journal of Youth and Adolescence*, 31(2): 123–36.

Flavell, J. H. (1977) *Cognitive Development*. Engelwood Cliffs, NJ: Prentice-Hall.

Fonagy, P., Gyorgy, G., Jurist, E. L. and Target, M. (2003) *Affect Regulation, Mentalization, and the Development of the Self*. New York: Other Press.

Fonagy, P., Bateman, A. and Bateman, A. (2011) The widening scope of mentalizing: a discussion, *Psychology and Psychotherapy: Theory, Research and Practice*, 84: 98–110 (doi: 10.1111/j.2044-8341.2010.02005.x).

Foulkes, S. H. (1983) *Introduction to Group-Analytic Psychotherapy: Studies on the Social Integration of Individuals and Groups*. London: Karnac.

Foulkes, S. H. (1990) *Selected Papers: Psychoanalysis and Group Analysis*. London: Karnac.

Foulkes, S. H. and Anthony, E. J. (1984) *Group Psychotherapy the Psychoanalytic Approach*. London: Karnac.

Fox, C. and Butler, I. (2007) If you don't want to tell anyone else you can tell her: young people's views on school counselling, *British Journal of Guidance and Counselling*, 35 (1): 97–114.

Frankel, R. (1998) *The Adolescent Psyche*. Hove: Routledge.

Freud, A. (1937) *The Ego and the Mechanisms of Defense*. London: The Hogarth Press and Institute of Psycho-Analysis (revised edition: 1966 [USA], 1968 [UK]).

Freud, S. (1916–17) The development of the libido and the sexual organizations. Introductory Lectures on psychoanalysis, in *The Standard Edition of the Complete Psychological Works of Sigmund Freud* (translated by James Strachey). London: Hogarth.

Freud, S. (1962) *Three Essays on the Theory of Sexuality* (translated by James Strachey). New York: Basic.

Friel QC, J. (1998) The impact of the European Convention on Human Rights on UK education law, *Childright*, 143: 6–7.

Garmezy, N. and Rutter, M. (1983) *Stress, Coping and Development in Children*. New York: McGraw-Hill.

Geddes, H. (2006) *Attachment in the Classroom*. London: Worth.

Geldard, K. and Geldard, D. (2004) *Counselling Adolescents* (2nd edn). London: Sage.

Gelso, C. J. and Carter, J. (1994) Components of the psychotherapeutic relationship: their interaction and unfolding during treatment, *Journal of Counselling Psychology*, 41: 296–306.

Gelso, C. J. and Hayes, A. J. (1998) *The Psychotherapy Relationship* (2nd edn). New York: Wiley.

Gelso, C. J. and Hayes, A. J. (2007) *Countertransference and the Therapist's Inner Experience*. London: Lawrence Erlbaum Associates.

Gendlin, E. (1978) *Focusing*. New York: Bantam.

Gerhardt, K. J. and Abrams, R. M. (1996) Fetal hearing: characterization of the stimulus and response, *Seminars in Perinatology*, 20 (1): 11–20.

Gerhardt, S. (2004) *Why Love Matters: How Affection Shapes a Baby's Brain*. London: Routledge.

Gibson-Cline, J. (1996) *Adolescents from Crisis to Coping*. Oxford: Butterworth Heinemann.

Gilbert, M. and Orlans, V. (2011) *Integrative Therapy: 100 Key Points and Techniques*. London: Routledge.

Gilmore, S. (1973) *The Counsellor in Training*. Englewood Cliffs, NJ: Prentice-Hall.

Goleman, D. (1996) *Emotional Intelligence: Why It Can Matter More Than IQ*. London: Bloomsbury.

Goodman, R. (1997) The Strengths and Difficulties Questionnaire: A research note, *Journal of Child Psychology and Psychiatry*, 38 (5): 581–6.

Graber, J. and Brooks-Gunn, J. (1996) Transitions and turning points: navigating the passage through childhood and adolescence, *Developmental Psychology*, 32 (4): 768–76.

Gray, A. (1994) *An Introduction to the Therapeutic Frame*. London: Routledge.

Gray, J., Galton, M. and McLaughlin, C. (2011) *The Supportive School: Wellbeing and the Young Adolescent*. Newcastle upon Tyne: Cambridge Scholars.

Green, H. (2004) *Mental Health of Children and Young People in Great Britain*. London: Office for National Statistics/Stationery Office.

Greenhalgh, P. (1994) *Emotional Growth and Learning*. London: Routledge.

Guishard-Pine, J., Hamilton, L. and McCall, S. (2007) *Understanding Looked After Children: An Introduction to Psychology for Foster Care*. London: Jessica Kingsley.

Hagell, A. (2009) *Changing Adolescence Briefing Paper*. London: The Nuffield Foundation.

Hagell, A. (2012) *Changing Adolescence: Social Trends and Mental Health*. Bristol: Policy.

Haine, R., Ayers, T., Sandler, A., Weyer, J. and Millsap, W. (2003) Locus of control and self esteem as stress moderators or stress mediators in parentally bereaved children, *Death Studies*, 27 (7): 619–40.

Hall, R., Tice, L., Beresford, T., Willey, B. and Hall, A. (1989) Sexual abuse in patients with anorexia nervosa and bulimia, *Psychosomatics*, 30: 73–9.

Hall, W. (2006) Cannabis use and the mental health of young people, *Australian and New Zealand Journal of Psychiatry*, 40 (2): 105–13.

Hamblin, D. H. (1974) *The Teacher and Counselling*. Oxford: Basil Blackwell.

Hamblin, D. (1993) *The Teacher and Counselling* (2nd edn). Hemel Hempstead: Simon and Shuster.

Hanko, G. (2002) Making psychodynamic insights accessible to teachers as an integral part of their professional task, *Psychodynamic Practice: Individuals, Groups and Organisations*, 8 (3): 375–89.

Hanson, J. W., Jones, K. L. and Smith, D. W. (1976) Fetal alcohol syndrome, *JAMA*, 235: 1458–60.

Harter, S. (1990) Self and identity development, in S. Feldman (ed.), *At the Threshold: The Developing Adolescent*. Cambridge, MA: Harvard University Press.

Harris, B. (2009) 'Extra appendage' or integrated service? School counsellors' reflection on their professional identity in an era of education reform, *Counselling and Psychotherapy Research*, 174–81.

Haugh, S. and Paul, S. (eds) (2008) *The Therapeutic Relationship: Perspectives and Themes*. Ross-on-Wye: PCCS.

Hawton, K., Rodham, K., Evans, E. and Weatherall, R. (2002) Deliberate self-harm in adolescents: self report survey in schools in England, *British Medical Journal*, 325: 1207–1211.

Hay, D. F. (1994) Prosocial development, *Journal of Child Psychology and Psychiatry*, 35 (1): 29–71.

Hedges, F. (2005) *An Introduction to Systemic Therapy with Individuals*. Basingstoke: Palgrave Macmillan.

Her Majesty's Government (HMG) (2010) *Working Together to Safeguard Children: A Guide to Inter-agency Working to Safeguard and Promote the Welfare of Children*. London: HMSO.

Herman, J. (2001) *Trauma and Recovery*. London: Pandora.

Heyno, A. (2009) Making the transition from school. In A. Perry, *Teenagers and Attachment*. London: Worth.

Hill, A., Cooper, M., Cromarty, K., Smith, K., Maybanks, N., Pattison, S., Pubis, J. and Coachman, A. (2011) *Evaluation of the Welsh School-based Counselling Strategy: Final Report October 2011*. Cardiff: BACP/Welsh Government.

Hoffman, L. (1993) *Exchanging Voices*. London: Karnac Books.

Holliday, C. and Wroe, J. (2012) *Forest of Feelings* (2nd edn). Cambridge: LDA.

Holmes, J. (2001) *The Search for the Secure Base: Attachment Theory and Psychotherapy*. London: Routledge.

Home Office (2004) *Bichard Inquiry Recommendations: Progress Report*. London: Home Office.

Horowitz, M. (1986) *Stress Response Syndromes*. Northvale, NJ: Jason Aronson.

Hovarth, A. and Symonds, B. (1991) Relation between working alliance and outcome in psychotherapy: a meta-analysis, *Journal of Counselling Psychology*, 38: 139–49.

Howard, S. (2010) *Skills in Psychodynamic Counselling and Psychotherapy*. London: Sage.

Howe, D. (2011) *Attachment Throughout the Lifecourse*. Basingstoke: Palgrave Macmillan.

Hughes, D. (1997) *Facilitating Developmental Attachment: The Road to Emotional Recovery and Behavioural Change in Foster and Adopted Children*. Northvale, NJ: Jason Aronson.

Hughes, D. (1998) *Building the Bonds of Attachment*. Northvale, NJ: Jason Aronson.

Hughes, D. (2006) *Building the Bonds of Attachment: Awakening Love in Deeply Troubled Children* (2nd edn rev.). Northvale, NJ: Jason Aronson.

Hughes, D. (2009) *Principles of Attachment and Intersubjectivity: Still Relevant in Relating with Adolescents*. London: Worth.

Hughes, D. (2000) *Facilitating Developmental Attachment: The Road to Emotional Recovery and Behavioral Change in Foster and Adopted Children*. Northvale, NJ: Jason Aronson.

Jacobs, M. (2010) *Psychodynamic Counselling in Action*. London: Sage.

Jaffee, S. R., Belsky, J., Harrington, H., Caspi, A. and Moffitt, T. E. (2006) When parents have a history of conduct disorder: how is the caregiving environment affected?, *Journal of Abnormal Psychology*, 115 (2): 309–19.

James, M. and Pollard, A. (eds) (2006) *Improving Teaching and Learning in Schools: A Commentary by the Teaching and Learning Research Programme*. London: ESRC/ TLRP.

Jenkins, P. (2010) Child protection and the case for a 'confidential space' in therapy, *Counselling Children and Young People*, March: 17–20.

Jenkins, P. and Palmer, J. (2012) At risk of harm? An exploratory survey of school counsellors in the UK, their perception of confidentiality, information sharing and risk management, *British Journal of Guidance and Counselling*, 40 (5): 545–59.

Jenkins, P. and Polat, F. (2006) The Children Act 2004 and implications for counselling in schools in England and Wales, *Pastoral Care in Education*, 24 (2): 7–14.

Johnson, M. and Lakoff, G. (2006) Why cognitive linguistics requires embodied realism, *Cognitive Linguistics*, 13 (3): 215–324. Available online at doi:10.1515/cogl.2002.016

Jones, E. (1993) *Family Systems Therapy: Developments in the Milan-Systemic Therapies*. Chichester: Wiley.

Kalff, D. M. (1980) *Sandplay: A Psychotherapeutic Approach to the Psyche*. Boston, MA: Sigo.

Kazdin, A. E. (1990) Psychotherapy for children and adolescents, *Annual Review of Psychology*, 41: 21–54.

King, G. (1999) *Counselling Skills for Teachers: Talking Matters*. Buckingham: Open University Press.

Klein, M. (1997) *The Psychoanalysis of Children*. London: Vintage.

Klonsky, E. M. (2008) Childhood sexual abuse and non-suicidal self-injury: meta-analysis, *British Journal of Psychiatry*, 192: 166–70.

Knight, G. E. (1985) Information processing and the development of co-operative, competitive and individualistic social values, *Developmental Psychology*, 27: 25–30.

Kohut, H. (1984) *How Does Analysis Cure?* Chicago: University of Chicago Press.

Kroger, J. (2004) *Identity and Adolescence*. London: Routledge.

Lakoff, G. and Johnson, M. (1980) *Metaphors We Live By*. Chicago: University of Chicago Press.

Lakoff, G. and Johnson, M. (1999) *Philosophy in the Flesh: The Embodied Mind and its Challenge to Western Thought*. New York: Basic Books.

Lamb, H. (2012) Thoughts from a school counselling manager, *BACP Children and Young People*, December: 36–9.

Laming, Lord (2003) *The Victoria Climbie Inquiry: Report of an Inquiry by Lord Laming*. London: HMSO.

Landreth, G. L. (2002) *Play Therapy: The Art of Relationship* (2nd edn). New York: Brunner Routledge.

Larson, R. (1996) Changes in adolescents' daily interactions with their families from age 10 to 18: disengagement and transformation, *Developmental Psychology*, 32: 744–54.

Larson, R., Bradford-Brown, B. and Mortimer, J. (eds) (2002) *Adolescents' Preparation for the Future: Perils and Promise – A Report of the Study Group on Adolescence in the 21st Century (Journal of Research on Adolescence)*. Ann Arbor, MI.

Layard, R. and Dunn, J. (2009) *A Good Childhood: Searching for Values in a Competitive Age*. London: Penguin/The Children's Society.

Lear, T. (ed.) (1984) *Spheres of Group Analysis*. London: Group-Analytic Society Publications.

LeSurf, A. and Lynch, G. (1999) Exploring young people's perceptions relevant to counselling: a qualitative study, *British Journal of Guidance and Counselling*, 27 (2): 231–43.

Lieberman, M. D., Eisengerger, N. I., Crockett, M. J., Tom, S. M., Pfeifer, J. H. and Way, B. M. (2007) Putting feelings into words: affect labeling disrupts amygdala activity in response to affective stimuli, *Psychological Science*, 18 (5): 421–8.

Liley, A. W. (1972) The foetus as a personality, *Australian and New Zealand Journal of Psychiatry*, 6 (2): 99–105.

Lloyd, G. (1999) Ethical and supervision issues in the use of counselling and other helping skills with children and young people in school, *Pastoral Care in Education: An International Journal of Personal, Social and Emotional Development*, 17 (3): 25–30.

Mabey, J. and Sorensen, B. (1995) *Counselling for Young People*. Buckingham: Open University Press.

MacKewn, J. (1997) *Developing Gestalt Counselling*. London: Sage.

Macksoud, M. S. and Aber, J. L. (1996) The war experiences and psychosocial development of children in Lebanon, *Child Development*, 67 (1): 70–88.

Madge, N., Hewitt, A., Hawton, A., de Wilde, E. Corcoran, P., Fekete, S., van Heeringen, K., De Leo, D. and Ystgaard, M. (2008) Deliberate self-harm within an international community sample of young people: comparative findings from the Child and Adolescent Self-harm in Europe (CASE) Study, *Journal of Child Psychology and Psychiatry*, 46 (6): 667–77.

Males, M. (2009) Does the adolescent brain make risk-taking more inevitable? A sceptical appraisal, *Journal of Adolescent Research*, 24 (3): 3–20.

Marcia, J. (1993) The relational roots of identity, in J. Kroger (ed.), *Discussions on Ego Identity*. Hillsdale, NJ: Lawrence Erlbaum.

Marsh, H., Bryne, B. and Shavelson, R. (1988) A multi-faceted academic self-concept: its hierarchical structure and its relation to academic achievement, *Journal of Educational Psychology*, 80: 366–80.

Maslow, A. H. (1943) A theory of human motivation, *Psychological Review*, 50 (4): 370–96.

Maughan, B., Collishaw, S., Meltzer, H. and Goodman, R. (2008) Recent trends in UK child and adolescent mental health, *Social Psychiatry and Psychiatric Epidemiology*, 43: 305–10.

McAdam, E. and Lang, P. (1994) *Appreciative Work in Schools: Generating Future Communities*. Chichester: Kingsham Press.

McGinnis, S. (2008) Counselling in schools, in M. Baginsky (ed.), *Safeguarding Children and Schools*. London: Jessica Kingsley. pp. 121–35.

McGinnis, S. and Jenkins, P. (2011) *Good Practice for Counselling in Schools* (4th edn). Lutterworth: BACP.

McLaughlin, C. (1993) Counselling in a secondary setting: developing policy and practice, in K. Bovair and C. McLaughlin (eds), *Counselling in Schools: A Reader*. London: David Fulton.

McLaughlin, C. (1996a) Critical issues in the field. In C. McLaughlin, P. Clark and M. Chisholm (eds), *Counselling and Guidance in Schools: Developing Policy and Practice*. London: David Fulton. pp. 58–71.

McLaughlin, C. (1999) Counselling in schools: looking back and looking forward, *British Journal of Guidance and Counselling*, 27 (1): 13–22.

McLaughlin, C. and Clarke, B. (2010) Relational matters, *Educational and Child Psychology*, 27 (1): 91–103.

McLaughlin, C., Byers, R. and Oliver, C. (2012) *Perspectives on Bullying and Difference: The Experiences of Young People with Special Educational Needs and/or Disabilities*. London: National Children's Bureau.

McLaughlin, C., Holliday, C., Clarke, B. and Ilie, S. (2013) *Research on Counselling and Psychotherapy with Children and Young People: A Systematic Scoping Review of the Evidence for its Effectiveness from 2003–2011.* Lutterworth: BACP. Available online at www.bacp.co.uk/admin/structure/files/pdf/11615_ccyp_systematic_review_2013.pdf

McNiff, S. (2004) *Art as Medicine.* Boston, MA: Shambhala Publications Inc.

Mearns, D. and Cooper, M. (2005) *Working at Relational Depth in Counselling and Psychotherapy.* London: Sage.

Mearns, D. and Thorne, B. J. (2000) *Person Centred Counselling Today.* London: Sage.

Meins, E., Fernyhough, C., de Rosnay, M., Arnott, B., Leekam, S. R. and Turner, M. (2012) Mind-mindedness as a multidimensional construct: appropriate and nonattuned mind-related comments independently predict infant–mother attachment in a socially diverse sample, *Infancy,* 17 (4): 393–415.

Meltzer, D. (1973) *Sexual States of Mind.* London: Karnac.

Mennella, J. (2013) Address given to The American Association for the Advancement of Science, Boston. (Report in *The Times,* 15 February 2013.)

Mental Health Foundation/Camelot Foundation (2006) *Truth Hurts: Report of the National Inquiry into Self-harm among Young People.* London: Mental Health Foundation.

Midgley, N. and Vrouva, I. (eds) (2012) *Minding the Child: Mentalization-Based Interventions with Children, Young People and their Families.* New York: Routledge.

Milne, A. A. (2002) *Winnie the Pooh: The Complete Collection of Stories and Poems.* London: Egmont.

Milner, M. (1950) *On Not Being Able to Paint.* Madison, CT: International Universities Press, Inc.

MIND (2005) *Children and Young People and Mental Health.* Available online at www.mind.org.uk

Ministry of Education (1963) *The Newsom Report: Half Our Future.* A report of the Central Advisory Council for Education (England). London: HMSO.

Mitchell, J. (ed.) (1986) *The Selected Melanie Klein.* Harmondsworth: Penguin.

Mitchell, J. (2003) *Siblings.* Harmondsworth: Penguin.

Moursund, J. and Erskine, R. G. (2003) *Integrative Psychotherapy: The Art and Science of Relationship.* London: Thomson/Brooks Cole.

Muir, E., Lojkasek, M. and Cohen, N. J. (1999) *Watch, Wait, and Wonder: A Manual Describing a Dyadic Infant-led Approach to Problems in Infancy and Early Childhood.* Toronto, ON: Hincks-Dellcrest Centre and the Hincks-Dellcrest Institute.

Mulye, T. P., Park, M. J., Nelson, C. D., Adams, S. H., Irwin, C. E. and Brindis, C. D. (2009) Trends in adolescent and young adult health in the United States, *Journal of Adolescent Health,* 45: 8–24.

Munro, E. (2011) *The Final Report of the Munro Review of Child Protection is Published: A Child-Centred System.* London: Department for Education.

Muris, P. and Field, A. P. (2008) Distorted cognition and pathological anxiety in children and adolescents, *Cognition and Emotion*, 22 (3): 395–421.

Music, G. (2008) Child and Adolescent Mental Health Services (CAMHS) in schools, in M. Baginsky (ed.), *Safeguarding Children and Schools.* London: Jessica Kingsley.

Music, G. (2009) Containing not blaming, *BACP Children and Young People*, June: 13–16.

Music, G. (2011) *Nurturing Natures: Attachment and Children's Emotional, Sociocultural, and Brain Development.* Hove: Psychology Press.

National Centre for Social Research (2005) *Smoking, Drinking and Drug Use Among Young People 2004.* Leeds: Health and Social Care Information Centre.

National Institute for Health and Clinical Excellence (NICE) (2005a) Latest NICE guidance sets new standards for treating depression in children and young people. Press release 022/2005, 29.09.2005, available online at www.nice.org.uk/newsroom/pressreleases/pressreleasearchive/press-releases2005/2005_022_latest_nice_guidance_sets_new_standards_for_treating_depression_in_children_and_young_people.jsp

National Institute for Health and Clinical Excellence (NICE) (2005b) *Post-Traumatic Stress Disorder (PTSD).* Available online at www.nice.org.uk/CG26

Nelson, E., Leibenluft, E., McClure, E. and Pine, D. (2005) The social re-organisation of adolescence: a neuroscience perspective on the process and its relation to psychopathology, *Psychological Science*, 4: 7–14.

Newsom Report (1963) *Half Our Future.* London: HMSO.

Nitsun, M. (1996) *The Anti-group: Destructive Forces in the Group and their Creative Potential.* London: Routledge.

Norcross, J. C. (ed.) (2002) *Psychotherapy Relationships That Work: Therapists' Contributions and Responsiveness to Patients.* New York: Oxford University Press.

NSPCC (2009) *Young People who Self-Harm: Implications for Public Health Practitioners.* London: NSPCC.

Nuffield Foundation (2012) *Social Trends and Mental Health: Introducing the Main Findings.* London: Nuffield Foundation.

Nurmi, J. (2004) Socialisation and self development, in R. S. Lerner (ed.), *Handbook of Adolescent Psychology.* New York: Wiley.

O'Brien, M. and Houston, G. (2007) *Integrative Therapy: A Practitioner's Guide.* London: SAGE.

Oaklander, V. (2006) *Hidden Treasure: A Map to the Child's Inner Self.* London: Karnac.

Orbach, S. (2009) *Bodies.* London: Profile.

Ougrin, D., Tranah, T., Leigh, E., Taylor, L. and Asarnow, J. R. (2012) Practitioner review: self-harm in adolescents, *Journal of Child Psychology and Psychiatry*, 53 (4): 337–50.

Panksepp, J. (1998) *Affective Neuroscience*. Oxford: Oxford University Press.

Panksepp, J. and Biven, L. (2012) *The Archaeology of Mind: Neuroevolutionary Origins of Human Emotions*: London: Norton.

Pattison, S., Rowland, N., Cromarty, K., Richards, K., Jenkins, P., Cooper, M., Polat, F. and Couchman, A. (2007) *Counselling in Schools: A Research Study into Services for Children and Young People in Wales*. Lutterworth: BACP.

Pattison, S., Rowland, N., Richards, K., Cromarty, K., Jenkins, P. and Polat, F. (2009) School counselling in Wales: recommendations for good practice, *Counselling and Psychotherapy Research*, 9 (3): 169–73.

Pearce, J. (1994) Consent to treatment during childhood, *British Journal of Psychiatry*, 165: 713–16.

Peirano, P., Algarin, C. and Uauy, R. (2003) Sleep-wake states and their regulatory mechanisms throughout early human development, *Journal of Pediatrics*, 143 (4): Supplement, 70–9.

Perry, A. (2010) *Teenagers and Attachment: Helping Adolescents Engage with Life and Learning*. London: Worth.

Perry, B. (2005) Applying principles of neuro-development to clinical work with maltreated and traumatised children, in B. Webb (ed.), *Working with Traumatised Youth in Child Welfare*. New York: Guilford.

Perry, B. (2006) *The Boy Who Was Raised as a Dog*. New York: Basic.

Piaget, J. (1966) *Psychology of Intelligence*. New York: Harcourt.

Pines, M. (ed.) (1983) *The Evolution of Group Analysis*. London: Routledge and Kegan Paul.

Popescu, E. A., Popescu, M., Wang, J., Barlow, S. M. and Gustafson, K. M. (2008) Non-nutritive sucking recorded in utero via fetal magnetography, *Physiological Measurement*, 29 (1): 127.

Pople, L. (2009) *The Good Childhood Inquiry: What Children Told Us*. London: The Children's Society.

Prior, V. and Glaser, D. (2006) *Understanding Attachment and Attachment Disorders: Theory, Evidence and Practice* (Child and Adolescent Mental Health Series). London: Jessica Kingsley.

Radwan, K. (2010) Regulation, regulation, regulation, *Adoption Today*, October, pp. 19–21.

Ray, D. (2011) *Advanced Play Therapy*. New York: Routledge.

Resnick, M. D. (2000) Protective factors, resiliency and healthy youth development, *Adolescent Medicine*, 11 (1): 157–65.

Roeser, R. W., Eccles, J. S. and Sameroff, A. J. (2000) School as a context of early adolescents' academic and social-emotional development: a summary of the research findings, *The Elementary School Journal*, 100 (5): 443–71.

Rogers, C. (1957) The necessary and sufficient conditions of therapeutic personality change, *Journal of Psychology*, 21: 95–103.

Rogers, C. (1965) *Client-Centred Therapy: Its Current Practice, Implications and Theory*. London: Constable.

Rothschild, B. (2000) *The Body Remembers*. New York: Norton.

Rowan, J. and Jacobs, M. (2002) *The Therapist's Use of Self*. Buckingham: Open University Press.

Royal College of Psychiatrists (2012) *Post Traumatic Stress*. Available online at www.rcpsych.ac.uk

Rudduck, J. and Flutter, J. (2004) *How To Improve Your School: Giving Pupils a Voice*. London: Continuum.

Rutter, M. (1991) Pathways to and from childhood to adult life: the role of schooling, *Pastoral Care in Education*, 9 (3): 3–10.

Rutter, M. and Smith, D. (1995) *Psychosocial Disorders in Young People*. Chichester: Wiley.

Rutter, V. (1995) Adolescence: whose hell is it?, *Psychology Today*, 28: 54–65.

Safran, J. D. and Muran, J. C. (2000) *Negotiating the Therapeutic Alliance*. New York: Guilford.

Salmon, G. and Dover, J. (2007) *Reaching and Teaching Through Educational Psychotherapy*. West Sussex: John Wiley & Sons.

Salmon, G. and Kirby, A. (2008) Schools: central to providing comprehensive CAMH services in the future?, *Child and Adolescent Mental Health*, 13 (3): 107–14.

Salzberger-Wittenberg, I., Henry, G. and Osborne, E. (1999) *The Emotional Experience of Learning and Teaching* (2nd edn). London: Karnac.

Samaritans, The (2012) Information Resource Pack. Available online at www.samaritans.org

Samuels, A. (1985) *Jung and the Post-Jungians*. London: Routledge.

Sandler, B. D. (1997) Developing linkages between theory and intervention in stress and coping processes, in B. W. Sandler (ed.), *Handbook of Children's Coping Processes*. New York: Plenum. pp. 3–40.

Saudine, K. J. (1996) Personality and behavioral genetics: where have we been and where are we going?, *Journal of Research in Personality*, 30 (3): 335–47.

Schaverien, J. (1992) *The Revealing Image*. London: Routledge.

Schore, A. (1999) *Affect Regulation and the Origins of the Self*. Hove: Psychology Press.

Schore, A. (2003a) *Affect Regulation and Repair of the Self*. London: Norton.

Schore, A. (2003b) *Affect Dysregulation and Disorders of the Self*. London: Norton.

Schore, A. (2010) *Projective Identification, Unconscious Communication and the Right Brain*. Available online at www.continuingedcourses.net

Schore, A. (2011a) From notes provided at the Cambridge Emotional Wellbeing Forum, Faculty of Education, University of Cambridge, 8 October.

Schore, A. (2011b) *The Science of the Art of Psychotherapy*. Cambridge: Cambridge University Forum for Children's Emotional Well-being.

Schore, A. (2012) *The Science of the Art of Psychotherapy*. New York: Norton.

Schore, A. and Schore, J. (2008) Modern attachment theory: the central role of affect regulation in development and treatment, *Clinical Social Work*, 36 (1).

Scroufe, L. A. (1983) Infant–caregiver attachment and patterns of adaptation in preschool: the roots of mal-adaptation and competence. In M. Perlmutter (ed.) *Minnesota Symposia in Child Psychology*. Hillsdale, NJ: Erlbaum. vol. 16, pp. 41–83.

Scroufe, A., Egeland, B., Carlson, E. and Collins, W. A. (2009) *The Development of the Person: The Minnesota Study of Risk and Adaptation from Birth to Adulthood*. New York: Guilford.

Sedgewick, D. (2001) *Introduction to Jungian Psychotherapy*. Hove: Psychology Press.

Semple, D. M., McIntosh, A. M. and Lawrie, S. M. (2005) Cannabis as a risk factor for psychosis: systematic review, *Journal of Psychopharmacology*, 19 (2): 187–94.

Sercombe, H. (2010) The 'teen brain' research: implications for practitioners, *Youth and Policy*, 103: 25–38.

Sharp, C., Fonagy, P. and Goodyer, I. M. (2006) Imagining your child's mind: psychosocial adjustment and mothers' ability to predict their children's attributional response styles, *British Journal of Developmental Psychology*, 24 (1): 197–214.

Shemmings, D. and Shemmings, Y. (2011) *Understanding Disorganized Attachment: Theory and Practice for Working with Children and Adults*. London and Philadelphia: Jessica Kingsley.

Siegel, A. M. (1996) *Heinz Kohut and the Psychology of the Self*. London: Routledge.

Siegel, D. (2010) *The Mindful Therapist*. New York: Norton.

Silverman, W. K. and Field, A. P. (2011) *Anxiety Disorders in Children and Adolescents*. Cambridge: Cambridge University Press.

Sinason, V. (1992) *Mental Handicap and the Human Condition*. London: Free Association.

Skynner, R. (1984) Group Analysis and family therapy. In M. Pines (ed.) *The Evolution of Group Analysis*. London: Routledge and Kegan Paul.

Smail, D. (1993) *The Origins of Unhappiness*. London: HarperCollins.

Smart, T. (2012) Engaging with Children's Networks. Seminar, Cambridge Forum for Children's Emotional Well-Being. Cambridge University Faculty of Education, 10 November.

Smith, D. (2006) School experiences and delinquency at ages 13 to 16. *Edinburgh Study of Youth Transitions and Crime, No.13*. Edinburgh: Centre for Law and Society, University of Edinburgh.

Sorenson, B. and Mabey, J. (1995) *Counselling For Young People*. Buckingham: Open University Press.

Stallard, P. (2005) *A Clinician's Guide to Think Good Feel Food: Using CBT with Children and Young People*. Chichester: John Wiley & Sons Ltd.

Stapert, M. and Verliefde, E. (2008) *Focusing with Children: The Art of Communicating with Children at School and at Home*. Ross-On-Wye: PCCS.

Steinberg, L. (2008a) A social neuroscience perspective on adolescent risk-taking, *Developmental Review*, 28: 78–106.

Steinberg, L. (2008b) *Adolescence* (8th edn). New York: McGraw-Hill.

Stern, D. (1985) *The Interpersonal World of the Infant: A View from Psychoanalysis and Developmental Psychology*. New York: Karnac.

Stern, D. (1998) *The Interpersonal World of the Infant* (rev. edn). London: Karnac.

Stiles, W. (2005) Vocal manifestations of internal multiplicity: Mary's voices, *Psychology and Psychotherapy: Theory, Research and Practice*, 78: 21–44.

Stinckens, N. (2002) The inner critic on the move: analysis of the change process in a case of short-term client-centred/experiential therapy, *Counselling and Psychotherapy Research: Linking Research with Practice*, 2 (1): 40–54.

Stolorow, R. D. and Attwood, G. E. (1992) *Contexts of Being: The Intersubjective Foundations of Psychological Life*. Psychoanalytic Inquiry book series, vol. 12. England: Analytic Press, Inc.

Sunderland, M. (2000) *Using Story Telling as a Therapeutic Tool with Children*. Oxford: Winslow.

The Samaritans (2012) Information Resource Pack. Available online at www.samaritans.org

Timimi, S. (2012) It's all about the outcomes, *Young Minds Magazine*, 115 (Spring).

Trevarthen, C. and Aitken, K. J. (2001) Infant intersubjectivity: research, theory, and clinical applications, *Journal of Child Psychology and Psychiatry*, 42 (1): 3–48.

Trevarthen, C. and Marwick, H. (1986) Signs of motivation for speech in infants, and the nature of a mother's support for development of language. In B. Lindblom and R. Zetterstrom (eds), *Precursors of Early Speech*. Basingstoke: Macmillan.

UNICEF (2007) *An Overview of Child Well-being in Rich Countries: A Comprehensive Assessment of the Lives and Well-being of Children and Adolescents in the Economically Advanced Nationals*. Geneva: UNICEF, Innocenti Research Centre.

Vaillant, G. E. (1992) *Ego Mechanisms of Defense: A Guide for Clinicians and Researchers*. Washington, DC: American Psychiatric Publishing.

Van der Kolk, B. (1994) The body keeps score, *Harvard Review of Psychiatry*, 1: 235–65.

Van der Kolk, B. (2003) The neurobiology of childhood trauma and abuse, *Child and Adolescent Psychiatric Clinics of North America*, 12: 293–317.

Van der Kolk, B., Perry, J. and Herman, J. (1991) The origins of destructive behaviour, *American Journal of Psychiatry*, 148 (12): 1665–71.

Verrier, N. N. (2009 [1993]) *The Primal Wound: Understanding the Adopted Child*. London: British Association for Adoption and Fostering.

Viorst, J. (1988) *Necessary Losses: The Loves, Illusions, Dependencies and Impossible Expectations That All Of Us Have to Give Up in Order to Grow*. London: Simon and Schuster.

Vygotsky, L. S. (1933) *Play and its Role in the Mental Development of the Child*. Kindle edition available at www.all-about-psychology.com

Vygotsky, L. S. (1978) *Mind in Society: Development of Higher Psychological Processes*, Cambridge, MA: Harvard University Press.

Waddell, M. (2000) *Inside Lives: Psychoanalysis and the Growth of the Personality.* London: Karnac.

Wadhwa, P. D., Sandman, C. A. and Garite, T. J. (2001) The neurobiology of stress in human pregnancy: implications for prematurity and development of the fetal central nervous system, *Progress in Brain Research,* 133: 131–42.

Wallin, D. J. (2007) *Attachment in Psychotherapy.* New York: Guilford Press.

Wampold, B. E. (2001) *The Great Psychotherapy Debate: Models, Methods, and Findings.* Mahwah, NJ: Lawrence Erlbaum Associates Publishers.

Watkins, C. (1999) Personal-social education: Beyond the national curriculum, *British Journal of Guidance & Counselling,* 27 (1): 71–84.

Welch, S., Doll, H. and Fairburn, C. (1997) Life events and the onset of bulimia nervosa: a controlled study, *Psychological Medicine,* 27: 515–22.

Welsh Government Social Research (2011) *Evaluation of the Welsh School-based Counselling Strategy: Stage One Report, July 2011.*

Wentzel, K. R. (1998) Social relationships and motivation in middle school: the role of parents, teachers, and peers, *Journal of Educational Psychology,* 90 (2): 202–9.

White, M. and Epston, D. (1987) *Narrative Means to Therapeutic Ends.* New York: Norton.

Williams, G. (1998) *Internal Landscapes and Foreign Bodies: Eating Disorders and Other Pathologies.* London: Karnac.

Williams, M. and Penman, D. (2011) *Mindfulness.* London: Piatkus.

Wilson, J. (1998) *Child-Focused Practice: A Collaborative Systemic Approach.* London: Karnac.

Winnicott, D. W. (1958) *Collected Papers: Through Paediatrics to Psychoanalysis.* London: Tavistock.

Winnicott, D. W. (1964a) *Deprivation and Delinquency.* London: Routledge.

Winnicott, D. W. (1964b) *The Child, the Family and the Outside World.* London: Perseus.

Winnicott, D. W. (1965a) *The Maturational Processes and the Facilitating Environment.* London: Karnac.

Winnicott, D. (1965b) The relationship of a mother to her baby at the beginning, in *The Family and Individual Development.* London: Routledge.

Winnicott, D. W. (1967) Mirror-role of the mother and family in child development, in P. Lomas (ed.), *The Predicament of the Family: A Psycho-Analytical Symposium.* London: Hogarth. pp. 26–33.

Winnicott, D. W. (1971) *Playing and Reality.* London: Routledge.

Winnicott, D. (2006) *The Family and Individual Development.* London: Routledge.

World Health Organisation (1998) *The World Health Report 1998 – Life in the 21st Century: A Vision for All.* Geneva: WHO.

Wright, K. (1991) *Vision and Separation between Mother and Infant.* London: Free Association.

Yalom, I. (1995) *The Theory and Practice of Group Psychotherapy* (4th edn). New York: Basic.

York, A. and Kingsbury, S. (2009) *The Choice and Partnership Approach.* Surrey: CAMHS Network. Available online at www.camhsnetwork.co.uk

Youell, B. (2006) *The Learning Relationship: Psychoanalytic Thinking in Education.* London: Karnac.

Zack, S. E., Castonguay, L. G. and Boswell, J. F. (2007) Youth working alliance: a core clinical construct in need of empirical maturity, *Harvard Review of Psychiatry* 15 (6): 278–88.

Legal references

(Admin) Gillick v West Norfolk Area Health Authority [1985] 3 A11 ER 402.

Axon, R. (on the application of) v Secretary of State and Anor [2006] EWHC 39.

Useful resources and websites

www.beatbullying.org.uk

www.childmentalhealthcentre.org.uk

www.selfharm.net.uk

www.annafreud.org

Agenda for Change: www.nhsemployers.org/PayAndContracts/AgendaForChange/NationalJobProfiles/Documents/Clinical_Psychologists-Counsellors.pdf

OOCAMHS: www.oocamhs.com/

Goodman's SDQ: www.sdqinfo.com/

CYPIAPT: www.iapt.nhs.uk/cyp-iapt/

www.iapt.nhs.uk/silo/files/a-practical-guide-to-using-service-user-feedback – outcome-tools-.pdf

Children's NSF can be downloaded at: www.dh.gov.uk/en/Publications andstatistics/Publications/PublicationsPolicyAndGuidance/DH_4089099

Index